Spirits of Resistance and Capitalist Discipline:

FACTORY WOMEN IN MALAYSIA

SUNY Series in the Anthropology of Work
June Nash, editor

Spirits of Resistance and Capitalist Discipline:

FACTORY WOMEN IN MALAYSIA

Aihwa Ong

State University of New York Press

Published by
State University of New York Press, Albany

© 1987   State University of New York

For information, address State University of New York
Press, State University Plaza, Albany, N.Y., 12246

Library of Congress Cataloging-in-Publication Data
Ong, Aihwa.
  Spirits of resistance and capitalist discipline.

  (SUNY series in the anthropology of work)
  Bibliography: p.
  Includes index.
  1. Peasantry—Malaysia—Selangor. 2. Selangor—Rural
conditions. 3. Social change—Case studies. 4. Labor and
laboring classes—Malaysia—Selangor. 5. Women electronic
industry workers—Malaysia—Selangor. 6. Economic
anthropology—Malaysia—Selangor.
I. Title.   II. Series.
HD1537.M27O54 1987   306'.36'095951   86-22980
ISBN 0-88706-380-2
ISBN 0-88706-381-0 (pbk.)   Rev.

10 9

To my parents

Contents

List of Abbreviations

ABIM   *Angkatan Belia Islam Malaysia* — Islamic Youth Movement of Malaysia

D.O.   District Officer

EJI   Electronics Japan Incorporated

ENI   Electronics Nippon Incorporated

FELDA   Federal Land Development Authority, government land schemes for the settlement of landless families

FMS   Federated Malay States

FTZ   Free Trade Zone

JCC   Joint Consultative Committee

JKK   *Jawatan Kuasa Kampung* — Village Committee

KEMAS   *Kemajuan Masyarakat* — Community Development projects for women

K.L.   Kuala Lumpur

MAS   Malaysian Airline System

MUZ   a manufacturer of musical movement components

NEP   New Economic Policy

PAS   *Partai Islam Se Malaysia* — Islamic Party of Malaysia

SSDC   Selangor State Development Corporation

TOL   Temporary Occupational License

UMNO   United Malays National Organization, the dominant party of the ruling National Front coalition

List of Tables, Maps, and Diagrams

TABLES

Preface

Why are Malay[1] women workers periodically seized by spirit possession on the shopfloor of modern factories? Educated Malays regard spirit beliefs a cultural relic which, like rustic speech and gestures, should have been left in departed villages. My aim in this book is to demonstrate how spirit attacks speak to the contemporary experiences of Malay women and their families as they make the transition from peasant society to industrial production.

To discover the meanings the market economy and industrial wage labor have for Malay women, it is necessary to talk about women as historical subjects and in terms of their subjective experiences. This inquiry deals with struggles over the means and meanings of gender in the context of exchange, disjunctions, and conflicts generated by land dispossession and the subjection of peasants to new forms of control and domination.

The proliferation of new disciplinary techniques, sexual images, and episodic outbreaks of spirit possession in the industrializing milieu leads me to ask: What is the relationship between work discipline and sexuality? What contradictions in the social experiences of factory women are mediated by evil spirits? In the new constellation of power relations, what do conflicting agencies and consciousness tell us about the nature of cultural change?

Capitalist development in Malaysia[2] engenders new forms of discipline in the everyday life of Malays, who up until recently were largely rooted in village (*kampung*) society and engaged in small-scale cash cropping. If "discipline" is taken to mean the effect of the exercise of power in the interests of capitalist production, then social control can be traced through a variety of cultural forms which enforce compliance and order within and outside economic enterprises. This inquiry will explore how changing relationships in the peasant household, village, and the global factory mediate divergent attitudes towards work and sexuality among Malays and within the wider society.

The extension of capitalist relations in Malaysia involves the simultaneous processes of agrarian transition and industrial capitalism which together are transforming Malay society in fundamental ways. In coastal Selangor, developmental change has produced not a classic proletarianization but a multiplicity of social strata. Caught in the flux of land dispossession, the majority of villagers are cast into unstable wage employment generated by the operations of transnational factories. What are the structural effects of centralized state power, on the one hand, and the decentralized operations of transnational corporation, on the other, on the nature of class power in the countryside?

The rise of a female Malay industrial force in Malaysian "free trade zones" is accompanied by divergent representations of female gender and sexuality in the ideological discourse of dominant political groups. Almost overnight, neophyte factory women barely out of their adolescence have become contradictory symbols in public commentaries on morality and "truth."[3] How do these conflicting images of their sexuality mediate the diverse interests of groups and classes? What do they tell us about the deployment of sexuality and hegemonic ideology?

Within the factory, working women confront industrial discipline as a manifold and wide-ranging network of overt and covert power relations. Marxists frequently assume that capitalist relations of production have an over-determined logic, based on the extreme separation of mental and physical labor, and the banishment of imaginative life from the factory floor. If that were the case, what is one to make of the production of "corporate culture" in transnational corporations? How are technology and cultural practices brought to bear in the production of "docile bodies," and a new subjectivity in female workers?

Caught between noncapitalist morality and capitalist discipline, some factory women alternate between states of self-control and spirit possession. The *hantu*, evil spirit of an archaic Malay world, is not alien to the sanitized environments of high technology factories. If one considers the complex *hantu* imagery as part of a noncapitalist critique of capitalist practices, what are the contradictory meanings of these nightmarish visitations in modern factories? Does the symbolism of possession episodes speak to an elegant opposition between the production of use values and of exchange values, as Michael Taussig has claimed for South American workers (1980)? Alternately, is the devil simply the shadow of a traditional belief system, or does it represent a contemporary assault on the Malay sense of humanity? Furthermore, does the *hantu* metaphor disclose an intense ambivalence in the factory women, their felt tension between old claims and new desires induced by capitalist culture?

To answer these questions, I have woven many narrative streams through the work. The voices of neophyte factory women, in counterpoint to corporate images and in protest against public abuse, articulate an intersubjective mode of apprehending the world. In their everyday vocabulary of moral piety, as well as in the possession indictments of male power, women workers seek to express new identities, to empower their relations with men and the wider society, and finally to diminish control by dominant power structures. This study is thus a composition in many discordant voices, claiming no final authority. It is an unfolding story that remains to be told more fully by young women living in the shadowy recesses undisclosed by the electronic gaze of the late twentieth century.

This book grew out of my meetings with hundreds of informants and friends in Kuala Langat, Selangor, where I spent fourteen months in the field (1979–80). I wish to express my gratitude to the people of the district — smallholders, factory workers, day laborers, petty traders, ordinary villagers, government officials, factory personnel — women, men, and children of different ethnic backgrounds who made my stay an enriching and unforgettable experience. In Sungai Jawa (a pseudonym, like all other village and personal names in the main text) Md. Naim b. Ahmad and Misripah bt. Hj. Ali welcomed me into their family as someone *kurang Jawa* (''not yet Javanese''), to be guided, with kindness, patience, and humor, through the intricacies of Malay-Javanese *kampung* life. My field assistant, Rageswari Balakrishna, competently conducted reams of time budget surveys. Villagers displayed warm hospitality and occasional impatience, breaking easily into conversations of remarkable interest and wit. I hope that by presenting their stories and daily experiences, which form the stuff of this study, I nowhere betray their trust or interest. May the book be of some satisfaction in particular to the young factory women whose quiet courage and steadfast loyalty to their families and themselves are yet to be appreciated by the wider society.

My training in the Department of Anthropology at Columbia University brought me, by a circuitous route, back to the heartland of Malaysia I had not known as a locally-born Chinese. My academic sensibility has been guided by Joan Vincent, Clive Kessler, Robert Murphy, and William Roff.

I am grateful to the following institutions for funding various phases of my dissertation research from which this book is derived: The National Science Foundation (grant no. BNS-787639) and the International Development Research Centre, Ottawa, which provided additional support for preliminary write-up at the Institute of Southeast Asian Studies, Singapore. I also wish to express my appreciation of research facilities at the following institutions: *Arkib Negara Malaysia* (The National Archives of Malaysia), Petaling Jaya, the University of Malaya, Kuala Lumpur, Universiti Sains Malaysia, Penang, and the National University of Singapore.

June Nash took an early interest in my dissertation and encouraged its metamorphosis into a book. Asraf Ghani's penetrating comments sharpened the contours of my argument as I began the task of revision for publication. Before it went to the press, this manuscript benefitted from critical suggestions by Brackette Williams. Different chapters were also read by Nancy Scheper-Hughes, Alan Dundes, Scott Guggenheim and Cristina B. Szanton. Finally, the Department of Anthropology, University of California, Berkeley, provided the necessary situation and diversions for time away from the task of writing. With such fine support, remaining flaws in interpretation are mine alone.

Berkeley, California
March 1986

PART I

Capitalist Development and Cultural Experience

Certain human realities become clearer at the periphery of the capitalist system . . . the meaning of capitalism will be subject to precapitalist meanings, and the conflict expressed in such a confrontation will be one in which man is seen as the aim of production, and not production as the aim of man.

Michael Taussig (1980: 10, 11)

[Under capitalism] labour must . . . be performed as if it were an absolute end in itself, a calling. But such an attitude is by no means a product of nature. It cannot be evoked by low wages or high ones alone, but can only be the product of a long and arduous process of education.

Max Weber (1958: 62)

Chapter 1

Spirits and Discipline in Capitalist Transformation

Writing this book is rather like opening Pandora's box: what kinds of spirits is one releasing? My inquiry into the meanings industrialization has for Malaysian society necessarily elicits the social significance of neophyte factory women not only for peasants but also for managers of transnational companies, government officials, Islamic zealots, school teachers, village children, and the wider society. Ethnographic knowledge builds upon a negotiated reality between the anthropologist and informants, and my claim to this alongside other possible interpretations rests on the inclusion of many voices seldom heard in the cacophony of academic and political exchanges. By documenting changes in rural society and weaving a multi-stranded, multilingual social reality into the account, this text discloses diverse reactions to an emerging Malay female proletariat, as well as their own eloquent descriptions of the disruptions and ambivalences of cultural change. Thus, while my interpretation may refract like a multifaceted lens, it preserves a dialectical tension vis-à-vis various particularistic views expressed about changing Malay society. In this account, the *hantu* (evil spirit), hovering over the passage of young Malay women into industrial modernity, becomes "an image which mediates the conflict between [non]capitalist and capitalist modes of objectifying the human condition" (Taussig 1980: xii).

The introduction of industrial capitalist discipline into Malay society involves both resistance and assent to change in work patterns, consumption, group identity, self-consciousness, and ultimately, a greater

1

synchronization of local life with the rhythm of advanced capitalist societies. The historical and ethnographic contexts lead me to ask: What are the effects of capitalist development on Malay peasant society? What are the possible connections between capitalist discipline and cultural discourse? How are the experiences of neophyte factory women and their images of vice and virtue mediated by the visitations of Malay spirits in modern factories?

To answer these questions, I take a dialectical approach by juxtaposing opposed or contradictory social phenomena. My descriptions will continually oscillate between the analysis of changing material relationships and the interpretation of cultural attitudes and practices both emerging and receding in the wake of Malay proletarianization.

This book seeks to illuminate cultural change in an industrializing society by talking about changing peasant beliefs and practices in a situation of shifting, complementary, and contradictory meanings. Previous analyses of Southeast Asian cultures have emphasized the syncretist paradigm of cultural streams (Geertz 1964) or the two-tiered model of great and little traditions (e.g., Scott 1976). Departing from this framework of society as a segmented system of cultural traditions, I consider divergent and discordant cultural forms in Malaysia where a complex network of bureaucratic mechanisms has been deployed to mobilize meaning in the discursive practices of everyday life, for the maintenance and reproduction of the political economy.

For too long, anthropological concepts of "culture" have been one-dimensional, overly comprehensive and extrahistorical. Clifford Geertz made a significant break when he urged that "culture" be taken as "webs of significance" (1973: 5), constituted by a system of shared meanings, symbols, and practices, to be read "from the native's point of view" (1979). What has been of less interest to Geertz is the question of power in the production, definition, and maintenance of dominant cultural patterns. More recently, Eric Wolf called for an examination of different cultural forms in specific social-historical contexts. He emphasized the importance of relating alternative symbol systems and practices to the "field of force" generated by the mode of production (1982: 387). The task of the analyst is to decode and understand changing cultural meanings, their making and unmaking, in relations of domination and resistance.

In this book, "culture" is taken as historically situated and emergent, shifting and incomplete meanings and practices generated in webs of agency and power. Cultural change is not understood as unfolding according to some predetermined logic (of development, modernization, or capitalism) but as the disrupted, contradictory, and differential outcomes which involve changes in identity, relations of struggle and dependence, including the experience of reality itself. Multiple and conflicting complexes of ideas and practices will be discussed in situations wherein groups and classes struggle to produce and interpret culture within the industrializing milieu. Raymond Williams has suggested that in class-divided societies hegemonic domination is not to be understood as merely controlling ideas and practices but as "a saturation of the whole process of living." By this he means that dominant meanings and practices shape the substance of everyday experiences: our lived expectations, meanings, and practices constitutive and constituting our sense of social relationships and of reality (1977: 110). Industri m m,sia

In Malaysia, industrialization has been accomplished through pervasive bureaucratic redefinitions of group identity and relationships in domains of public and private life, including the constitution and boundary-marking processes which define these. Such processes are currently intensified in many third world states undertaking capitalist development. Since hegemonic attitudes and practices are necessarily incomplete (at any time, oppositional forms exist), continual activities through education, media, and employment structures are required to defend, modify, and even incorporate countercultural tactics of subordinated groups (Williams 1977: 121–27).

Taussig (1980) and Williams thus emphasize the cultural construction and reconstruction of divergent meanings and action which embody a specific distribution of political and economic forces. Such a formulation enables us to deal with cultural change without a false opposition between ideology and practice. Michel Foucault's explication of the varied forms modern power takes is pertinent for our understanding of how social organization and realities are being reconstituted in some third world societies. By suggesting that the operations of modern power are in fact productive rather than repressive (i.e., effectuated through repression) he argues that schemes of discursive practices are involved in the complex production of rituals, objects, and "truth" (1979: 194). The effects of power/knowledge relations (e.g., scientific managment) are to implant disciplinary techniques in bodies and human conduct, thereby complementing more overt forms of control in everyday life. In transnational corporations, we see that relations of domination and subordination, constituted in scientific terms, operate not only through the overt control of workers' bodies but in the ways young female workers come to see themselves. In their changing positions within the family, the village, the labor process, and wider society, they devise counter tactics for resisting images imposed on them and come to construct their own images.[1]

A heightened sexuality attributed to Malay female workers by the Malaysian public can be considered the contradictory cultural constructions of a society intensely ambivalent about the social consequences of industrial development. In looking at the complex relation between sexuality and gender, it is necessary to eschew the assumptions of received concepts such as ''women's roles,'' ''sexual inequality,'' and ''patriarchy'' either in their implied sense of ''achieved states'' (Williams 1977: 11–20) or as suitable starting points of analysis. Many ethnographies written about ''women's status/role'' in third world societies often lack this critical understanding of gender as cultural constructions, both imposed and increasingly self-defined, in particular historical situations. Even more rare, as Marilyn Strathern has pointed out, is the recognition that in some societies, gender may not be the primary organizing code of sexual difference but rather an idiom for other kinds of social differentiation, such as prestige ranking (1981). Perhaps most critically, the preoccupation of ''women's studies'' with statistical measurements of structural ''inequality'' overlooks the self-formative activities of women which partially structure their identities and the immediate relationships within which they are enmeshed in daily life. As a consequence, they leave underanalysed the dialectical relation between processes out of which constraints are developed and within which gender is culturally formed and transformed. This inquiry asks why sexuality should become a key image/construct in Malay transition to industrial capitalism; what does it tell us about culture as a dialectical construction? It is a major contention of this work that local meanings, values, and practices have been reworked within the operations of administrative organs, capitalist enterprises, and civil institutions.

In Malaysia, capitalist discipline operates through a variety of control mechanisms in social, political, and work domains both to regulate and legitimate unequal relations which sustain the process of industrial modernization. By ''discipline'' I mean the effects of the exercise of power on the subjugated, and the enforced and induced compliance with the political, social, and economic objectives, considered rational and functional for capitalist production. The development of political mechanisms of control, whether in state offices, development projects or factories, necessarily involves changing material relations as well as an altered sense of reality, changing self-knowledge, and cultural justification of the social order, in times of noncrisis.

The following section will discuss how the cultural construction and reconstruction of meaning, gender relations, and sexuality are involved in new disciplinary systems and forms of resistance generated in rural Malay society. It will be argued that class formation is not the only process whereby new consciousness and practices emerge or are superseded.

The concept of "proletarianization" is fraught with Marxist assumptions derived from Lenin's discussion of the transition from Czarist feudalism to agrarian capitalism in Russia (1964). The situation in the corner of Peninsular Malaysia I am concerned with is not representative of the classic case of rural differentiation into a small number of agrarian capitalists and a multitude of rural laborers. Rather, the on-going dispossession of Malay peasants in Kuala Langat will be considered in relation to (i) an expanding state bureaucracy for the integrating fractions of the peasantry loosened from the land, and (ii) global corporate strategies based upon the fragmentation of the labor force dispersed throughout the world system. In other words, we are talking about circumstances in which the changing conditions of production and reproduction are less ordered by merchant capital than commanded over by the state apparatus and by global capital. This centralization of bureaucratic control over local reproduction processes is not limited to the production of exchange values but extends to the production of cultural values as well.

The crisis is seen in processes involved in the social reproduction of the *kampung*, the basic community, territorial unit, and the social matrix of everyday life. In Kuala Langat, *kampung* households exhibit differential capacities to reconstitute the labor process in smallholding production as more households come to control smaller parcels of land. But the formalism of landownership categories is only one (and often misleading) dimension of changing peasant-capital relationships. The making of new class relations is dependent not only upon access to land but also upon the ability of households and individuals to realize new forms of linkages with the state machinery and modern labor markets. Furthermore, recognition of the domination by the state and capital over the labor process is politically justified in terms of development *in the interest of* rural Malays. This is a form of "misrecognized" domination Pierre Bourdieu calls "symbolic violence" (1977). However, as I will try to show, complicity in their own social domination, if an obstacle to group interests, can also be a hidden channel to individual upward mobility.

As more *kampung* folk become wage workers, downward mobility is more commonly endured by the majority than upward mobility into the ranks of bureaucratic or industrial employment. Increasingly, individual educational and occupational trajectories beat a path out of *kampung* society, a structural effect of market and bureaucratic disciplining operating selectively on individuals rather than on groups. Such individuated grassroots reactions to the changing economy make doubtful the significance of peasant responses such as household strategizing (White 1976) and resistance to market and state policies (Scott 1976) which have been claimed for rural societies elsewhere in Southeast Asia. As my description of *kampung* society will demonstrate, group strategies adapted to changes in the local economy are not very effective for class mobilization when the field of conflicting interests becomes integrated within wider structures of political coercion and labor market manipulation. Dispossessed peasants, set upon different trajectories of survival and mobility, are individuated as much by gender, education, village origin, and political affiliation as by social class aspirations.

As productive activities on the land give way to the sale of labor by household members, the power configuration of domestic relations is continually realigned, both in cooperation and in conflict. In this transition to industrial labor, special pressures are brought to bear on women, but especially daughters, in the Malay *kampung* family. Parents' attempts to set sons and daughters on different career paths, in accordance with selective market demands, are often fraught with conflict and ambivalence. Pierre Bourdieu notes the cumulative structure of dispositions (*habitus*) cultivated through education, acquired values, and practices — symbolic capital — in individual and collective pursuit of upwardly mobile pathways (1977; 1984). The acquisition of symbolic capital in particular families thus mediates the relationships which restructure emotions between parents and children, brothers and sisters, as well as govern those relationships which distribute individually acquired material resources within and between generations. In this new configuration of day-to-day relations, what women and men come to mean to each other in the domestic domain, and how they perceive the household, are aspects of their cultural history too often overlooked in ethnographic accounts.

In the new milieu of their production activities, neophyte factory women and men experience power as a manifold, everchanging, and elusive force. Much of the literature on third world women and multinational corporations has neglected to recognize the multiple forms and foci of power relations which constitute the social domains of these industrial workers. State linkages to foreign investments and to labor control condition the constellation of power relations exercised over the nascent working classes. Political disciplining of the rural population involves support for the privileged few who can be integrated into the state apparatus, on the one hand, and political and material constraints on the majority, on the other. The Malay laboring poor, subjected both to bureaucratic culture and to the call of Islamic revivalism, consider themselves politically informed Malay-Muslims rather than a class in the Marxist sense. Female workers express in the culture of their everyday life the ambiguous images and practices of a fragmented, mobile, and ultimately dispensable labor force harnessed to global industrial production.

Induction to capitalist relations of production generates profound contradictions in the Malay peasant's orientation towards work and life. Hitherto, village life was ordered by the rhythm of agricultural cycles, daily Islamic prayers, and *kampung* tasks largely carried out according to personal cumpulsion; everyday life was decidedly non-capitalist. The over zealous villager seen cycling to his garden on a hot afternoon is mocked as "devil-driven" by neighbors jealous that he is "planting capital" while they take their customary nap. More critically, *kampung* folk expect to work at their own volition, be their "own boss," and not be ordered around by others. In daily life, it is often only young girls who are supervised, if at all, in their domestic tasks by female relatives. Thus, I would argue, the trauma of industrial labor for village women is in the rigidity of the work routine, continual male supervision, and devaluation of their labor in the factory. Spirit possession episodes, in which women become violent and scream abuses, are to be deciphered not so much as a noncapitalist critique of abstract exchange values (Taussig 1980) but as a protest against the loss of autonomy/humanity in work. Six or more years of elementary schooling have not dampened the carefree spirit of peasant girls for whom corporate control and labor discipline is a continuing personal and social crisis.[2]

However, contrary to some Marxist assertions (e.g., Burawoy 1979), capitalist relations of production cannot be assumed to have an inherent logic, operating as they do in diverse situations of the multiple and shifting play of power relations. I maintain that the series of disciplinary mechanisms brought into play in the transnational corporation combine both labor control and management techniques disguised and reworked into a ''corporate culture'' which pervades the workaday life. Drawing on Foucault's insights, I argue that in the labor process, young women are being reconstituted as instruments of labor and as new sexual personalities. Foucault has observed that the deployment of sexuality, as part of the expanding political technology of modern power, unavoidably induces self-management in the subjected, who, in becoming a self-affirming subject, ''opens up the possibility of a substantial shift in tactics'' (1980: 130). The elaboration of a culture of consumption or a cult of purity by different groups of Malay factory women must be seen in this light of differentiated resistance and cultural maneuvers in changing power domains.

For the Malaysian public, the sexuality of these new working women in transnational factories becomes the focus of anxiety over the social effects of capitalist development. This study therefore seeks to understand the industrial transformation of rural Malay society by looking at the predicament of young *kampung* women. In the public eye, neophyte factory women have become the mediating images of truth, the currency of discourse for parents, brothers, factory managers, male workers, politicians, Islamic revivalists, and themselves. I will talk about the varied coinage of sexuality in the home, the workplace, and the public forum, alternating between external representations of gender roles and sexual meanings and the self-constitution of identity by the neophyte factory women.

In the rural household, the cash-earning unmarried daughter becomes a challenge to the local ideology of male protection: what are the changed perceptions of fathers, brothers, and ''boyfriends'' (a new category) to the working girl-woman no longer accommodated under a unified concept of "maiden"? How do factory women handle the contradictory experiences of economic autonomy from kinsmen and political coerion by men in the corporation and the wider society? ~~Sexism~~

Are the *hantu* hallucinations a residual image of remembered village, a present shadow in their industrial life, or both? This sense of affliction is induced as much by a particular corporate surveillance as by a general public gaze of disapproval. In the proliferation of consumer culture, how do neophyte factory women come to reimagine power relations and the public perception of women as sexual/moral threat? What can notions of counter tactics and alternative self-images contribute to our analysis of their attempts to redefine themselves, restructure gender relations, and form different linkages to class and economic power?

~~order~~

This book is arranged in three parts. Chapter 2 deals briefly with the colonial history of Malay peasants, composed of local inhabitants and immigrants from the wider Malay archipelago who established cash cropping villages in coastal Selangor. The rest of the study draws upon fieldwork investigation conducted in 1979–1980.

Part II takes the reader into a contemporary subdistrict (*mukim* Telok) of Kuala Langat to observe changes in the daily life of Malay villagers, mainly of Javanese ancestry. Primary focus is on the reworking of domestic relations, the structuring of feeling and family strategies in a situation of rapid proletarianization.

Part III concerns the experiences of Malay peasant women in transnational electronics factories located in a nearby "free trade zone." Management techniques of control in the labor process include the management of emotions and the production of a new sexuality. In analysing the rearrangements of power relations, I will discuss the symbolic meanings of the *hantu*, and of the neophyte factory women, for the various participants in this local drama which momentarily suggests the universal features of cultural change in the late twentieth century.

Moving through this threefold study is the theme of cultural resistance among rural Malays at different phases of their encounter with and incorporation within the world capitalist system. Over the last one hundred years, the introduction of new relations of production and exchange into rural Malay society has involved the cultural reconstructions of ethnicity, family, female, male, and morality within changing configurations of power relations. In the transition from cash cropping to industrial labor, preexisting meanings, values, and practices were reformulated by Malay peasants in their everyday acquiescence in and resistance to larger structures of domination. This is a story of cultural struggle in which the dialectic between spirits of resistance and new forms of discipline is the key refrain of rural Malays as they enter into the world of laboring by the clock.

Chapter 2

Malay Peasants from Subsistence to Commodity Production

Through centuries of seafaring trade, immigration, and foreign conquest, coastal Selangor on the Malay Peninsula was one of many landing points on the Straits of Malacca (see Map 1). This study of changing Malay society explores the particular outcomes, at the individual, domestic, and regional levels, of the interplay between local culture structure and external influence through successive waves of integration into the world system. It is also the untold story of immigrant and local Malays who over the past hundred years have been reconstituted as cash cropping peasants and laborers in the transnational companies of late capitalism.

Drawing on colonial records, the present chapter traces changing relations of production and cultural practices as Malay society in Selangor became the object and subject of British colonial policies within the local and international contexts of industrial capitalism. Through "indirect rule" of the Malay States (1874–1957), British officials introduced politico-legal changes governing native land, cultivation, and populations of diverse origins. Colonial policies also gave birth to a discursive existence of the "native," ideologically differentiated from immigrant Chinese and Indian populations. The actual experiences of immigrant Malay populations in pioneer *kampung,* rice fields, and new rubber holdings have to be gleaned from colonial accounts. Politically situated by colonial practices, buffeted by market forces, the Malay household economy evolved flexible strategies, not to accumulate wealth but to ensure survival in economic crisis origi-

11

nating elsewhere in the world system within which they were now integrated.

Rural Malay Society on the Eve of British Intervention

> The people lead strange and uneventful lives. The men are not inclined to much effort except in fishing or hunting, and, where they possess rice land, in ploughing for rice . . . The women were lounging about the house, some cleaning fish, others pounding rice; but they do not care for work, and the little money which they need for buying clothes they can make by selling mats or jungle fruits. . . .
>
> Isabella Bird (1967:138-39)

In the nineteenth century, the coastal regions of the Malay Penin-sula were loosely controlled by unstable tributary systems. These petty systems were given political legitimacy, Islamic aura, and cultural focus by Malay sultans, momentarily the strongest monarchs, who were ensconced in royal towns situated at river mouths. Below the sultan, conceived in native terms as the source and concentration of all wealth (Milne 1982), local "big men" (*orang besar*) extracted tribute from territories (*Negeri*) conveniently shaped by rivers, the main lines of trade, cultivation and hence control. The *rakyat*, as direct producers on the cleared land, paid out taxes, levies on riverine trade, and cor-vée labor to "big men" who administered local justice and defense (Gullick 1958: 36). Under the *kerah* system, "big men" could demand unlimited customary services from villagers to carry out large proj-ects of jungle clearing or construction. Debt slaves and war captives also provided labor for the nonproducing class (Sadka 1968: 297).

Malay cultivators in small settlements held usufruct rights to land from the sultan in return for such tributes in kind and labor. Royal grants to Peninsular Malays and Muslim peoples from elsewhere in the Malay archipelago were the means for accumulating, retaining, and replenishing the cultivating population. Once land was cleared and developed by a Malay settler, it could be transferred to family members, so long as they continued to cultivate and occupy the land, while meeting their customary rents to "big men" and sultan (ibid., 340).

Thus a tension was engendered between village production for sub-sistence needs and production for surplus extraction by the non-

Map 1
Selangor: Districts, Pre-1942 Boundaries

producing class. *Kampung* production was accordingly curtailed, the level determined by individual domestic subsistence needs, surplus payments, or the ability to evade such customary exactions. The locale and size of settlements, consisting of 20 to 50 households, were determined by the possibility of wet rice cultivation along swampy river banks. Despite the low level of technology, villagers exploited different ecological niches — jungle, river, and sea — which provided produce for self-sustenance, tribute, and sometimes small-scale trade.

Given the particular combination of easy access to abundant jungle land and not uncommon peasant attempts to evade heavy exactions, families remained small in size (often consisting of less than five individuals) and dispersed over scattered settlements. There was little incentive to accumulate land since land not improved by labor was "dead land" (*tanah mati*) (Maxwell 1884: 173). Only cultivated land, which could be tended and passed on by family members, was "live" (*tanah hidup*). Since uncultivated land was in abundant supply, family formation and dissolution were influenced by the early departure of children to make new plots in the jungle. Furthermore, the combination of low yields and high corvée demands would have induced the early dispersal of children, contributing to scattered, lightly-populated settlements.[1] Indeed, given the mode of extraction, wealth accumulation by the *rakyat* would have invited the unwelcomed attention of rapacious lords. The peasant household thus strove to be small, self-sufficient, and structurally adapted to easy relocation or dispersal of members, as required by ecological or political contingencies. Individual domestic groups did not require sustained exchanges with other households or with the market to ensure simple reproduction.

As cultivators living on the edge between jungle and river-sea, daily activities were carried out according to a simple division of labor between men and women, adults and children. Women worked on rice fields and raised garden produce and poultry. Among immigrant groups like the Javanese and Minangkabau, peasant women took up petty trading in regional markets (Winstedt 1981: 131). To supplement their meagre production, men, women, and children turned to fishing and the gathering of wild vegetables and animals. As village society was not divided into occupational groups, the family head furnished household and farm implements from jungle material. There was almost no need for cash, although occasionally, cash was earned by ferrying travellers across rivers (Gullick 1958: 30–31). A small quantity of surplus products was sold to Chinese tin-mining camps which gradually became a feature of the Malay Peninsula from midcentury onwards.

Throughout the latter half of the nineteenth century, as British mercantile interests were drawn by tin deposits in the Malay Peninsula, coastal Selangor was disrupted by intermittent warfare between rival kinsmen for the Bugis royal seat. Village settlements, if never stable before, became "consciously impermanent" as villagers turned *en masse* to flight, a customary response to heavy exactions and invasions by overlords (ibid., 29). By 1874, when agents of the British East India Company intervened to stabilize conditions for the tin trade, many villages in the region had been depopulated, and the inhabitants fled to other parts of the Peninsula (Rathborne 1898: 117–118).[2]

It was in such circumstances that rural Malay society first came under the scrutiny of British administrators and visitors. Following the imposition of a Residential system,[3] British colonial officials handsomely pensioned off the sultan and gained administrative control of the territory under his sovereignty for the systematic collection of revenue. In the early 1880s, passing through the Malay Peninsula, Isabella Bird observed that Malay men were "not inclined to much effort except in fishing and hunting, and, where they possess rice land, in ploughing." She commented that Malay women could use more of their time making artifacts to sell for cash (1967: 138–139). Viewing the precapitalist society with market lenses, she found the work patterns and time allocation of Malays wanting. In the next few decades, British perceptions of Malay peasants evolved into an image of the "indolent native," part of a colonial ideology which obscured actual changes wrought within rural Malay communities by British rule and capitalist transformation of the wider society. Politico-legal changes in land control and immigration broke the economic self-sufficiency of the Malay peasantry, integrating their production activities within the circuit of the embryonic capitalist economy. As peasant access to land became restricted, and they turned increasingly to cash cropping, the reproduction of the domestic group as a unit of production and consumption came to be governed by world market forces.

Colonial Rule: Malay Immigrants and Peasants

> The Malay never works if he can help it, and often will not suffer himself to be induced or tempted into doing so by offers of the most extravagant wages.
>
> Hugh Clifford (1927: 19)
> British colonial official in Malaya

Indirect rule by the British India Office enabled British mercantile interests to undertake primitive accumulation in Malay territories. This process of capital expropriation was twofold — the subjugation and consolidation of the Malay peasantry, and the exploitation of primarily non-Malay immigrant labor in capitalist enterprises. First, a nascent capitalist economy was built upon British and Chinese capital and the large-scale influx of male immigrant labor from China and India. Chinese and Indian immigrants cleared the land, built towns and the infrastructure necessary for capitalist development. They also provided cheap labor for tin mines, plantations, and urban services. Second, British policy towards Malays was one of mutual accommodation with the royal elite; a structure of colonial administration and preserved royal privilege for the reconstitution and domestication of a peasantry artificially shielded from capitalist disruptions. Thus the colonial state, through a dual policy of selective peasantization and immigration, deployed local and immigrant populations in differentiated sectors of the emergent "plural society." This "divide-and-rule" strategy complemented the process of "uneven and combined development" in the colonial territory.

In Selangor, an immediate task of British administration was the fortifying of the diminished peasant population. At the time of British Intervention, only about 5,000 Malays were left in the state (Rathborne 1898).[4] Under colonial administration laws governing land, immigrant labor, and market activities enabled the colonial power to increase the peasant population in allotted spaces within the changing economy. During the first decade, revenues generated by the fast-expanding tin industry enabled the colonial administration to lift the taxation burden from other sectors of the economy. In 1879, Frank Swettenham, the Assistant Resident of Kuala Langat, formulated his land policy by asserting "we do not seek revenue but population" (Sadka 1968: 331). He felt that the main need was to get a permanent population onto the soil so that the expansion of a food-producing peasantry would ultimately produce indirect revenue (ibid., 343).

Thousands of immigrant Malays from the Dutch East Indies were encouraged by rent remissions and small loans to settle in the district. Javanese, Sumatrans, and Outer Islanders arrived in groups, often led by leaders who applied for state land for their followers.[5] By 1886, two-thirds of the Malay population in Selangor consisted of immigrants from the Netherlands East Indies (ibid., 1968: 327–328). These immigrants were considered potential peasants; they were given land grants in swampy coastal areas to found *kampung* on the borderlines of the interior dominated by towns, plantations, and mines. These were quickly connected by a network of road and rail paid for by tin revenue. In the next few decades, the majority of immigrant Malays arriving in the Federated Malay States (FMS)[6] were Javanese.

By the new century, the demands of Western capitalist economies for rubber propelled the FMS into the mainstream of the world market. Javanese immigration into the Malay States has to be seen in this context. Built upon indentured laborers from Tamil Nadu,[7] the Malayan rubber plantation industry also engendered a small stream of Javanese contract workers from the Dutch East Indies, many by way of Deli, North Sumatra.[8] There were two systems for imported Javanese contract laborers. From 1926 through the 1930s, plantations made formal arrangements to import Javanese workers on three-year contracts. After their term expired, many applied for land grants to settle down as "Malay" smallholders. Under the second system of labor importation, Muslim shipping agents — called "sheiks" — recruited and paid the passage of impoverished Javanese to Singapore, where they were handed over to labor contractors (*tukang tebus*). Bonded workers (*wong tebusan*) made verbal contracts with their *tukang*, agreeing on a period of servitude as debt payments (T. Shamsul 1967: 238; Khazin 1980: 10–11). In practice, many *wong tebusan* were undoubtedly exploited beyond the contract period and awarded varying shares of the land grants they helped develop. An informant recalls that in the 1930s he was a bonded laborer for ten years. During that time, he developed a 15-acre lot for his *tukang*, for which he received a 3-acre plot. Finally, many "free" Javanese immigrants, attracted by land grants and the quick wealth rubber represented, attached themselves to patrons — earlier settlers who were relatives and friends — until they could acquire their own *kampung* holding.

British colonial authorities considered Javanese immigrants, together with Banjarese, Minangkabau, and other Muslim peoples from the Dutch territories as "immigrant Malays" who could apply for *kampung* land and settle down as peasants. Thus, in the southern half of the Malay Peninsula, scores of *kampung* came to be founded by immigrant Malays who had entered both as free individuals and as contract workers. These villages took root in the interstices of rubber estates and mines or established themselves along trunk roads, their gardens miniature homemade versions of the great plantations within which they were enclosed. By the Second World War, immigrant Malays comprised almost half the total Malay population in coastal Selangor, and a majority in Kuala Langat (see Table 1).

Table 1

Malay Population in Selangor, 1891-1957

Year	Local Malays	Immigrant Malays	Total
1891*	23,750**	2,828	26,578
1901	34,248	6,392	40,640
1911	45,474	19,588	65,062
1921	63,995	27,826	91,821
1931	64,436	58,502	122,938
1947	103,456	83,868	187,324
1957	194,506	96,905	291,411

(Source: Dodge 1980: 463)

*This was the first census conducted in the state. In that year, there were 75,000 Chinese in Selangor because of the tin mining industry based in and around Kuala Lumpur (Jackson 1964: 45–51).

**Immigrant Malays were probably also entered under this category; it was mentioned earlier that immigrant Malays comprised some two-thirds of the total Malay population in 1886.

Constructing A "Malay Yeomanry"

Colonial rule profoundly changed the relationship of Malay cultivators to the land and to the wider society. For the majority of local and immigrant Malays, the most immediate effect on their social situation was the introduction of the Torrens system of land registration. Under the land code, village lands and new holdings developed by Malays were entered into subdistrict (*mukim*) registers. Thus Malay land, formerly not an item for exchange, thereby became a commodity which could be bought, sold, mortgaged, or transferred, as the registered titleholder so pleased. The rapid development in a market for Malay-held or Malay-developed land soon threatened the continued existence of *kampung* society and raised the spectre of a landless class that would challenge its sultan's rapprochement with the British colonial masters. District land officials feared that once the Malay peasant sold his land to go on the hajj, he soon "ceased to be a Yeoman and [became] at best [a] day labourer and at worst, a vagabond" (SSF 3170/10, no. 37).

During the first decades of the twentieth century, the expansion in the Malayan rubber plantation industry set off a scramble for areas not yet claimed by capitalist interests, i.e., *kampung* lands. Tempted by land speculation, local and immigrant Malays sold their existing land and newly developed holdings to Chinese planters, Chettiar money lenders, and European companies. Villagers were induced to sell their holdings by the offer of high prices or because neighbors had sold land and departed (ibid.). Throughout the FMS, Malays exercised their new power to participate in commercial land dealings in return for quick sums of ready cash (Jackson 1968: 195–197).

In Selangor, district officers were alarmed that a total of 1,584 *kampung* holdings (some 7,567 acres) were disposed of by Malays to non-Malay merchants and capitalists between 1909–1910. A report from the Kuala Langat district office noted that twenty Javanese families had recently moved out after selling over 28 lots (state grants ranged from 4 to 7 acres); another 150 lots were going on the market. Similar sales of village holdings were reported in other districts; where the plantation industry was expanding, Malay lands were purchased by large holdings or joint-stock companies. By the time of the first rubber boom, the fringe areas remaining for Malay settlement had already become very limited (SSF 3170/10, no. 37).

This potential dissolution of the *kampung* society and influx of landless Malays into the capitalist sector threatened the colonial framework for administering a plural economy. The district officer of Kuala Langat warned that

> from the government point of view not only does the disappearance of the Malay *Kampongs* (villages) diminish the prospect of a future agricultural population but it defeats the very aim and object of which we are "protecting" the Malay States. It also upsets all land administration . . . for a collector who has been trying to keep European Estates, Chinese rubber and Malay *Kampongs* each in their proper place, to find the whole arrangement upset by the buying up of a flourishing Malay *Kampong* to float a rubber company. . . . (ibid.)

To arrest the uprooting of local Malays and fix peripatetic immigrant Malays to village land, colonial officers introduced paternalistic land and cultivation regulations to restrict the commercialization of Malay land and labor. Educated in public schools, Cambridge, and Oxford, British colonial officers saw Malays as "a race of yeoman-peasantry

. . . deluded by visions of present but transitory wealth." These self-appointed caretakers of native populations felt that they had to exercise better judgement on the behalf of "the Malay yeoman-peasant" in order to prevent his "extinction" by the market economy (SSF 10/12).

Consequently, the colonial administration in 1913 signed into law the Malay Reservation Enactment. This setting aside of special areas for Malay cultivations required a colonial legal definition of who constitued a "Malay." In 1913, the Malay Reservations Enactment Committee defined "Malay" as "a person belonging to any Malayan race who habitually speaks the Malay language or any Malay language and professes the Muslim religion" (FMS Enactment no. 15, 1913). Accordingly, quit-rent of different classes of land was reduced to encourage increased immigration by settlers from the Netherlands East Indies (SSF 3170/10, no. 37). In pressing for passage of the legislation, the Legal Adviser to the FMS argued that

> the present measure purports to provide for the protection of Malays against the temptation to divest themselves of their land. It is really a measure to provide protection for the Malays against themselves (FCP 1913: 23-25).

Thus, in the name of "the continuation of the Malay race," the reservations act was passed.

Throughout the British-controlled states, Malay Reservations were established in remnant, unsettled areas, the choicest lands already having been claimed by plantation and mining interests (Lim T.G. 1977: 114). Any land within a gazetted Malay Reservation could not be sold, leased, or otherwise disposed of to a "non-Malay." Thirty-five Reservations, ranging from 300 to almost 4,000 acres in size, were established in Selangor. In setting aside this relatively small area, the Reservations Enactment Committee declared that it was "not to prevent any Malay that had the acumen to acquire land with a view to profitting" (SSF 10/12). The official position was "to secure to his heirs their hereditary rights . . . (the enactment) would at the same time be a strong inducement towards permanent settlement in the State" (SSF 3170/10, no. 37). Thus colonial policy intervened to safeguard the political economic conditions whereby local and immigrant Malays, threatened with the loss of land, could be reconstituted into a land-owning peasantry sheltered from the more disruptive forces of the nascent capitalist system.

Other measures to ensure a "Malay yeomanry" included restrictions on cultivation of cash crops in order to "preserve" the purported *kampung* character of Malay lands and reinforce the assigned role of Malays as food-producers. Such rules governing cash cropping in fact arrested a self-generated movement among Malay smallholders to grow rubber in places unsuitable for rice, and, more critically, to benefit from the high prices for the commodity. In Selangor land offices, the registrations of Malay "ancestral lands" (*tanah pesaka*) were accompanied by a "non-rubber" condition. District officers claimed that this restriction made Malay lands less attractive to non-Malays, thus forestalling the temptation to sell or purchase *kampung* holdings (SSF 3170/10). Planting restrictions were reinforced by a graded system of taxation for cultivated plots in Malay Reservations; newly alienated plots with rubber trees were most highly taxed (Lim T.G. 1977: 116). Despite such legal constraints, rural Malays over the next decades took up production of rubber and coconut, which provided the cash needed by peasants increasingly dependent on the market economy.

British "Protection" and the Image of "Indolence"

The Reservations Act not only set aside Malay lands and ensured the Malays' continued existence as a peasantry, but it also gave political-legal substance to Malay ethnic identity, thus shaping the Malays' role and location within the political economy for decades to come. As early as 1900, the Resident-General of the FMS had elaborated this role vis-à-vis the colonial master:

> The principal industry, that of mining, being practically controlled by the Chinese and a few Europeans, it has been asked what has British protection done for the Native peasantry, "the real Malay." The reply is that it has given him security for life, and property, unknown before to the common people, when wives, daughters and orchards were at the hands of the aristocracy. . . . In return, the only contribution he makes to the Government revenue is a very small annual quit-rent, if he is a landowner. . . . The only complaint he can make is that the British advisers have not *forced* him to become industrious by making him work after the manner of the Dutch with their natives in the East Indies. (FMS AR 1900: 10)

Thus political gratitude and servitude came together in the legal construction of a specific set of relationships between Malays, the land, and the market economy. Colonial hegemony structured the circumtances of Malay life but also conditioned discourse on the "indolent Malay." In the sport of native watching, colonial officials were continually struck by the self-determination Malays displayed in the conduct of their everyday life. *Kampung* activities, unregulated by disciplinary procedures in which British civil servants felt at home, were viewed as evidence of cultural backwardness and natural dependency befitting subject populations. Swettenham, drawing upon the cumulative weight of colonial soul-searching, declared firmly that the Peninsular Malay was "unquestionably opposed to continuous work." He attributed this "inherent laziness" to precolonial experiences in which wealth accumulation invited expropriation (S. Hussein Alatas 1977: 44–45). Another colonial officer, Hugh Clifford, saw Malays as a thirteenth century people propelled so forcibly into the nineteenth century that they were "apt to become morally weak and seedy." Such colonial observations of native disregard for clock-time and the assumed equation of unregulated activity with moral laxity echoed bureaucratic warnings about policing the "lower orders" back home in Great Britain.[9] However, hegemonic constitution of the social attributes of subject populations operates in complex ways, depending on the particular alignment of relations of domination and subordination. Whereas in England enclosures, poor laws and new institutions such as mass education gradually bent the freeborn Englishmen to the requirements of industrial discipline, in nineteenth century British Malaya, the reconstituted "Malay yeomen," sheltered within legally-demarcated Reservations, were celebrated for their self-directed activities as "Nature's gentlemen." There is a grudging respect in Clifford's complaint that "the Malay never works if he can help it, and often will not suffer himself to be induced or tempted into doing so by offers of the most extravagant wages" (1927: 19).

A Malay scholar, S. Hussein Alatas, maintains that the "myth of the lazy native" was "merely a veiled resentment against Malay unwillingness to become a tool for enriching colonial planters" (1977: 81). On the contrary, I would argue that the simultaneous images of Malays as both indolent and free, outside the constraints of colonial capitalist transformation, were part of an elaborate, racist ideology lending powerful moral legitimation to British "Protection." An urban intellectual writing *The Malays in Malaya: By One of Them* in 1928 employed native symbolisms to Malayize what was essentially a

British construction. Haji Abdul Majid b. Bainuddin warned:

> It is dangerous for the featherless young chickens like ourselves,
> they would say, to move about alone when there are hawks and
> eagles hovering about ready to pounce upon them (1928: 93).

The colonial master was essential for guarding Malays from ''predatory'' aliens in the changing wilderness wrought by capitalism. It is within the British ''divide-and-rule'' framework — the Malays to be food-producing peasants and not traders or wage laborers — that the image of native indolence must be examined (including racist images of alcoholic Tamils and brutish, drug-addicted, and grasping Chinese). Indeed, within the artifically shielded peasant society, Malay daily activities were attuned to a rhythm different from the forced-march pace of capitalist development which controlled and regulated the lives of Chinese and Indian laborers.

Malay Peasants Under Colonialism: the View from Below

Colonial records have often lent themselves to varied interpretations of changes in the dominated society, whether the subject is native ''character,'' female status, or grassroots protests against imposed rules and regulations. Thus, an Ester Boserup can claim, despite contradicting evidence, that European rule of African and Asian societies brought about the decline of women's participation in agricultural production (1970). In Malaysian historiography, it was not until recently that local historians challenged the accepted view that Malay peasants had been politically passive under colonial rule and capitalist domination.[10]

To avoid the distortions of the top-down view of gender and power relations under colonialism, it is necessary to seek out local practices buried within the imposed coherence of colonial records. The cumulative effect of colonial policies governing Malay settlers, land, and cultivation was to reconstitute rural Malays into petty commodity producers dependent on the market for their survival and long-term reproduction. This transition was not merely a shift along the continuum from subsistence production to market specialization, as some scholars have argued (Firth 1966; Lim T.G. 1977), but a qualitative change in the social character of the peasantry. Most critically, colonial legalization of land as private property set into motion differential access to land, enforcing the peasant transition from the production of use values to the production of exchange values (commodities and labor-power) destined for capitalist circuits of exchange. How did village women, men, and children adapt to market forces and colonial control? What were the tactics and strategies they employed to survive in circumstances beyond their control?

Cash Cropping Smallholders: Surviving Economic Crises

Ecological conditions and colonial policies shaped the patchwork of Malay crop cultivations in Selangor (and elsewhere in the Malay states). As small-scale producers of rubber, coconut, and even rice, *kampung* households were now reproduced within the matrix of an expanding capitalist system. Exposed to the fluctuations of the world market, village households evolved a set of practices which enabled families to respond in a flexible manner to economic crises. Domestic labor deployment was finely tuned to local contingencies and price fluctuations. However, the very ability of *kampung* households to balance multiple economic activities and survive depressions instilled a false sense of peasant autonomy which persisted even as local Malay society became internally differentiated.

In Kuala Langat, where ecological conditions were unfavorable to rice cultivation, most of the communities founded by immigrant Malays established smallholdings of coconut, coffee, and rubber (see Table 2).[11] Since these settlers did not produce the staple, they were much more vulnerable than rice-growing peasants to volatile market forces. Rubber/coconut smallholders had to be flexible in their responses to changing prices for their cash crops, food, and other consumer items. It became imperative for peasant households to allocate limited resources and labor among different economic activities so that they could shift between limited food production and wage work to minimize losses to the domestic economy throughout the decades from the 1920s to the 1950s when the rubber market went through spectacular swings from very high to low prices. Such alternation between different tasks generated an increasing individuation of interests within the household economy.

Smallholding production of rubber itself was an individual operation which could be alternated with other *kampung* activities. The crop was easily adopted by Malay peasants because it entitled little starting capital — seedlings, tapping knives, cups, buckets, and perhaps

Table 2

Crop Acreage in Selangor, 1933–1948

Crop Grown	1933	1938	1948
Rubber (e,s)	503,000	511,977	503,704
Coconut (e,s)	111,900	117,905	119,707
Oil palm (s)	20,300	21,404	21,723
Tea (e)	790	1,680	2,137
Rice (s)	30,000	15,646	51,186
Kampong crops	23,000	24,536	15,996
Coffee (s)	6,600	8,148	n.d.
Pineapple (s)	7,500	6,560	3,333

(Source: SAR 1933, 1938, 1948)
  e: estate crop
  s: smallholder crop
  n.d.: no data

hand-mangles for rolling sheets. The trees could be scattered among other tree crops and, with little attention, would produce latex for twenty or more years. The procedures of bleeding trees every other day, collecting the milky liquid dripped into cups, and coagulating the latex for flattening into sheets were simple repetitive activities which could be done by individuals on their own. Wet rubber sheets were treated in smokehouses operated by Chinese dealers or left on roads to be dried. The possibility of collecting and selling rubber every few days, and the "short-term labor elasticity" of the peasant rubber enterprise, enabled the peasant family to shift to other cash-earning activities whenever rubber prices fell, without incurring major loss (Ooi 1959: 147).

Thus, world commodities prices, rather than credit-hunger, were the primary determinants of supplementary activities pursued by rubber and coconut peasants.[12] The survival strategy of the rubber peasant family is inscribed in its *kebun*, where rubber stands gradually merged into fruit and spice trees surrounding the homestead. In times of bad rubber prices, the household increased its stock of minor crops for sale and for home consumption. The elliptical space — *karangan* — of minor crops was by custom and preference women's responsibility. Javanese settlers had from the earliest days intercropped pineapple, bananas, and coffee among their maturing cash trees. By the late 1930s, over 10,000 coconut holdings had been intercropped with coffee in Kuala Langat (SAR 1936: 37). Peasant women tended and harvested the coffee trees. They also helped the men to depulp and dry the cherries in order to gain better prices for their secondary crop. These peasants were thus less badly affected by falling copra prices than local Malay families who derived all their income from coconut alone.

Food crops were even more critical whenever low market prices and government ban on rubber production drove cash cropping peasants back into subsistence production. Throughout the depression years (1929–33), many peasants cut down their less productive rubber trees to grow tapioca, sweet potatoes, and bananas. In some cases, almost three-quarters of rubber holdings were replaced by garden crops tended by women (SAR 1932: 15). Coconut smallholders in Kuala Langat who had neglected to raise minor crops were forced to subsist on only one meal a day (Lim T.G. 1977: 197-199). During the Japanese Occupation 1942–45), many rubber stands were abandoned while peasants reverted to the production of food crops and rice cultivation in the swamps of Kuala Langat.

The prior demands of activities meeting home consumption needs rather than market demands were reflected in domestic reorganization of labor. Women and men turned to food-production and fishing, leaving the old and very young to tap rubber trees which were sometimes multilated in attempts to extract more latex (SAR 1932: 15). Peasant women also dominated the "eight flourishing markets" where they sold eggs, tobacco, poultry, and homecooked foods (SAR 1932: 20; SAR 1938: 199). This pattern of oscillating between cash cropping and raising foodstuffs continued into the postwar depression, when Malay rubber smallholders produced about two-fifths of their own food requirments (Bauer 1948: 84).

Colonial records seldom contain references to village children, except those concerning rural hygiene and nutrition. In going over rural health records, I found this rare reference:

> (O)ne very often comes across an isolated house in charge of a little girl aged eight or nine. The father and mother are away at work during the day. She scarcely moves from the house until the parents return at night. She cooks and washes for three

or four younger brothers and sisters, their only food being rice and sauce and occasionally a bit of dried fish or a few green vegetables (SAR 1936: 20).

In the same year, a separate report on ''schoolboys'' in Sungai Jawa noted that in a number of households fresh fish was eaten once a week, but meat or eggs were seldom consumed (being reserved for the market). Rice was taken garnished with greens, but many children went to school without a meal.

Besides not consuming food which could be sold, young children helped in household chores as well as in tending livestock, fetching firewood and water, and in different field tasks, thereby releasing their parents for wage work. Women engaged in domestic industries — such as making thatch (*atap*), preparing soybean cakes (*tempe*), and cooking palm sugar (*gula jawa*) — were assisted by their children (SAR 1935: 19; SAR 1936: 144–145). During *Ramadan*, when younger children did not fast, they helped their mothers in tapping rubber trees while the men undertook heavier work in the fields (Bauer 1948: 67).

With children taking over house chores, adult men and women could participate in different kinds of short-term employment within and without the village economy. *Kampung* women took in sewing and laundry for richer households. Others earned additional income as midwives (*bidan*) or bridal attendants, but these skills required prior training. Women abandoned by men may have been forced into domestic service in nearby towns. Men brought in additional cash by working as temporary village barbers, part-time carpenters, or taxi-drivers. Others operated outside *kampung* society as itinerant peddlers, marketing agents for Chinese merchants, and even engaged in clandestine trade with the Sumatran coast. Others joined road crews, transportation workers, or plantation labor gangs whenever additional cash was needed. Such extraordinary income-earning activities could be started up or folded up easily, depending on the family need for cash and the current price of cash crops. Given limited peasant capital and perception of these activities as stopgap measures, few households pursued sideline occupations for long. Once market prices for their crops improved, these activities were phased out.

The ability of the Malay village household to adapt to fluctuating market prices by allocating family labor among multiple subsistence and cash-earning activities ultimately minimized losses and ensured the long-term survival of the domestic economy. Since the production of minor crops, petty trade, and irregular wage work were elements in a strategy for surviving market fluctuations and government curtailment of peasant rubber production, village Malays were not able to accumulate capital to bring about the rise of Malay capitalist farmers. Instead, the short-term multiple activities of peasant women, men, and children contributed to a false sense of household autonomy from market forces and accounted for the relative political quiescence of Malay peasants throughout the colonial period of boom and bust in the rubber industry.

Rubber, Peasant Protest, and Incipient Social Differentiation

Rubber, the tree crop that perpetually bleeds latex-wealth, provided the basis for the great British plantation industry in the Malay States. Even a few Chinese and Indian immigrants, stripped of all but their labor power, lived through the transformative effects of the rubber industry to become capitalist farmers. For local and immigrant Malays, rubber gave germination to a sprawling checkerboard of miniature cash tree holdings. They ultimately formed the verdant reserve of an irregular labor reserve for capitalist enterprises in the waning years of colonial rule.

The expanding rubber industry and immigrant flows from the Netherlands territories planted the seeds of social differentiation within Malay reservations. Small divisions existed between local Malays and paupers from the archipelago, between "free" immigrant Malays and those who arrived as contract laborers.[13] However, severe colonial restrictions on smallholding rubber production and the growth of a Malay civil service simultaneously limited capital accumulation while fostering the rise of a small number of Malay rentiers in *kampung* society.

S. Husin Ali observes in his study of "social stratification" in Kampung Bagan, Johore, that early Javanese settlers who gained control over large tracts of land could utilize *wong tebusan* came to constitute the first village landlord group. Later arrivals and contract workers receiving small parcels or no land at all formed the landless poor (1964: 37). For a number of reasons given in the oral histories of Javanese settlers in Kuala Langat, I would argue that this early pattern of differentiation was relatively unstable. The operation of Islamic inheritance rules, frequently modified to award equal shares of property to daughters and sons in the pioneer settlements, reduced extreme inequality in land access by the second generation. Also, daughters with landed property attracted landless but able-bodied immigrants who were absorbed by marriage into families rich in holdings. Finally, many of the earlier settlers sold off part or entire holdings to undertake the pilgrimage to Mecca (see also Ramsay 1956: 122; SAR 1936: 142). I maintain that neither prior arrival by settlers nor rubber-wealth deepened incipient differentiation within Malay Reservations during the colonial period. It was rather the progressive penetration of the state system and the rise of a class of Malay civil servants which on the eve of independence came to provide structural continuity in differential access to village resources and power.

Under colonial rule, cash cropping Malays not only learnt to survive market crises but also had to continually defend their ground against administrative policies which worked against their interests. The linked cycles of economic depression and colonial restrictions on peasant rubber-production prevented Malay rubber-growers benefitting from the rubber boom. Throughout the 1920s, world market prices fell while British Malaya faced stiff competition from other rubber-producing countries. The colonial government introduced two schemes which restricted the extension of planted acreage as well as overall production output, discriminating more severely against the peasant sector than the plantation industry in both cases. The Stevenson Restriction Scheme (1922–28) prohibited new planting of rubber except on reserve land, which the estates held in supply. Malay peasants, who had almost no reserve land, engaged in illegal planting of the crop (Bauer 1948: 14). From 1928 until the war broke out in 1941, only a very small number of lots were alienated to peasants for rubber growing (in 1928–30 and 1939–40); otherwise, new planting was banned.

Smallholder rubber output was also drastically curtailed by planters underassessing smallholding capacity and authorizing very low levels of peasant output (Lim T.G. 1974: 139–154). Malay peasant resistance to cultivation restrictions not only took the form of widespread illegal plantings and sales[14] but also of petitioning the British Resident. In 1924, 26 Malay villagers from Klang, including nine women, signed a letter protesting

> (w)e are the people of this country. . . . By hard labour we have managed to open up a few acres of land, which is life and death to us, and we consider ourselves now worse off than before the

> rubber restriction. . . . We do not mean to say that those Euro-
> pean planters who have inspected our areas are bad-hearted
> people, but they should be sympathetic in our case, for our
> "kebun" could not be so well and cleanly kept as their own
> estates (SSF 1138/24).

In fact, as Bauer points out, "when production (of rubber) was un-
restricted annual average yields per mature acre on Malayan smallholdings were 12–30 percent higher than on estates" (1948: 80). The
low cost of peasant rubber production posed a formidable challenge
to the plantation industry, with its heavy overcosts and huge resident
labor force (see also Lee 1973).

Thus, while rubber, more than any other crop, could have provided
the basis for the emergence of an indigenous class of capitalist farmers, complex schemes of restrictions on land alienation, peasant production quotas, and the wild fluctuations of rubber prices (see Table
3) meant that the peasant advantage in production costs did not
become the means for indigenous capital accumulation. Ultimately,
the low cost of peasant production contributed to the extraordinary
rubber revenues of the colonial state and the extended reproduction
of the colonial capitalist economy.

By the late colonial period, differentiation in access to village resources deepened, not because of rubber ironically, but as a result
of the growing state system. Although the vast majority of Malay peasants continued to operate holdings of under five acres (SAR 1935: 19),
a very small group of Malay civil servants had become medium-sized
(over ten-acre lot) landowners in village society. Their special connections to the state bureaucracy enabled this salaried elite — teachers,
health inspectors, policemen, and a few businessmen — to participate
in land speculation and live off rent as absentee landlords. Besides
providing regular incomes, government service was also a means of
access to state subsidies for rubber replanting. This emergent Malay
bureaucratic elite, basking in the glow cast by official and landowner
status, did not invest capital to increase labor productivity on village
land. Neither did they engage in the reorganization of rubber production; instead they merely rented their holdings to sharecroppers
who had to supply their own knives, buckets, and sickles (Bauer 1948:
28–29). In effect, land speculation and absentee landlordism led to
poor cultivation techniques and low quality in village rubber output.
Retiring government officials settled in their village houses while rent-

Table 3

*Prices Obtained by Kampung Malay Smoked Sheet Rubber,
Selangor, 1932-1958*

Year	Price Range (M dollars) per picul (133.3 lbs)
1932 (Depression)	$ 5.00 – 10.00
1933	5.50 – 19.00
1934	17.65 – 31.00
1935	22.00 – 28.00
1936	25.00 – 44.00
1937	n.d.
1938	24.00 – 35.00
(World War II years)	n.d.
1948	42.50 – 56.60
1951	133.00
1952	113.00
1955 (Korean War boom)	127.00 – 185.68
1958	93.00

Sources: *Calculated from the Selangor Annual Reports* (1932-38), The *Federated Malay States Annual Report* (1951-1955), and Ooi 1959:155 for the 1958 figure. (Average rubber price for that year was estimated at 70 cents per pound).
n.d. — no data

ing other properties, thereby contributing to the spread of rentier parasitism on peasant society. Michael Swift points out that this process of differentiation, induced by the penetration of the state bureaucracy, accelerated after independence in 1957, when land concentration in Malay Reservations continued "the transfer of peasant land to an upper official class" without effecting the transition to capitalist agriculture within Malay society (1967: 254).

In the postwar years, communist insurgency (officially known as "the Emergency," 1948–60) against the reimposition of British rule dramatically increased wage employment for rural Malays in the capitalist sector. As early as the 1930s, the public works department of the colonial bureaucracy had begun to recruit village Malays to supplement their teams of Tamil workers (SAR 1936: 61). It was, however, the communist insurgency which, by violently disrupting labor or-

Table 4

Ethnic and Sexual Division of Estate Workers,
Selangor, 1948

Ethnic Group	Men	Women
Indians	21,668	18,742
Chinese	5,292	7,272
Javanese	2,362	737
Others	34	29
Total	29,356	26,780

(Source: SAR 1948:20)

ganization in capitalist enterprises, provided the conditions for drawing rural Malays more deeply into wage employment. In Selangor, peasant men left *kampung* holdings in the care of women while they joined the Special Police or military forces. During the first year of "the Emergency," repeated guerilla attacks on smallholdings and the withdrawal of rural men for lucrative jobs in the security forces caused the rate of tapping in the smallholding sector to decline from 75 percent to 62 percent. In Klang, labor strikes by Chinese dockworkers led to the recruitment of 150 Malays as stevedores (SAR 1948: 19). Similarly, Chinese plantation workers suspected of being infiltrated by communists were repatriated to China and replaced by Javanese workers in Klang and Kuala Langat district. Among the Malay-Javanese workers employed in Selangor plantations, almost 30 percent were female (see Table 4). Thus it took severe disruptions of the operation of the "plural economy" for Malay peasants to be released on a large-scale into the capitalist sector. As a colonial bureaucrat blandly noted, the prewar "Malay reluctance" to work in plantations and mines had been replaced by "an ever increasing interest in local industry and commerce . . . The Emergency gave a slight impetus to this tendency to engage Malays in preference to Chinese" (SAR 1948: 35). Malay entry into sustained wage employment involved substituting for members of the other two major ethnic groups already well-entrenched in capitalist production.

From the perspective of the *kampung* household, short-term wage employment in the plantation economy made most sense in relation to fluctuations in commodities prices on the world market. Low rubber prices at the beginning of "the Emergency" helped to push many peasant men into estate work. In contrast, during the Korean War boom in the early 1950s, the number of Malay workers in plantations throughout the Malay States fell from 70,000 to 66,000 because of a "movement back to self-employment in the *kampong*" (FMAR 1950). It was estimated that rubber production in smallholdings increased by 42,000 tons, which would have required over 30,000 additional workers. Thus, when commodities prices were high, cash cropping peasants could earn good incomes and perhaps accumulate some wealth, without having to resort to wage employment. Even sharecropping earnings in *kampung* exceeded those paid in plantations, where female tappers were paid at 75 percent of male wages (FMAR 1952: 36–37).

Thus, as long as Malay peasants still controlled village resources, they could resist being utilized as a major labor reserve for the plantation economy. Such a situation could prevail only as long as progressive social differentiation was held in check by land fragmentation through Islamic inheritance rules, sharecropping practices, and the low productivity of peasant holdings. However, since the 1960s, the greater integration of *kampung* society into the wider economy and state system has accentuated forces for irreversible dispersal of Malay rural workers throughout the wider society, even if still attached to *kampung* moorings.

The imposition of British colonial rule over the Malay States drew Malay peasants into the volatile circuits of the capitalist world economy. Despite strenuous policies to remake local and immigrant Malays into a "food-producing yeomanry," sheltered within Reservations and celebrated for their "indolence" as well as "natural inclinations," rural Malays became producers of rubber and coconut demanded by world markets. Even as colonial authorities benefitted from the vast rubber revenues, successive attempts were made to arrest the expansion of the peasant rubber sector at the expense of the foreign-dominated plantation industry. Colonial policies limited alienation of jungle land and curtailed rubber production but failed to halt the progressive transformation of rural Malays into petty commodity producers. Increasingly dependent on the market to sell their crops and to buy manufactured goods, village households evolved multiple-occupational strategies to spread risks and minimize loss; few were able to accumulate wealth. As peasant men fanned out in search of wage employment in the wider economy, salaried bureaucrats gained increasing control of village land for speculation and for rent. By the eve of independence, which was itself negotiated for by aristocratic Malay officials, the local residence and power of Malay civil servants had begun to increase social differentiation within rural society.

PART II

The *Kampung* Society of Coastal Selangor

The process, humourously designated by statisticians as 'the tendency of the rural population towards large towns,' being really the tendency of water to flow uphill when forced by machinery.

Thomas Hardy
Tess of the d'Urbervilles

But what was the use of beauty to farmers' daughters. . . . Men did not look for beauty when they asked for a wife. Let those daughters of hers grow dark. Let the soles of their feet grow pale and have a thousand cracks. People would still ask for their hands.

Shahnon Ahmad
Malaysian Novelist
No Harvest but a Thorn

Chapter 3

Tropical Confluences: Rural Society, Capital, and the State

Driving into *mukim* Telok, Kuala Langat, one passes into the stagnant spaces of endless plantations. Obliquely receding rubber trees are interrupted at intervals by estates of equidistanced oil palms, the favored postwar industrial crop. Relief is in sight when the agribusiness monotony is broken by coconut trees like welcoming banners disclosing Malay *kampung* nestled within the plantation country.

This chapter delineates the changing pattern of village life within the structures of corporate capitalism and state intervention. In the two decades since independence from Great Britain, the fabric of *kampung* society has become more firmly woven into the broader cloth of national society and capitalist economy. We will consider how village land in Kuala Langat is no longer simply the basis for *kampung* livelihood and social order. The expansion of the state bureaucracy, political parties, and capitalist enterprises, facilitated by a fine communications system, has elaborated disparate mechanisms of control, channels of mobility, and new modes of thinking for *kampung* folk in the district.

A New Tropical Configuration: *Kebun, Ladang,* and Free Trade Zone

In official parlance, village holdings or *kebun,* usually under five acres, are designated "smallholdings," while any agricultural enterprise beyond 100 acres in size is labeled "estate/plantation" (*ladang*). Kuala Langat in the 1970s still bore the stamp of its colonial landscape: Malay cash cropping *kampung* along the coast and margins of Euro-

37

pean and Chinese plantations which form a thick belt along the foot-
hills further inland. A winding trunk road feeding off the four-lane
highway between Kuala Lumpur and Port Klang leads into the plantation country. Its destinations are Telok Datok, the district capital, and
its uneasy Chinese twin, Banting, which expanded almost overnight
from the influx of squatter Chinese during the Emergency. (see Map 2)

The tertiary and commercial networks linking *kampung* and *ladang*
are complemented by the system of state bureaucracy. A parallel political structure has been established by the United Malays National
Organization (UMNO) party, the dominant Malay faction of the ruling National Front coalition in Kuala Lumpur (K.L.), the national
capital. From the District Office of Telok Datok, the day-to-day administration is in the hands of the *penghulu*. As the lowest state official, he oversees land and rural development projects and acts as
a political broker in his *mukim* (subdistrict).

Map 2
Kuala Langat: Land Use, Towns and Transportation Lines to the Klang Valley

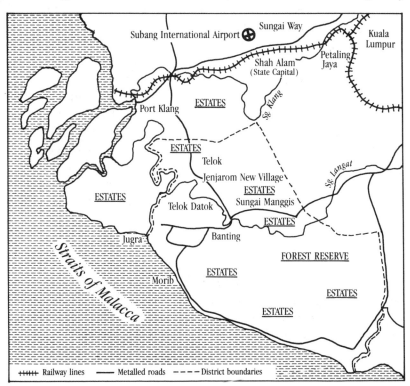

The penetration of the UMNO party and its inseparable identity with local government is reflected in rural political organization. Since 1972, villagers can no longer elect their own headman or village committee. Instead, the District Officer (D.O.), as the most important UMNO leader in the district, selects UMNO members as village headmen (*ketua kampung*). These are informal but critical grassroots links between ordinary people and state party officials. In turn, the *ketua kampung* favors UMNO members in his nomination of village elders to sit on the village committee (JKK, i.e., *Jawatan Kuasa Kampung*). A village identified as "pro-UMNO" is assured favored considerations in the distribution of government resources. Furthermore, UMNO village leaders receive a cut of state subsidies, construction projects, and other programs for the "development" — *pembangunan* — of rural Malays under the New Economic Policy.[1]

Between 1979 and 1980, I conducted field research in Telok, a subdistrict of some 32,000 acres under Malay Reservations, estates, and residual forest reserves. There are five *kampung* in the *mukim*. I resided in Sungai Jawa (a pseudonym), the focus of my field investigation, made regular visits to the other *kampung*, and travelled to communities throughout the district and along the coast.

Within the *mukim*, Kampung Telok is the miniature commercial and administrative center. Malay teachers and civil servants reside there, while Chinese and Malabari merchants handle their marketing, retailing, and credit businesses. A rural flavor still adheres to Kampung Telok: Malay stilt houses, orchards of *rambutan* and *durian*, and the truncated line of two-story shophouses. However, the township is newly girded by rows of concrete houses, the anonymous blocks which have come to stand for "development" in so many third world cities. Across an open space of red earth, the "low cost housing" points, as if indicating its intended center, to a palm oil factory, owned by Malay aristocracy, and a "free trade zone" (FTZ).[2] Road services have been improved to connect the town to Port Klang and the International Airport. The biggest village crop seems to be schoolleavers who have been identified as a labor reserve for Malaysian industrialization. In the bureaucratic language of the state development agency:

> Industrialization on the periphery of the Klang Valley . . . would put the vast pool of rural manpower to good use and would help

diversify an economy traditionally dependent on export of primary commodities (SSDC 1976: 19).

The FTZ has been sited to attract transnational capital, to invest not in agriculture but in manpower. Since 1972, three Japanese microcomponent assembly factories have sustained a labor force of 2,000. These are predominantly young women from the *kampung*, recruited to turn out millions of microcomponents every day. Administered urbanization has thus arrived in this region of declining Malay smallholder economy. The district has become a contested terrain between Malay villagers, national corporate interests, and foreign capital. The story of the industrial impact on *kampung* life and culture is told from Chapter 4 onwards, following our mapping of changes in agrarian relations and political life in the district.

A Colonial Legacy

> The most important thing [about my job] is to control labor.
>
> The workers are so encaged that if given freedom, they would not know how to take care of themselves.
>
> It is sad the laborers are so oppressed but you get used to it.
>
> > A Malay field assistant, an Indian field assistant, and a Chinese engineer on a British plantation.

In the postwar decades, changes in the world commodities market have been reflected in the local reorganization of plantation industry and *kampung* economy. From the late 1960s onward, declining prices have led to the reduction of total rubber acreage in the district from 66,670 acres in 1966 to just 12,800 in 1978 (see Table 5). Plantations initiated the shift to oil palm production as prices for the product rose steadily. Besides, oil palm cultivation does not require a permanent labor force, as was the case with rubber estates.

The shifting regime of different tree crops in the district masks the progressive loss of *kampung* land to urbanization and expanding capitalist enterprises. The total cultivated area of the district became roughly divided between plantations and smallholdings in the ratio of 6 to 4 (see Table 5). It is necessary here to sketch a picture of the plantation system which encircles Malay smallholding villages and remains the heart of the Malaysian economy.

Table 5
Acreage Under Cash Crops in Kuala Langat, 1966-1978

Crops	Estates		Smallholdings**	
	*1966**	*1978*	*1966**	*1978*
Oil palm	21,254	41,184	2,948	14,825
Rubber	39,377	9,825	27,300	2,978
Tea	1,162	645	—	—
Coconut	1,276	—	18,455	15,984
Coffee	—	—	7,141	8,984
Cocoa	—	69	—	2,970
Totals	63,069	51,723	55,844	45,741

Sources: *Laporan Tahunan: Jabatan Pertanian Selangor,* 1966 & 1978.

*The total land ara of the district was larger in 1966 than in 1978 because the redrawing of coastal lines had reduced the Kuala Langat share by about 6,270 acres. However, change in acreage under various crops was caused by changing patterns of land use rather than by boundary adjustments. Coffee and cocoa were intercrops and occupied the same land space accounted for coconuts.

**Smallholdings included commercial gardens under one hundred acres owned by Chinese and Indians as well as Malays.

Table 6
Estimated Average Monthly Incomes from Malay Holdings, Kuala Langat, 1979

Crop	Income/Acre
Coconut-coffee	M$ 100
Rubber	80
Oil Palm	160–250*
Cocoa	160*

Source: Agricultural Extension Officer, Telok Datok, Kuala Langat.

*When regularly infused with chemical fertilizers (which cost about M$ 350 each year at government-subsidized prices).

There are over 21 major European plantations in Kuala Langat, operated by companies which control estates elsewhere in the Peninsula. For instance, just offshore is Carey Island which, except for tiny *orang asli* (aboriginal) and forest reserves, is entirely owned by Harrisons and Crosfield. The company operates three plantations (80 percent under oil palm) covering some 26,000 square miles. As a bastion of colonial days, the island is equipped with offices, mill, clinics, school, a golf course, a sports club with a Tudor facade, and English cottages.

The plantation system is stratified into at least seven tiers of occupational rank, almost color-coded by ethnicity. Two of the estates are still headed by British managers, followed by a senior assistant, three field assistants (each in charge of a division), field conductors (administering the work force and pay budget), and field *mandur* (leaders of labor gangs). Whereas the supervisory staff is multiethnic, the last two categories consist mainly of Tamils. However, the plantation labor composition is rapidly changing because of changeover to oil palm and cutback on labor cost. Compared to the tens of thousands of workers required for rubber production in the 1960s, only a remnant labor force of 277 Tamil workers and their families continues to reside in barracks on each estate. In September 1979, the average take-home pay of the general laborer was M$120 per month, thus making the resident estate worker the true rural proletariat in the country (see e.g., Kusnic and DaVanzo 1980:66 for statistical measures of household incomes).

Increasingly, the plantations rely on outside labor groups brought in by 16 labor contractors (mainly Chinese) to harvest and transport heavy bunches of the scarlet nuts twice a month. Each gang consists of 25 male laborers, many Malay, who are paid 20 percent of the collective wage, or 15 cents for cutting down each bunch. Thus, one-third of the plantation labor force (400 out of 1,231) is now recruited from the surrounding *kampung*, which have become a labor reserve for the plantation industry.

Within these villages, the average *kebun* is getting smaller; in Sungai Jawa, most coconut-coffee holdings are 3.5 acres in size. Government statistics for poverty among coconut growers in the country is around 50 percent (*Third Malaysia Plan* 1976: 72). In Kuala Langat, many of the coconut trees are old and peasants have been encouraged to rely on secondary crops for additional income. In 1979, the estimated monthly incomes from the various crops grown by peasants put oil palm at the top of the list: M$160 per acre (see Tabel 6). This means that a family would still require at least a two-acre holding to live on the edge of "poverty" — officially defined at living below the national standard of nutritional health and the satisfaction of basic needs in clothing, housing, and education (ibid.). Besides, most families in Sungai Jawa, for which I conducted four major surveys, had around six to seven members, i.e., those who engaged in some form of sharing and joint, if episodic, residence. Obviously, the declining importance of *kampung* holding, as a basic source of livelihood or means for structuring critical production relations, is a reality which is at the very heart of the crisis Malay villagers confront.

Rural Malays, Land Hunger, and Bureaucratic Capitalism

> What happens to my family? Do we have to live in the sea? Here I am, a man who has served the King and country for 16 years, without an inch of land to my name. I am clearly a deserving case for land. But to whom does the land go? Rich people, that's who! It makes my blood boil to see wealthy people and people who have not even stayed in this area get land while landless people like us have to suffer.
>
> Malay villager and ex-serviceman
> Darat Batu, Kuala Langat
> *New Straits Times,* Oct. 5, 1979

Despite a decline in the immigrant flows immediately following independence,[3] the rural Malay population in the Peninsula has been increasing rapidly ever since. By 1976, there were a total of 5.5 million Malays (including immigrants from the Indonesian islands), of whom 82 percent resided in the countryside, where the rate of population growth was the highest (*Third Malaysia Plan* 1976: 1949-50). Kuala Langat was no exception in this general demographic trend. During "the Emergency," many rural Chinese and Indians were forcibly relocated into "New Villages"; and after 1960, many non-Malays voluntarily resettled in Klang Valley as urban wage workers. Within twenty years, as Malays came to constitute half of the population in the district, demographic and economic pressures intensified competition for resources within and without the Reservations.

At the *kampung* level, two processes made for constraints in peasant access to land: (i) the operation of Islamic inheritance rules, and (ii) the increasing aggregation of village holdings by civil servants and capitalists. Under the Islamic rules of devolution, holdings are divided, usually after the death of both parents, into equal shares for sons and half shares for daughters.[4] The effects of these rules were to reduce holdings to uneconomical parcels by the second or third generation. A common situation is the legal fragmentation of single lots into so many shares that it is no longer feasible to physically divide the holding or renew the crops. In that case, coinheritors simply share-crop the joint property and share the rent. Alternately, married sisters living elsewhere would let their brothers manage the undivided property in return for a small portion of the farm income.

My survey of 242 households in Sungai Jawa shows that the average holding in 1979 was just below 3.5 acres. However, this figure disguises the fact that almost 24 percent of the sampled housholds owned no land or only had a house-lot. Only 27 percent of households owned properties between two and five acres, the farm size which would sustain a family of six. Fifty-four percent of the total acreage surveyed was controlled by 12% of the households (see Table 7, Chapter 4).

Since Malays are Muslims, all families are affected by the process of land fragmentation through the implementation of Islamic inheritance law. However, villagers or new arrivals with access to external sources of income can counteract this levelling effect on the distribution of village resources over time. Rich villagers can use surplus farm incomes, savings from trade, and interest from loans to purchase additional holdings, locally and elsewhere. Sixteen of the richest households together controlled 343 acres (about 40 percent of which lay outside Sungai Jawa but in nearby villages) dispersed into more than fifty separate and noncontiguous parcels. One copra merchant owned eight separate lots, totalling 22 acres. Although most of his coconut trees were old, he recently used his savings not to renew his crop but to buy low-quality rubber land in lower Perak, renting it out to local sharecroppers.

Like rich peasants, civil servants also acquire village land in piecemeal fashion for speculation. No attempts have been made in Sungai Jawa to consolidate multiple holdings, nor do landowners take a consistent interest in improving the quality of the crops and soil. The *kebun* are tended by sharecroppers whose main intent is to maximize extraction of the products. Whether civil servant or rich villager, landlords tend to place less importance on the quality of the tree crops than on the acquisition of multiple holdings, a practice which in itself is a measure of *kampung* prestige.

Population pressure, parcellization of holdings, and land accumulation have contributed to land hunger (*lapar tanah*) throughout the district. Men would scrutinize holdings rumored to be up for sale, comparing the relative value of the soils and tree crops. Coffee shop speculations revolve around which official or rich peasant would be the successful bidder for which piece of property.

By the 1970s, competition among the growing number of officials for *kampung* lands has overtaken the randomness of fortuitous purchases to produce a coordinated pattern of shared privileges. New land lots opened up under the "green revolution program" (*rancangan revolusi hijau*) intended for landless families in the district became prizes to be fought over through patron-client networks. In one case, a government clerk petitioned the land office to allocate 160 acres on the fringe of Kampung Telok to local applicants. Applicants were interviewed and selected through a lottery system. Nevertheless, the lots were eventually awarded to the clerk's relatives and friends — 62 Malays and 18 Chinese, many of whom were already property owners. A few of the successful applicants, unable to pay the premium (M$190), resold their land titles to rich villagers. In such fashion, some civil servants, teachers, and businessmen came to acquire additional property under the "green revolution program."

By the end of the decade, demand for land had built up to the degree that illegal squatting on plantation and state reserves was a widespread practice. The state government stepped up its plan to clear the remaining jungle reserves for the settlement of landless families.[5] In *mukim* Telok, the remaining 2,000-acre reserve was divided into two-acre lots for distribution to Malay residents in Sungai Jawa, Kampung Telok, and other villages. A village elder pointed out that the new lots could only settle one thousand families, whereas the actual number of landless families was much larger. As it was, many young couples with children were compelled to reside with their parents. But again, the distribution of new land lots ostensibly for landless families with many young children brought intense competition from the landrich few. To maximize their chances in the land lottery, *kampung* folk beat a path to the house of the local assemblyman (himself a large landowner). They recited a litany of past acts of loyalty which secured him his office; they appealed to his sense of Islamic fairness to sponsor their deserving applications. In a more subdued manner, members of the village JKK committee, who were assured of land grants, squabbled over the relative merits of individual parcels.

The growth of a market in village land has dramatically raised land values beyond any hope of purchase by most villagers. Even as early as 1962, the breakup of a 744-acre estate in the *mukim*, which went for M$800–M$1,200[6] per acre, was beyond the reach of the majority of local Malays and Indians. Most of the buyers of the two-, five-, and ten-acre lots were local Chinese and others from Klang. As one peasant remarked, the only "gain" of the estate breakup for local Malays was to be hired as laborers in the newly constituted smallholdings.

However, more recent sales of *kampung* holdings and newly cleared lots, confined to Malay buyers, have not benefitted the majority of Malay villagers either. In 1979, a scrub-covered three-acre lot in the recently cleared jungle reserve cost about M$8,000. A similar holding, already planted with young oil palm, fetched M$17,000. In Sungai Jawa, where the soils were richer and village life more attractive, a three-acre palm holding would cost over M$24,000, i.e.. M$8,000 an acre. These prices kept most but the salaried villagers out of the land market. Indeed, buyers included Malay civil servants from Klang and even Kuala Lumpur looking for bucolic settings to build second homes.

As the last reserves in Telok *mukim* were being divided up, competition for scarce land elsewhere in the district brought forth angry protests and confrontations between Malay peasants and state officials. The inequitable distribution of new land lots — 460 in the late 1970s — did not slake the land thirst. In 1981, for instance, the awarding of 120 four-acre lots to residents in Darat Batu and Darat Kundang was challenged by villagers who claimed that only 79 applicants had qualified under conditions set by the land office at Telok Datok. The protesters claimed that some of the successful applicants already owned houses and land. At least six of them, all teachers, were drawing salaries of over M$1,000 a month.[7] Confrontations with the state have also appeared over squatting and residential rights throughout the district.

Clandestine squatting has been a form of protest against the changing land market since the 1960s. Illegally cultivated plots are a fairly common feature in state lands such as areas marked off for road construction, housing, and jungle reserves. Before the current land crisis, state officers had turned a blind eye to squatters and been amply awarded with tea money, fresh vegetables, and exaggerated deference.

One such 500-acre tract, sandwiched between a Malay reservation and Brooklands Estate, had been planted with oil palm for the past decade. To forestall impending eviction and loss of a valuable crop, the 150 Malay and Chinese squatter families had filed for temporary occupational licenses (TOLs) from the district land office. State officials frown upon squatter cultivation of permanent crops like oil palm, because it would be difficult to evict them without paying compensation.

In October 1979, forest officers and police forcibly evicted the squatters by razing their huts and crops to the ground. Shocked by this brutal onslaught, the squatters complained to the press that their estimated material losses amounted to M$9,000 per family. Many had used their wives' jewelry or high-interest loans to purchase the palm seedlings. They had laborered over clearing the land. One squatter, harking back to a remembered custom, protested

> I persuaded my friends to leave the area peacefully as we had no choice although we couldn't take it . . . We are poor people and we believe we should be allowed to own the plots of land opened up by us.[8]

Throughout the district, this sudden eviction of squatters was widely believed to be linked to the impending exploitation of rich tin deposits (conservatively valued at M$4 billion in 1980) in the area. In 1979, a mining agency, the *Kumpulan Perangsang Selangor*, had been formed by 70 percent state interests and wealthy Malays to acquire 4,200 acres of Brooklands Estate for initial mining operations. Thus far, tin deposits have been discovered in 40,000 acres within the district, an area larger than the Kinta Valley, the major tin mining region in Malaysia.[9]

The contested terrain lies in the constituency of the Selangor Chief Minister who was on a pilgrimage to Mecca when the squatters were expelled. The eviction thus prevented the squatters' plight from developing into a major political issue. Furthermore, the suddenness of the takeover caught villagers by surprise and forestalled any move to raise the prices of *kampung* land. Increasingly, landless and land-poor Malays who seek informal access to land come into direct conflict both with the interests of the local Malay officials and new forms of corporate power held by state and national Malay bourgeoisie.[10] Thus the latest phase of competition for village resources in the region is primarily a result of market speculation and investment moves on the part of the external Malay elite, and not the result of changes in village relations of production. We will now consider some of the mechanisms whereby Malay professionals and politicians mobilize other kinds of resources intended for "development of the Malays" (*pembangunan orang Melayu*).

Administering Rural Development and Bureaucratic Culture

> The population is the subject of needs, aspirations, but it is also the object in the hands of the government, aware vis-à-vis the government, of what it wants, but ignorant of what is being done to it.
>
> Michel Foucault (1979a: 18)

In this section I will trace the bureaucratic–party diffusion of modern strategies of government which in redefining social relationships, discourses, and identities, constitutes a transformation that is culturally singular in rural Malay society. Since the early 1970s, *kampung* life has been the target of large-scale governmental intervention which, by focusing on the economy, identifies problems specific to the Malay population for increasing management. Besides the political patronage which ramifies the overlapping state and UMNO party systems, social policies produce a bureaucratic culture, fraught with political calculation and tactics, in the socialization of the younger *kampung* generations.

UMNO Politics

For a rural district, Kuala Langat is peculiarly well-connected to the Federal government: it contains the constituencies of an ex-Chief Minister of Selangor and of the Minister of Social Welfare, a powerful female Member of Parliament. It was largely due to their efforts as state officials and UMNO leaders that the national government located the first rural-based FTZ in the district. This "brainchild" of strategically positioned politicians is regarded by *kampung*folk as the centerpiece of a whole series of govenment awards, from piped drinking water and macadamized roads to mosques and low-cost housing, in return for regularly voting UMNO. UMNO enjoys support from about two-thirds of the voters in the district. Its major contender is the Islamic party PAS (*Partai Islam Se Malaysia*). Charismatic leadership and concrete UMNO support has thus gained the district a reputation as "the showcase of rural development." Foreign dignitaries from "less developing" countries (e.g., Papua New Guinea) are frequently taken for a tour of Kuala Langat, perhaps not unexpectedly, since it is within easy reach of the Subang International Airport.

The elaboration of a bureaucratic style among civil servants, teachers and even barely educated village leaders is immediately evident in their adept practices and languages of "development" (*pembangunan*). Under the New Economic Policy, the introduction and administration of various rural development programs fostered an expanded state apparatus as the mode for the proliferation of UMNO organizations of the grassroots level. Civil servants were often selected for their UMNO loyalty, or expected to demonstrate the proper party credentials whatever their hidden loyalties. This accounts for the control of development resources by the state assemblyman *(wakil rakyat)*, the D.O., and his subordinates, technical experts and teachers, who are also the leaders of local UMNO organizations. In the everyday scramble for state largess, these brokers openly poclaim their support for UMNO either in words or deeds, despite a state injunction requiring civil servants to abstain from party politics. A district official and leader of the UMNO Women's Faction (*Wanita* UMNO) says

> As a member of the District Council I cannot play politics in front of government servants, but I may do so behind their backs. I operate as part of the political machinery, becoming involved for the sake of the party (UMNO) strength . . . But even though I play politics, the development of (Malay) society is also important.

She is part of the new educated elite outside *kampung* society who have arisen through secular schools, the state bureaucracy, and UMNO party channels. Within the district, the interlocking membership of leaders in the main UMNO committee, UMNO Women (*Wanita*), and UMNO Youth (*Pemuda*) divisions who hold positions in the state system is striking. In 1978–79, the District Officer was the UMNO leader for the district. The *Pemuda* Executive Committee in Kampung Telok, for instance, was headed by a clerk from the state Islamic Office, while most of the other eleven members were also government officials, teachers, and dockworkers at the state-owned Port Klang Board. Other local *Pemuda* and *Wanita* executive positions were also filled by employees from various state agencies. In Sungai Jawa, UMNO leadership of the tripartite executive committees had become a family affair: the village head was the UMNO president, his daughter the *Wanita* leader, and her husband head of the *Pemuda* section.

The intermeshing roles of political leaders in state and party organizations provide them with a strategic position to intercept and control the flow of *pembangunan* funds and tap them for political as well as economic gain. Local politicians manipulate state-funded community projects with the finest calculation of voting returns to party investment. Sungai Jawa has been a favored UMNO constituency. It is the largest administrative village in the district, but its size alone cannot account for its emblems of "development" — a bus-stop shelter, a maternity clinic, a primary school, and short lines of macadamized roads fed by piped water and electrical wires. Forlorn-looking villages down the road advertise their stigma as PAS strongholds. Within Sungai Jawa, the otherwise inexplicable termination of piped water, electrical lines, and widened tracks marks the beginnings of recalcitrant neighborhoods which did not vote UMNO in the last election.

Besides the hamlet by hamlet doling out of government resources, the implementation of development funds was also carefully timed to wrest the highest political return. Months prior to the 1978 state elections, cement courts costing M$800–M$1,000 were constructed in the house compounds of UMNO leaders in Sungai Jawa. Every week the courts blossomed with festivities as young men playing ball were watched by female spectators while food vendors did a brisk business. The political-sports arena drew attention to UMNO's ability to deliver the goods, especially to the growing population of restless and hostile youths. The opposition PAS has appeal for petty businessmen, religious teachers, unemployed students, and disaffected laborers, i.e., people who are not occupationally linked to governmental agencies and who have given up hope of every being so. Limited to private contributions, PAS was unable to indulge in public displays of material progress and instead emphasized Islamic asceticism by holding meetings "underground." Villagers, wise to the ways of both parties, threw their support behind UMNO as the party best able to tap state and Federal sources for "development"; the UMNO incumbent was returned.[11]

Sometimes, the desire for enhancing personal symbolic and economic capital overrides the careful adjustment of state resources to promised votes. In the same year, the incumbent assemblyman diverted materials allotted for improving access to the primary school to pave the track leading from the main road to his house. This action probably cost him some votes and, perhaps, even won him a few for his audacity and enhanced prestige. Despite whispered accusations of corruption, many civil servants and village leaders expect to receive a "cut" of any major state project (e.g., land development, low-cost housing) which they can attract to their community. They also expect to get a large share of routine government credit for fertilizers, replanting, and loans from the Farmers' Bank (*Bank Pertanian*). For instance, when the FTZ was first opened, a rich UMNO supporter obtained a bank loan to buy two secondhand buses. With his son, he ferried factory women between village and FTZ. Thus, ultimately, the channeling of government resources and the controlled transmission of vital information in UMNO meetings serve to exclude most ordinary non-UMNO and even lapsed UMNO members from sharing in the benefits of *pembangunan*.

It is important to mention that party patronage occasionally roped in the less educated or the growing numbers of "fence-sitting" youths and displaced traditional religious teachers (*kijaji*). For instance, a school gardener was able to break into local UMNO party leadership when he was asked to stand in for a teacher in a meeting of the *Pemuda* Executive Committee in Kampung Telok. The gardener, despite his illiteracy, cultivated UMNO leaders and articulated received party truths. He was soon elected to the committee, in the process garnering a portion of the tenders for local government projects. He thereby gained an additional income as a labor broker. For those without white-collar credentials, individual maneuvering and positioning within the party structures can provide access to government forms, licenses, and contracts which may be accordingly milked.

Social Policies: Village Clinic and School

In the spaces between the overlapping governmental and party systems, specific policies governing issues of the population as a whole come to constitute an administrative reality making the state UMNO domination of society both intelligible and self-evident to rural Malays. By what Foucault terms "bio-politics," disparate policies regulating a plurality of problems such as health, family, education, and religion induce conformity to a particular ordering of society (1979a). In their technical competence, officials, teachers, and party functionaries pronounce the goals of governmental policies, specify the critical problems, and isolate the perceived threats to people and development, thereby domesticating rural women and men to the norms and techniques of political culture.

For the majority of villagers, whose daily lives exist outside the activities of state offices and party organizations, the experience of state party domination is less apparent but nonetheless real. An important example is the Community Development Program (*Kemajuan Masyarakat*: KEMAS), organized through the Ministry of Agriculture, which furnishes a bureaucratic base for mobilizing illiterate women in adult education classes. In 1978, the district supervisor of KEMAS (an acronym which means "tidy-up") women's classes was a young *Wanita* leader. Her formal responsibility was to implement classes in childcare, nutrition, general hygiene, sewing, and home budgetting. As Wanita leader, she selected 32 pro-UMNO villages in Kuala Langat for these classes, and handpicked 35 village women, each of whom had had six years' education, to be instructors at M$150 per month. The village instructors in turn recruited about 30 favored women as students. The localized clusters of rural women were linked in a district-wide network which operated simultaneously as a channel of resources, a means for instructing peasant women in "correct" attitudes and behavior, and a structure of mobility. In fact, the *Wanita* supervisor admitted that "the politics (of the village instructors) is to carry out government orders, thus strengthening the government."

Few questions were raised when, in celebration of the 1978 UMNO victory, those KEMAS instructors who had recruited most women voters through their classes were each awarded M$1,000 to take a vacation in Sumatra. Thus, it is in joining sewing bees and lessons in elementary hygiene and handicrafts that the lives of village women are progressively regulated and transformed through public policies. It is perhaps not irrelevant to add that the current Chief Minister of Selangor began his political career in the district as supervisor of adult men's classes, a position from which he could organize supporters scattered in many villages throughout Kuala Langat. It was a meteoric rise for a village man who started out as a labor contractor. But the daily practices of ordinary village women who will never attain official positions are transformed in more subtle ways.

Social welfare practices constitute women in particular as the guardians of the Malay family, culture, and future by focusing on specified problems of female sexuality: the risks of family planning, the dangers for women working in the factories, and the problem of female consumerism. Sungai Jawa is well-known in public health circles for its resistance to family planning organized by the maternity clinic located in the village center. Only 85 couples sign up for contraceptives, in a *kampung* of about 1,700 families (and population of over 7,000). Many women have said that they wished to reduce or space the number of their children but came up against their husbands' resistance. The pill is believed to induce dizziness and "laziness" in women, and village men are said to refuse other forms of contraception.

What is interesting here is an inversion of the national family planning program (up until 1984) by local politicians and teachers who seek to link the personal activities of rural couples to "development" problems of the Malay population. Local UMNO leaders, whatever their own private practice, present the family planning program as risky to women's health, a challenge to the marital relationship, anti-Islamic, and ultimately a threat to the Malay race. The extraordinary manipulation of technical information by various religious groups, including the *dakwah* (proselytizing Islamic fundamentalists), impresses upon village women that "the pill" (unfortunately the main contraceptive proffered) destroys fetuses. *Dakwah* advocates have insisted upon the Prophet's injunction against killing unborn children, although older religious teachers question whether preventive measures are against Islam. Whatever their private wishes regarding children, most village couples believe that family planning is contrary to Islamic teachings and thus contrary to Malay interests. A male teacher at the local primary school observes that educated Malays are ideologically opposed to family planning because of its implicit assumption that Malay parents are unable to raise many children. To an increasing number of Malay white collar workers, family planning poses the threat of increasing ethnic imbalance in urban constituencies which are dominated by non-Malay populations. As the teacher remarked ironically, "We plan our families as well as plan the country."

His words were unintentionally prophetic. In late 1984, the federal government turned family planning on its head and reprogrammed the national agency for "family development." National economic planning calls for accelerated population growth to reach the target of 70 million (from a total population of 14 million) by the year 2000. "Manpower" needs in an expanded industrial economy yet to be constructed will be met by natural increases in the Malay population and immigration from the Indonesia islands.[12] Thus, the "political economies" of bureaucratic discourse have produced new government practices for constituting a new demographic reality. In the emergent set of strategic practices, rural Malay women are obligated, by a combination of religious, ethnic, and governmental injunctions, to produce more children for realizing projected economic goals through the rest of the century.

In a campaign speech, a *Wanita* leader and schoolteacher reminded village women that their special role in ensuring the educational success of their children was inextricably linked to the preservation of the UMNO heritage of their grandchildren. The *Wanita* motto warned that "The defeat of UMNO is the defeat of the entire Malay race." Thus, primary and secondary education for rural Malays is a key institution for constructing the mentality and shaping the behavior of not only boys and girls but also their parents. Throughout the year, school officials, teachers, and political leaders symbolize power, allocate funds, and provide critical contacts, thus generally establishing the norms of bureaucratic conduct in rural society. At school celebrations, the main speakers are invariably UMNO state assembly members whose lists of monetary contributions (drawn from government funds) are meticulously read to the gathered crowds. Speeches enjoin parents and students to be grateful for government support of their local schools and to be loyal to Islam as well as to teachers (the local UMNO representatives). Thus parents learn that education excellence depends upon cultivating UMNO goodwill to ensure the continuing flow of scarce resources.

The school system itself, socializing students to bureaucratic values and the demands of the labor market, becomes a channel for individual mobility. Nevertheless, there are divergent effects on boys and girls. Social pressures, family sentiments, and educational practices (which will be dealt with in Chapter 5) have a more adverse effect on the performance of female than male students in secondary school. Rural girls who do poorly in Form 3 are just the right age for employment (16 years old); not surprisingly, many end up as factory operators in the local FTZ. Students in the Upper Forms, mainly boys, are streamed into vocational schools, while the brightest students are sent on, equipped with scholarships, to matriculation, teacher-training, or university education in the capital.

Besides attaining above-average grades, deferential relations with schoolteachers and other UMNO functionaries provide contacts and guidance for the ambitious student on his/her trajectory through the educational-bureaucratic channels. By the Upper Forms and college years, the ethic of government patronage has become so instilled in upwardly mobile students that they are propelled into bureaucratic jobs which seem to be awaiting them upon graduation. For the less adept and lucky, any job outside of government (*kerajaan*) is considered merely temporary until they get "the real thing" in civil service. Some older Malays remember their first experience of government service in the armed forces after the War. They point out that those *kampung* Malays who earn salaries in a government office enjoy other social privileges: they can sit at a desk in an air-conditioned office and perhaps be assisted by typists and peons. The latter two jobs in some government outfit are the cherished goals of village boys and girls who have ended schooling at the secondary level. Finding themselves with the job options of factory worker (*pekerja kilang*), or worse, manual laborer (*kuli*), many young men prefer unemployment. They also resist work on their parents' holdings. Young men hang around homesteads or drift through nearby towns until, feeling the acute need for liquid cash, they reluctantly join older *kuli* in oddjobbing around the countryside.

Kuala Langat, as a showpiece of administered development, is being reconditioned by political technologies which operate in the webs of government bureaucracy and party system. In the specified spheres of social welfare, sexuality, and education, to name only a few, the everyday lives of village Malays are being reconstituted according to new concepts, language, and procedures. The *kampung* family is gradually becoming the target of policies of regulation and surveillance. Alongside state and party functions, social policies provide supplementary channels for the inculcation of particular attitudes and practices for individual strategizing. UMNO members frequently justify their manipulation of positions and funds as an unavoidable part of the technical procedures necessary to ensure the "development of race, religion, nation" (*pembangunan bangsa, ugama, negara*).

For ambitious villagers, the internal linkages to state bureaucracy and the modes of disciplining embodied in the bureaucratic culture are channels for individual mobility out of the countryside. It is such bureaucratic elaboration of mobility trajectories which account for limited rural group resistance from below.[13] The conflicts between different categories of upwardly mobile Malays are a different dynamic expressed in religio-political terms (see Chapters 8 and 9). We can now take a closer look at the distribution of life-chances in Sungai Jawa as *kampung* families become more tightly integrated into the wider political and corporate structures.

Chapter 4

Sungai Jawa: Differentiation and Dispersal

> Every immigrant knows in his heart of hearts that it is impossible to return. Even if he is physically able to return, he does not truly return, because he himself has been so deeply changed by his emigration. It is equally impossible to return to that historical state in which every village was the center of the world.
>
> John Berger (1984: 64)

The *kampung* resides in the minds and hearts of Malays as a "garden of culture," the seat of simple yet enduring wisdom, an unadulterated haven against non-Malay worlds. It is also the home from which they are departing in unprecedented numbers. In this chapter, we will enter the village to discover why rural Malays are leaving, even when they claim continuing, if sporadic, residence in rural homesteads.

I begin by tracing the statistical universe of a *kampung* increasingly differentiated by access to land and divergent linkages to labor markets and the state bureaucracy. By the selective use of quantitative data, I intend to discuss the limits of economic models of "household strategizing" in accounting for changes in agrarian societies. In Kuala Langat, and elsewhere in the Malaysian countryside, class differentiation into relations of capital and labor involves the active participa-

57

tion of the state. Through their particular access to different labor markets and the state bureaucracy, *kampung* folk are reconstituted into a localized version of the Malay proletariat, or a fraction of the emergent Malay middle class.

Tanam Modal, Jual Tenaga: Planting Capital, Selling Labor Power

An anthropologist seeking the social terrain of a *kampung* staked out for "fieldwork" is readily provided with the homemade microsociology of "poor folk" (*orang miskin/susah*), "ordinary people," the middle majority (*orang biasa/sederhana*), and "the rich" (*orang kaya*). (See, e.g., S. Husin Ali 1975: 87–90). As a cluster of symbols for guiding navigation, such native categories are easily misapplied by the anxious cartographer bent upon imposing a "scientific" grid on fluid waters. The statistical tables presented below should be read in the light of this caution; at best, they distort and reconstitute, by the very act of measuring, the very fleeting reality they hope to arrest. Thus, quantitative data on village landownership, occupations, household composition, and time budget[1] are meant to be taken as momentary and, alas, possibly misleading approximations of social situations in flux. Such measurements are also intriguing reminders that native terminologies stand askew to social scientific concepts, questioning our assumptions and referring to native schemes of meaning which we may ignore, but at the peril of ending up in deep water.

Unlike some of their would-be analysts, Malay villagers distinguish between "family" (*keluarga*) and "household" (*rumah tangga*). Given the choice, village Malays prefer to live as nuclear families in separate but clustering dwellings. Since *kampung* houses are elegantly, and sensibly, raised on stilts, the household, which may at any one time contain an assortment of nonnuclear kin, is characterized as "sharing one stairway." The household implies some degree of sharing: in residence, earnings, consumption, and perhaps claims to property. Land, the inherited estate (*pesaka*), is individually owned by women and men, and can be claimed only by blood descendants (special provisions have to be made for adopted children). Sometimes, household membership is limited only to occasional coresidence, contingent upon continuing affection and perhaps sporadic contributions to the family budget.

In 1978, I undertook an on-the-ground census of 242 households in Sungai Jawa, approximately one-third of the total number recognized in official records. The richly varied nature of my findings puts to rest at once the notion that village Malays derive most of their living from crop cultivation. Although many other "facts" slipped my net, the quantitative measures gathered reveal that the multi-occupational household economy predominates, suspended in webs of overlapping concentric labor markets, with nodes as nearby as the local FTZ and as distant as Saudi Arabia. I will provide snapshots of such divergent socio-economic relationships by discussing differential household access to land resources, the constraints on use of child labor, and patterns of resource sharing within the household.

Table 7

Distribution of Households by Land Access, Sungai Jawa
(Sample of One-Third of Total Population), 1979

Households		Farm Size (acres)	Total Acreage	
Landless	57 (23.8%)	0.0 – 0.5	10	(1%)
Landpoor	91 (37.4%)	0.6 – 2	132	(18%)
Smallholder	65 (26.7%)	2.1 – 5	226	(28%)
Middle	13 (5.3%)	5.1 – 10	92	(11%)
Rich	16 (6.6%)	10.1 – 70	343.5	(42%)
Totals	242		803.5	

Although native categories recognize only three social strata — poor folk, ordinary people, and the rich — I have made finer social distinctions in Table 7. My categories are divided according to whether land-ownership *alone* permitted self-sufficiency (i.e., about five acres for a family of six). For the landpoor, are wage incomes the primary source of livelihood? For the landrich (ownership of more than ten acres), does land operate mainly as a form of investment? On this basis, I distinguish five social categories in Sungai Jawa: landless, landpoor, smallholders, middle landowners, and rich landowners. These are merely analytical devices to demonstrate the divergent and fluid changes in rural property relations. At any point in time, some households are upwardly mobile while others are slipping into the pool of laboring poor.

Table 7 represents a snapshot of a moving rural scenario: 24 percent of the total sample of 242 households fall within the landless category. From another perspective, 88 percent of the households have access to holdings under five acres, i.e., they depend to some degree on nonagricultural earnings for their sustenance. Some 5 percent of the total, the middle landowners, can live entirely off farm income, while about 7 percent can certainly use part of their property, not as a means of livelihood, but for market speculation.

Table 8

*Primary Occupations of Household Heads by Land Access,
Sungai Jawa, 1979*

Occupation	Landless	Landpoor	Small	Middle	Rich
Farm operator	0	11	24	6	6
Kampung professional*	2	8	6	1	
Trader	3	2	2	1	5
Landlord			1	1	3
Sharecropper	9	5			
Casual laborer	20	35	19		
Steady wage-worker	20	24	10	3	1
Salaried worker	3	5	3	1	1
Totals	57	90	65	13	16

Kampung professionals such as Malay spirit-healer *(bomoh)* and midwife *(bidan)*.

The Limits of Household Strategizing

Like a number of other Southeast Asian societies, increasing land parcellation has not given rise to a significant landlord class within rural Malay society. This configuration indicates that land *by itself* is not a major source of class differentiation. Relations of production within the *kampung* economy are no longer the fundamental means whereby rural Malay households are being reproduced. A glance at

Table 8 reveals the critical importance of wage employment to household heads and working adults residing in Sangai Jawa. The primary occupation of household heads (mainly male) is determined by land access: in the landless, landpoor, and smallholding categories, the majority of family heads are (irregular) wage laborers. As might be expected, household heads in the middle and rich landowning strata are independent farm operators. However, the process of differentiation by landownership is being supplanted by the dynamic of class formation contingent upon access to wage employment and corporate capitalism.

The Domestic Deployment of Labor

In recent years, the "rediscovery" of the "household unit" by the "New Home Economics" school, and the fashionability of statistical models in the social sciences, have promoted studies which treat households as autonomous units operating independently of the

Home of a squatter family.

Home of a well-to-do village woman.

wider social contexts. The basic assumption is that "the household" operates like a capitalist firm in allocating scarce resources — measured in time units — among competing activities in order to maximize productivity/utility (Becker 1965). Similarly, recent time budget studies undertaken to account for demographic processes in Asian societies have treated the domestic group as a unit of decision making, with no attention to internal and external relations of domination and expropriation (see some examples in Bingswanger et al. 1980).

Of particular appeal has been the "value of children" model which draws upon the Chayanovian notion that the peasant household, at different phases of family development, is "a distinct labor machine" (Thorner 1966: 60). The argument is that in the technologically backward Asian countryside, rural families depend on a large number of children for maintaining a tolerable standard of living (Mamdani 1973; White 1976). While this may indeed be the case for food-producing households in some countries, the labor contributions of children should not be assumed to be of similar significance for domestic groups in all levels of agrarian society.[2]

In Kuala Langat, social differentiation and divergent linkages to external institutions, rather than agrarian demand for labor, are seen to have an important limiting effect on household use of the family labor. In addition, "development" processes such as mass education and wage employment in service and manufacturing industries have placed severe limits on rural household strategizing through the control of child labor.

In conducting a time-budget survey[3] of forty households in the landless, landpoor, small, and rich categories, three sets of economic tasks are distinguished. These daily activities are "household maintenance" (childcare and house chores), "farm work" (self-employment), and "wage labor" (sale of labor power). The tables below will show that, depending on their access to village resources, *kampung* households are devoting less time to cash cropping, making minimal use of child labor in agriculture, and expending more time in wage employment.

Table 9 shows that among families in four social strata, the distribution of daily time by adult men and women (age seventeen years and above) in different work categories is weighted towards wage employment and most insignificant in farm chores. Among the landless households, over 60 percent of the total work activities are spent in wage earning, whereas among the landrich, only 29 percent of their daily work time falls within that category. Women in landless households alone account for more labor time in wage employment than the combined rate of man and women in rich households.

Household location in relation to village resources also influences the kind of wage employment household members can participate in. Among the landless, women tend to spend more time in steady jobs, i.e., factory employment at the local FTZ, whereas their men are primarily involved in casual labor on nearby estates. Landpoor households, still holding on to small plots, expend most time in casual wage labor and job contracts which may take them away for months on end. Among the households with 2.1 to 5 acres of land, time in casual labor decreases in importance to time spent in steady wage employment, usually in government service departments and factory work. Not surprisingly, men in landrich households rarely engage in casual work, and even their participation in steady employment is at a lower rate than those of the other *kampung* strata.

Labor time invested in wage employment is inversely related to time

Table 9

Average Daily Work Time (in Hours) by Men and Women*
in Forty Households, Sungai Jawa, 1979

		Household Chores	Farm Work	Wage Labor Casual	Steady	Total
Landless						
Men	(11)	0.89	0.71	2.82	3.97	8.39
Women	(13)	4.26	0.44	0.84	4.71	10.30
Totals		5.15	1.15	3.66	8.68	18.60
Landpoor						
Men	(20)	0.70	1.09	3.35	2.28	7.42
Women	(22)	4.61	0.50	0.65	2.40	8.16
Totals		5.31	1.59	4.00	4.68	15.60
Small						
Men	(23)	1.11	2.29	0.92	2.63	7.73
Women	(29)	4.66	1.07	0.46	2.14	8.33
Totals		5.77	3.36	1.38	4.77	15.70
Rich						
Men	(18)	0.63	3.85	0.42	1.42	6.42
Women	(18)	4.99	1.06	0.02	2.45	8.52
Totals		5.62	4.91	0.44	3.87	14.90

*Age seventeen years and older.

expended in farm work. As expected, landless households spend negligible time on farm work, and the rate increases along with the degree of land access. Only among the landrich households do both women and men expend about one-third of their average daily work time in farm-related activities. These time budgets confirm field observations that coconut and coffee, and even rubber, require limited attention

Table 10

Average Daily Work Time (in Hours) by Girls and Boys*
in Forty Households, Sungai Jawa, 1979

	Household Chores	Farm Work	Wage Labor	Total
Landless				
Girls (11)	2.02	0.20	0.52	2.74
Boys (11)	1.28	0.51	0.78	2.57
Totals	3.30	0.71	1.30	5.31
Landpoor				
Girls (16)	2.25	0.20	0.24	2.69
Boys (18)	0.71	0.44	1.10	2.25
Totals	2.96	0.64	1.34	4.94
Small				
Girls (9)	2.30	0.16	0.26	2.72
Boys (13)	0.48	1.08	0.18	2.34
Totals	2.78	1.24	0.44	5.06
Rich				
Girls (7)	2.12	0.36	0.00	2.48
Boys (6)	0.17	1.50	0.20	1.69
Totals	2.29	1.86	0.20	4.17

*Age between six and sixteen years.

from the smallholders. For those who own oil palm holdings, farm work is limited mainly to supervising day laborers in harvesting and pruning. Since farm incomes are proportionately higher for the land-rich than for households in other land categories, men and women in rich families shun manual labor in the fields. Prestige derives from living off farm products/rents, doing office work, or teaching.

In all households, an average of five to almost six hours a day is spent on household chores such as cooking and cleaning, i.e., the daily physical and emotional care of children and adults which ensures the biological and social reproduction of the population.[4] Such domestic chores are largely performed by women, but among the landless, women spend almost as much time seeking wage earnings. Wives in the richest households, who do not seek any kind of wage employment, expend most time in cooking, childcare, and cleaning the house, the only activities deemed prestigious for women in land-rich families. Taking the overall view, one notes a definite correlation between degree of land access and total average working time: the poorest families spend most time in various work tasks, whereas the richest families expend the least amount of time in work activities (a difference of almost 4.5 hours). Young women from the poorest households have the longest working day.

What about the children sixteen years and under? Do they undertake farm chores while their parents seek wage employment? On the average, children in the sampled households contribute about 30 percent of the total labor time expended by adults. However, by breaking down the households according to land access, we see that children's work activities follow the pattern of their parents' time allocation in activities other than household chores (see Table 10). Girls and boys from landless and landpoor families expend most time in wage work, whereas in the small and rich households, children spend more time on farm work.

In other words, children in *kampung* society almost never engage in work activities outside of parental direction and supervision. If we were to test the "value of children" model, we would see that in Sungai Jawa, the deployment of child labor is more or less significant depending on the access of their families to land resources and/or job opportunities in agriculture. Children in farm families can help their parents by weeding, collecting palm nuts, tending livestock, and other such tasks. In the well-to-do families, older children in their late teens may begin to take over responsibility for harvesting and marketing the crops in their parents' holdings (see Table 13). Thus, only those families in effective control of land can utilize the labor of children. In such cases, grown children demand a wage, revealing the degree of economic individuation within an apparent joint production unit (see below).

Rural laborers from the landless and landpoor categories in some sense have greater control over their young children's labor and the fruits of that labor. Day laborers working in plantations may take along their sons to help cut down and carry palm nuts. By helping their parents, boys still too young to be considered full laborers can boost their father's day wage, which is calculated according to the number of bunches collected. Boys can also scatter through the undergrowth looking for fallen nuts which can be surreptitiously sold for additional income. Within the village economy, the coconut gatherer is usually aided by his son or some young male relative. A village woman seeking some cash income may organize her children, especially the girls, into a party for picking coffee cherries and drying the beans for a rich family. Although the acreage under rubber has declined greatly, some villagers still supplement their farm incomes by hiring themselves out as tappers, with their children tagging along to carry latex buckets and collect scrap rubber. Children are almost never employed on their own, i.e., hired directly, except by a kinsman, and then they are only paid a child's wage. The above work activities, in which the children seldom receive a payment, account for the labor time boys and girls from landless and landpoor households expend in "wage labor." Not unexpectedly, children from rich households make no significant contribution to "wage labor."

What is significant about Table 10 is the limited amount of time *kampung* children spend in farm work and rural wage labor. The largest amount of time is devoted to household maintenance chores, i.e., from about 50 to 68 percent of their total work time. Young girls play a significant role in the daily tasks of laundry, cooking, and cleaning the house, while boys sometimes assist by gathering firewood or picking fruits and wild vegetables. Reflecting the work patterns of adults, children in poorer houses work harder than those in well-off families.

My discussion of the time allocation of adults and children is not intended to claim an overdetermining relationship between land access and the deployment of family labor by *kampung* households. As mentioned earlier, the social categories are essentially analytical constructs to illustrate that differential access to land resources and employment opportunities requires a diversity of income-generating activities which often do not depend on parental control of children's labor power. In Kuala Langat, changing *kampung* society places limits on a household strategy which is based upon the control and supervision of children's labor by their parents. Already, in the younger families, fathers engaged as wage workers in urban private and public industries are rarely able to take along their children as additional labor power. The "value of children" model assumes that domestic groups will benefit from child labor because of the agrarian context. Insufficient attention has been given to the effects of rural differentiation and wider labor markets on changing relations of production within and without the household. Furthermore, we will next see that the "demand for child labor" model cannot account for variations in domestic composition and pooling of resources in Sungai Jawa.

Household Composition and the Sharing of Resources Between Generations

"Every child has its own fortune" *[Tiap tiap anak ada rezekinya]*

Malay proverb

As *kampung* society becomes a labor reserve for the wider economy, domestic organization in Sungai Jawa produces a range of structural forms. Building upon relationships of kinship and marriage, house-

A grandmother and her grandson.

Credit: International Development Research Centre (IDRC), Social Sciences Division, Ottawa

hold formation is dictated more by interests in joint consumption and coresidence than by joint production activities.

As mentioned above, rural Malays prefer nuclear family residential units, but Table 11 shows that 20 percent of 242 households are three-generational arrangements. These complex domestic structures are better represented in the small and rich landholding strata than in other categories. Besides, Tables 11 and 12 indicate that the retention or expulsion of grown children by itself does not account for household composition and size. In the landless, landpoor, and small categories, families with children 18 years and older tend to retain about 40 percent of their grown children in the house, although their average household size hovers around 6.2 to 6.4 (see Table 11). Domestic groups in the middle category retain most of their grown children (78 percent), whereas the rich households exhibit the highest rate of dispersal (63 percent) and yet continue to maintain the largest units (see Table 12).

In deciphering these structural configurations, one must attend to the ways relations of consumption and dependency influence household composition. Domestic composition is a dynamic process continually readjusting to the arrival of infants, the departure of grown children and the recruitment/expulsion of other dependents and/or income earners. Two households, headed respectively by a middle-

Table 11

*Composition and Size of 242 Households,
Sungai Jawa, 1979*

Number of Households	Number of Generations			Average Household Size
	One	*Two*	*Three*	
Landless: 57	2	50	5	6.2
Landpoor: 91	3	72	16	6.2
Small: 65	2	45	18	6.4
Middle: 13	0	11	2	7.5
Rich: 16	0	11	5	8.3
Totals 242	7	189 (78%)	46 (19%)	6.92

Table 12

*Retention and Dispersal of Children 18 Years and Older
in 138 Families, Sungai Jawa, 1979*

Families With Children 18+		Total Number Children 18+	Living in 131 Households	Departed from Parental Household
Landless	15	60	24	36
Landpoor	51	269	108	161
Small	49	217	91	126
Middle	10	32	25	7
Rich	13	70	26	44
Totals	138	648	274 (42%)	374 (58%)

aged man and woman, reveal contrasting patterns of resource sharing found in Sungai Jawa. The pooling of cash incomes and balancing claims between generations within the same household are at best provisional measures.

Halim[5] owns a half-acre holding which is taken up by his houseplot and a miniature coconut-coffee garden. He and his wife have six children at home: five daughters between the ages of ten and 21 years, and a twelve-year-old boy. Although his crops bring in less than M$30 a month, the combined earnings of Halim, an office peon, his wife, a coffee-picker, and three daughters, all factory workers, provide the family with a monthly income of M$365, quite adequate for their expenses. Besides, their simple wooden house is cluttered with formica-topped furniture, a television set and a radio. Halim has a motorbike; his family shares a bicycle.

Another family also owning a half-acre farm is very much poorer. Divorcée Hayati barely manages to make ends meet from her aging rubber trees and meagre earnings as a tapper on other people's holdings. She has a 20–year–old daughter in factory work who makes a monthly contribution of M$45 and supports her two younger siblings in school. Hayati attempts to limit monthly expenses to M$80 for the family of four. She worries about the immediate future whenever her daughter keeps a tryst with her boyfriend.

For domestic groups with decreasing access to land, the presence of grown daughters and sons who will make "voluntary" cash contributions to the family fund is a distinct advantage. A number of households in the landpoor, small, and middle categories manage to have a fair standard of living because at least two daughters and sons agree to pool part of their earnings in the family fund. However, such strategies, depending not on the control of children's labor but on receipt of their earnings, are ad hoc and easily subverted by rebellious children (see Chapter 5).

When the pooling of resources occurs between parents and married children, stem-family structures of varying duration are established. Among households with holdings between 2.1 and 5 acres, almost one-quarter are stem-family arrangements. Six households include married sons and sometimes married daughters (and families), and the rest only married/divorced daughters (and families) and unwed children. In a few instances, parents no longer able-bodied needed sons or sons-in-law to help manage the farm and supplement household incomes. In other cases, married sons or married/divorced daughters unable to support their families, have returned to the parents' household for short- or long-term support.

In one family where the father has retired from farm work, the son, a stevedore at Port Klang, takes care of all household expenses, supplemented by income from the father's 3.5-acre plot, which is tended by his mother and wife. In two other examples, where the parents have larger holdings, the flow of resources is in the opposite direction. In the first case, the son with a wife and two children live with his parents, who provide for all daily expenses. The son merely pays the utility bills (M$16/month) and will only help his father on the farm if he receives a wage in return. This is work on the property which he will one day inherit in part, according to Islamic law. What is especially illuminating about this case is that the son, a married man and factory worker, does not consider his labor power at the disposal of his father, despite coresidence on the father's land. The young man thinks that he should receive a wage like any other hired laborer if he helps his father harvest the palm. Familial relations are salient *not* as relations of production but as relationships through which the different generations can meet their housing needs, make material claims, and receive moral support.

Stem-family arrangements also occur when married daughters

return to their parents' household after divorce or widowhood. These women are often accompanied by their children, who will be raised in their grandparents' home. If their mothers remarry, they move out, and the stem-family is reduced once again to the nuclear form. In some stem-family formations, married daughters with husbands and children coreside with the maternal grandparents. Most of these arrangements involve married women who are youngest daughters fulfilling their customary role of caring for parents in old age. The son-in-law usually contributes a substantial amount of the daily expenses, since his children are the main dependents and free housing is provided. In the majority of such units, the daughters will inherit the parents' house after the old folks die.

As the above cases demonstrate, the nurturing of grandchildren is usually the basic reason for complex family formation. Extended households involve both temporary and indefinite arrangements. Newly married daughters prefer to return home in the late stages of their first pregnancy for comfort and support, often at the time when their husbands are in the process of saving for or building their own house. These are temporary but critical episodes whereby parents help the young family ride through their first crisis before they begin householding on their own. Other cases of in-living married children and families are more long-term arrangements for raising the grandchildren, a practice common among the landrich households. In two cases, grandparents have taken in grandchildren because the childrens' own parents are too poor to take care of them as well. The old folks contribute food, lodging, and pocket money in return for housework, general care, and the company provided by the children. The richest man in Sungai Jawa, for instance, has a household of seventeen, including two wives, ten (out of fifteen) unmarried children, and four grandchildren whose parents are not coresident. Rich *kampung* families tend towards complex household formation because they have the resources to shelter and raise grandchildren, receiving in turn company, help in household chores, and perhaps management of their property.

Household composition in Sungai Jawa thus results from a multiplicity of practices for the sharing of resources within and between generations. In nuclear formations, the retention of wage-earning children accounts for the persistence of large households over a longer duration than was the case in earlier generations. In stem-family arrangements, married sons and daughters coreside with their parents, often not so much to care for the former as to receive a stream of tangible and intangible benefits from the older generation. The well-off aged may recruit grandchildren and others for housework or simply the satisfaction of having the house ring with the voices of children. Finally, household size fluctuates with the assortment of nuclear and non-nuclear kin who are in various stages of dependence, e.g., grown children still in school, unemployed sons, daughters waiting to get married, and other dependents.

A Note on Labor Time

As long as we are in the statistical realm, what other reading can we make of rural time budgetting and what can it tell us about villagers' experience of changing relations of production?

In the past decade, time-budget studies have been used to discover the effects of increased market participation on time alloted to housework and childcare (Minge-Kalman 1978; Evenson 1978; Schultz 1980). In a survey of time-allocation studies drawn from agrarian and advanced capitalist countries, Minge-Klevana maintains that with the transition to industrial wage labor, "there is . . . overall increase in labor time inside the home, that is, in activities pertaining to the maintenance of the family itself" (1980: 287). I wish here to merely point out that in agrarian transitions, changing patterns of labor utilization can seldom be generalized even within the same community, much less in gross comparisons across cultures and time spans.

In Sungai Jawa, the total average time expended by children and adults indicates that sustained participation in wage relations does not necessarily increase time in household maintenance chores (see Table 13). In landless and landpoor households, which exhibit the highest rates of wage employment, reduced agricultural self-employment has been compensated for by increased time in wage labor. In other words, as the poor spend less time in farm activities, their overall work day has become lengthened by wage employment. Among the rich adults, only 33 percent of total labor time is spent in wage work, and yet time spent in household chores remains about the same rate as for all other social strata.

In other words, the table indicates that in the Sungai Jawa experience, proletarianization has led to an increase in labor time "outside" rather than "inside" the family (Minge-Klevana's terms). As

Malay villagers spend less work time on the land, more labor time is devoted to wage-earning activities, contributing to overall increase in market work. In addition, labor time in self-employed activities such as farm work and household maintenance is reduced, especially for landpoor work households.

In the explosion of time budget studies, the human implications of the transition from "nonmarket" to "market" labor time are almost never considered. However unintended, time units can also be the dumb but eloquent measure of a qualitative alteration in the experience of work. To discuss the actual "market" and "nonmarket" costs of the shift from self-employment to sale of labor power, one must put flesh and blood on these statistical structures, making them speak of the lived experiences of social groups in the making.

Emergent Class Structure

The above abstractions regarding property and wage employment are merely analytical snapshots of a situation of structural instability as *kampung* households devise alternative strategies of mobility. Furthermore, by using the same time-budget method, I demonstrated that models narrowly based on quantitative measures of household labor demands miss critical external relationships which reconstitute relationships within and without domestic groups. In Sungai Jawa, changing relations of production have been shown not to be a consequence of basic transformation of the *kampung* economy but to have emerged out of the intrusions of state institutions and the labor markets linked to the world system. This increasingly complex division of labor spans rural and urban sectors, giving rise to or recombining fractions of the bureaucratic elite, professionals, and entrepreneurial elements who may continue to plant capital in the *kampung* but sell their services elsewhere.

How may we understand these processes of transformation in both class and cultural terms? Do native constructs necessarily mystify changing relations of production, speaking in counterpoint and perhaps offstage to the main "objective" events? Prior to the Second World War, the occupational system in Kuala Langat was directly linked to land and agriculture. Rural Malay population was almost universally village folk (*orang kampung*), and in the local terms of *kuli* (laborer), *orang miskin, orang biasa* and *orang kaya*, their point of ref-

Table 13
Average Labor Time Spent by Children and Adults in Household and Income-Earning Activities Sungai Jawa, 1979

Land Strata		Household Chores	Income Work Farm Work	Wage Labor	Total
Landless					
Children	(22)	1.64	0.35	0.65	2.64
Adults	(24)	2.57	0.67	5.04	8.28
Totals		4.21	1.02	5.69	10.92
Landpoor					
Children	(34)	1.33	0.33	0.70	2.36
Adults	(42)	2.84	0.88	4.03	7.75
Totals		4.17	1.21	4.73	10.11
Small					
Children	(22)	1.61	0.72	0.24	2.57
Adults	(52)	3.00	1.62	3.20	7.82
Totals		4.61	2.34	3.44	10.39
Rich					
Children	(13)	1.22	0.87	0.01	2.10
Adults	(36)	2.86	2.42	2.30	7.58
Totals		4.08	3.29	2.31	9.68

erence was land tenure and the wealth derived therefrom. Since differentiation within village society was limited, the term ''*orang kaya*'' was almost exclusively reserved for the small class of aristocratic retainers at the sultan's palace. Despite the introduction of private property under the colonial system, the *rakyat* continued to view the sultan as the suzerain of *Tanah Melayu* (Malay lands).

The term *"orang kaya"* was also on occasion applied to non-Malays who came into contact with village folk. The ubiquitous Chinese trader, or an occasional Malabari shopkeeper, may be mockingly addressed by that term. In the rural townships, Chinese and Indians operated dry goods stores, provided credit, and marketed cash crops gathered in from the *kampung.* In back country roads, village Malays sometimes passed Tamil Indians, the majority of whom were sequestered in plantation barracks. Also rarely glimpsed at a distance was the British civil servant, followed dutifully by his Eurasian or Indian clerk on some inspection tour. To *orang kampung* these were all *orang luar* (outsiders), whose alienness was doubled by their perceived cultural differences from village folk.

In the postwar decades, closer integration of the district with the national society and wider economy has expanded the range of occupations and social groups which are somehow encapsulated in native categories. Malay villagers came to see the fundamental dis-

Coconut plucker.

A village woman picking coffee in her garden.

A hired worker in a cacao smallholding.

Food vendors at the Saturday morning market.

tinction as being between self-employment and wage employment: *kerja kampung* as opposed to *makan gaji* ("living off a salary"). These terms are encrusted with layers of implicit meanings which define for villagers the fundamental gap between them and others; a gap which they now consider as a matter of personal accomplishment and ethnic pride, and one which it is essential to narrow. To *makan gaji* is to derive steady monthly income from a white-collar job, to enjoy lifelong employment which culminates in a pension, to be well-situated for making contacts essential to further advancement and prestige. In contrast, "self-employment" (*kerja sendiri*) means living with the uncertainty of farm income (because of commodities prices, the weather, aging crops), manual work under the hot sun, and having no opportunities to forge linkages within the bureaucratic network. Unskilled wage labor is not encompassed under *makan gaji* but designated by specific terms such as sharecropping (*bagi dua*), oddjobbing (*ambil upah*), contract work (*kerja kontrak/kerja borong*), and being a hired farm laborer (*buroh tetap*). Clearly, local terminology recognizes clear-cut distinctions between self-employment on one's property, different forms of manual wage labor, and salaried work. Why has *makan gaji,* preferably *"kerajaan"* (a shorthand way of saying government employment), taken on such social significance in rural society?

The expansion of local government offices in administration, education, health, social services, religion, and development have brought in Malay white-collar workers and families, mainly from outside the district, to constitute a local Malay elite. While a number of the younger bureaucrats and teachers reside in towns like Telok Datok and Port Klang, most of the officials live in rural centers such as Kampung Telok. Their local residence and participation in UMNO activities and government rituals are critical in the rural production of a bureaucratic culture.

In almost daily contact with students, teachers (*guru*) are highly regarded for their learning, their *kerajaan* stamp, and orientation towards national Malay society. They set local standards for aspiring *kampung* boys and girls, the majority of whom seek career paths out of agricultural work. *Guru* not only display the accoutrements of urban lifestyle such as cars, plastic-sheathed furniture, electronic gadgets, and expensive clothes, but they also speak in authoritative tones about Malay problems, sprinkling their speeches with technical terms and English phrases. As the varied representatives of a rural intelligentsia, teachers, policemen, office clerks, and party functionaries furnish rural folk with workaday knowledge of the wider society, a bureaucratic elaboration of the increasing diet of *Televeshen Malaysia* and popular magazines eagerly consumed by village families. Situated in government offices and public institutions, *guru* and official are strategic nodes in the bureaucratic system linking rural Malays to the national society. Their technocratic image and political contacts overshadow the customary deference accorded leading *kampung* families, but with whom marriage alliances are sought to intermesh the dual bases — salaried employment and landed wealth — of the new Malay middle class.

Young officials coming into the district may not yet own village resources, but by effecting marital ties with landrich families they stand to benefit from two simultaneous processes of differentiation. As civil servants they derive their primary source of income from state positions, not land. Their eventual acquisition of local land properties has a different use and mode of deployment from village practice. The holdings they do come to control are not the cause of their occupations but the result of external sources of income, contacts, and prestige. Some break into local commercial activities such as catering, coffee milling, house construction, etc., because of their superior access to government credit. Others, and these include the *ketua kampung*, enter into covert alliances with Chinese contractors (*pemborong*) who pay fat commissions and give a cut in business projects ostensibly won through competitive bidding. We thus see in the official *kampung* elite the convergence of multiple economic and symbolic capitals whereby fractions of urban and rural Malays can consolidate their middle class position.

Chinese traders, building contractors, and labor recruiters are the critical commercial networks which interface with the bureaucratic structure channelling contracts, goods, and funds. Although there are a few Malay grocery stores struggling to keep in the black within *kampung* communities, and the occasional Indian spice-and-rice shop in rural townships, Chinese operate businesses as different as hawking fish and vegetables, vehicle repair shops, import-export trade, cinemas, transportation, and the construction industry. Chugging into *kampung* on their scooters, Chinese traders buy and transport farm crops, as well as provide liquid credit to their regular customers. The debt is gradually repaid by claiming price deductions on future produce (*tolak hasil*). Some rich Malays also loan money in this manner, earning a disguised interest (*bunga*) and thus circumventing the Koranic injunction against taking interest. Except for the major capitalists who enjoy special arrangements with Malay officials, most Chinese retailers are tightly knit ino their own exclusive networks and have little noncommerical contact with people outside the trading class.

Other non-Malays in the district are connected with the major capitalist industries. The estate managers and technical staff are socially and spatially K.L.-centered, some travelling by helicopter, others by cars, at least once a week to escape plantation doldrums. The professional, supervisory, and even clerical workers at the local FTZ daily take the highway back and forth to towns in the Klang Valley. In their wake, the slow eddies of plantation life swirl around a residue Tamil labor force. Other ex-plantation Tamil workers, either laid off or voluntarily resigning, are squatter-cum-laborers on Chinese and Indian holdings. Their daily lives are still conducted in the green shadows of tree crops, on the periphery of Malay *kampung*, plantations, and rural townships. Gradually, Tamil men and women are appearing as laborers in the Chinese *pemborong's* work crews. They have trickled out of the plantations to join Malays in the informal labor market.

Since the 1960s, some Malay boys and girls can escape this fate through education. The *guru,* as gatekeepers to officialdom, have guided a steady flow of bright children into urban schools on special government scholarships. Some of these *kampung* students, having graduated from teachers' colleges or universities, choose to remain in K.L. or have been sent as civil servants to other states in the country. Remittances from these transplanted professionals are rare and usually come on Hari Raya, the post-Ramadan celebrations when town-dwelling Malays make their annual pilgrimage back to the villages (*balik kampung*). The maintenance of networks between town and country provides younger siblings with urban bases (usually the home of a married older sister) if they seek further education or wage employment in towns like Shah Alam, Sungai Way, or K.L. Contacts with *kampung*folk also keep the migrants abreast of village land sales. A few professionals have returned to their home villages in the *mukim* and have begun to play an important role in local politics. Although the majority of rural men and women will never reach even the lower rungs of the state bureaucracy, most realize the strategic benefits of *kerajaan* and compete even for jobs as gardeners and peons in some government or UMNO office.

The drawing off of *kampung* Malays into the Klang Valley and beyond has been greatest at the level of wage laborers. The first postwar influx of Malays from the district occurred in the 1960s, when industrialization in the Klang Valley drew off mainly male migrants to work in Port Klang, as well as in private and public enterprises. Decreasing access to *kampung* land and declining productivity of smallholding compelled villagers to seek off-farm wage work on a more regular basis than before. Some of the migrants have since settled in town, becoming part of the nascent Malay urban working class. However, the majority of unskilled workers continue to commute daily on motorbikes, buses, and trucks to urban and plantation jobs (travelling some 10 to 35 miles). Others join labor gangs and have become absorbed into migration circuits which connect many *kampung* with work projects elsewhere in Malaysia and even overseas. The draining off of rural labor by manufacturing, construction, and transportation industries is paralleled, on a small scale, by the resettlement of villagers on government land development schemes in different parts of the country. About fifty families from Sungai Jawa have left the area to become pioneer farmers in government FELDA[6] land schemes.

In my survey of 242 households in Sungai Jawa, over two-thirds of all adult (17 years and older) working men are casual and permanent laborers working as road crews, dockworkers, and construction laborers (see Table 14). Whether they work within the district or outside, all of them have their home bases, usually attached to a small holding, in the village. Some older men work on the *kebun* in the morning and seek casual wage jobs in the afternoon. Others leave their wives and children to tend the gardens and may be gone with labor gangs for weeks or months on end. Still other younger, better-educated men who have landed skilled jobs in Klang Valley commute to work daily and take care of their cash crops on weekends. A young married man may hold three or more jobs, as dockworker, marketing agent, and weekend farmer; carrying village produce on his motorbike, he drops them off at the Klang market on his trip to the harbor. Employment at Port Klang is highly desired by most village men because one can progress through the ranks and enjoy all the benefits of a government job. Access to jobs is jealously guarded by patron-client networks controlled by the older permanent workers. Some village men work as "casual" cargo handlers for many years before they gain access to "permanent" employment. These are terms in which *kampung* men explain their constant attempts to negotiate their way into a strategic position within the port system.

The outflow of male workers has been joined by rural women since the early 1970s. In Sungai Jawa, the majority of working adult women (70 percent of the total) are wage workers either in factories or agriculture (Table 14). Most are young unmarried women living with their parents who commute daily to work in the local FTZ (a distance of about five miles). Rural women seldom commute long distances to work; those who are employed in industries in Shah Alam, Petaling Jaya, or even Port Klang stay with relatives or in rooming houses in town, returning on some weekends. Thus, Table 14 shows that of the 525 working adults (17 years and older) in my sample, 76 percent of the men and 78 percent of the women are engaged in casual, factory, and state employment outside the *kampung*, but they return daily, weekly, and at longer intervals to village households. In other words, the working population whose primary occupation remains cash

Table 14
Primary Occupations of Men and Women,
One-Third of Total Population, Sungai Jawa, 1979

Occupation	Men	Women	Total
Farm operator	54	23	77
Kampung professional	3	3	6
Peddler	13	7	20
Entrepreneur (market agent, store or business operator)	11	2	13
Landlord	3	2	5
Sharecropper	10	4	14
Casual laborer (day, contract)	111	41	152
Shop assistant	6	8	14
Factory worker (steady & temporary)	42	70	112
Steady wage-worker (government & port)	77	0	77
Government employee (clerk, teacher, official)	28	7	35
Totals	358	167	525

Kampung professionals such as Malay spirit-healer (*bomoh*) and midwife (*bidan*).

cropping has been reduced to about 15 percent, a fact disguised by the garden appearance of many Malay villages.

In this situation of downward mobility, a localized version of the widespread proletarianization of rural Malays, we see a curious inversion of *kampung* symbolic structure. Whereas in the recent past, only *kuli* (manual laborer) status was shameful, among the younger generation today, the term *tani* (farmer) has also taken on a pejorative gloss. Indeed, household strategizing on the basis of control over family labor is fast becoming an outdated practice. Parents attempt instead to enforce some collectivization of children's wage earnings, but they are more successful with daughters than with sons, as we shall see in the next chapter. The overwhelming majority aspire to *makan gaji* (earn a salary) and are willing to be *pekerja kilang* ("factory worker," a status viewed as a mixture of manual and white-collar elements) or even unemployed while waiting to receive the bureaucratic ticket to *kerajaan*.

The reproduction problematic remains: bureaucratic culture and the mystification of *makan gaji* are increasingly out of tune with the realities of downward mobility for the many and upward strategizing by the favored few. Production and reproduction of bureaucratic discourse in the domains of education, public agencies, government officers, and UMNO gatherings both mystify and discipline local aspirations. Dissonance between official images and the distribution of chances, though muffled, becomes louder as one moves closer to the ground of everyday life. The structure of demand for rural labor, increasingly selective on the basis of gender and skill-grade, channels parental attempts to place sons and daughters on divergent educational and occupational pathways; few parents expect, or even want, their children to grow up to be *tani*.

Kampung culture is fundamentally decentered, and the ongoing subdivision of holdings has converted many *kebun* into mere housing lots. For the laboring poor, staking their houses on a *kampung* plot is the final claim to a security which rarely exists in their spatial-social dispersal as wage laborers. The cultural and structural reconfiguration of relationships between parents and children, brothers and sisters, male and female is fraught with new needs and conflicts. As it will be shown, the social reproduction of the reconstituted *kampung* society, now firmly situated in the circuit of capitalist development, is more discontinuous than one may assume.

Chapter 5

Domestic Relations: The Reconfiguration of Family Life

Sungai Jawa at dusk: women stroll over to neighbors' homes, sit in cozy circles imbibing coffee and gossip while keeping an occasional eye on the "tele," which is turned on to an Islamic choir program (*nasyid*) or "Charlie's Angels." Infants in sarong hammocks dangle from the rafters and men commiserate on the stairs as children chase after a ball in the lengthening shadows.

Noraini is the mother of eight children. Every Friday evening relatives and friends, children in tow, gather in her house. Under her husband's guidance, young children recite the Koran. A daughter-in-law, visiting niece, or some other young woman frees her from household chores to sit with her guests. At one such gathering, Noraini was nursing a feverish granddaughter when her 16–year–old son flung himself into her lap and cajoled her for money. He was the family athlete and had recently sprained his ankle. Earlier that day he had picked two gallon-drums of coffee cherries for the inflated "wage" of M$10 and was asking for M$20 more to buy a pair of track shoes. Shifting her granddaughter onto one lap, Noraini rubbed her son's ankle while indulgently negotiating his request. She was the main character in an evening drama of women and children; her husband had an occasional walk-on part. Daughters brought refreshments and confided worries, while sons lolled on mats, now and then addressing a comment or question to her. Most family affairs and problems of extended kin are talked over and settled in such matrifocal gatherings.

85

In this chapter, we look at changing relations and sentiments in the domestic domain as children are streamed into secular education and diverging career paths. I begin by discussing family power relations and gender images prior to the widespread participation of *kampung* daughters in wage employment. Next, the experiences of boys and girls in school are related to their differential integration into the wage market. The changing sense of obligation between children and parents is revealed in a series of cases on household budgeting. Conflict as much as cooperation ensues as *kampung* life quickens to the ring of the cash register and time is no longer embedded in social relations.

Families, Spirits, and Other Familiars

> Although in Islamic life, men are considered more important, for example, in tracing descent, the influence of the mother is greater (within the family).
>
> Kadi, Telok Datok

*Kampung*folk understand their culture in terms of a localized world view encompassing both *adat* (customary sayings and practices) and Islamic principles.[1] These are historically produced concepts which take on different meanings in particular social contexts.[2] Under Islamic injunction, Malay parents are morally obliged (*wajib*) to provide for their children up to the age of fifteen. The moral obligations of children to support their parents is unemphasized and more often enforced according to *adat*. Thus, customary practice instills in the youngest daughter (often born when her mother was in her early forties) a special emotional attachment to her parents which will ensure her caring for them in old age. Similarly, although Islamic principles vest formal authority in the father, *adat* enforces dependence on women and the maintenance of kin relations through womenfolk. It is in the spiritual realm that Islam and *adat* have come into severe conflict in recent years. Exposed to Middle-Eastern and Pakistani Islamic trends, Malay-Muslim intellectuals would like to expunge beliefs in spirits, sorcery, and animistic rituals from Malay culture. Nevertheless, villagers continue to be influenced by ''non-Islamic'' but indigenous Malay values and practices. Despite pious public denials, tensions between Islamic rules, *adat*, and social conduct repeatedly break through in the course of daily life. Intolerable contradictions are produced when these belief systems, abruptly challenged by changing social relationships, have to be modified and reinterpreted to contend with the seduction of alternative worldviews.

In ordinary *kampung* society, Malays believe that men enjoy moral superiority over women because men embody more reason and self-knowledge (*akal*) than women, who are overly influenced by carnal desires (*hawa nafsu*). Young unmarried women are situated at the juncture of these authority structures built upon age and gender hierarchies: male honor hinges upon protecting the doubly junior status of pubescent girls. Whereas young unmarried men (*bujang*) are encouraged to assert their independence and roam near and far, their female counterparts are carefully trained to concern themselves with activities directly tied to family needs. Furthermore, their negotiation through adolescence is considered one fraught with danger to their own person and the honor of their male kin. Thus, constrained by decorum and clothing to be shy (*malu*) and pliant in nature and body (*lemah lembut*), nubile girls are further hedged-in by rules which prohibit them from wandering into ''dangerous'' spaces.

After dinner, a father talks while his children listen.

88

Customary [...]od as
necessary pro[...] to be
particularly w[...]dition
which makes [...]ehav-
iour. Young gi[...], (jinn
and *hantu*) dw[...]: Tres-
passing into f[...]omen
by angry spir[...]spirit-
healers (*bomo*[...]nce in
the victim. Ir[...]uence
of spirits bec[...]*mpung*
paths (by "de[...]" their
community. Besides, the intelligentsia's reinterpretations of Islam have cast shame on spirit-beliefs and the *bomoh*. In any case, such ideas remain powerful in the social monitoring of young virgins. Fearful (*takut*) of strangers and unfamiliar surroundings, young girls are socialized to accept the moral custody of father, brother, and other male kin.

Malay-Islamic practice governing marital relationship also places the wife under the shelter and moral authority of the husband. As long as they remained married to each other, the husband is required by Muslim marriage law to be totally responsible for his wife's maintenance (*bagi nafkah*) — shelter, food and clothing — and for the children they bear together. This custom formally frees the married woman, no matter how well-off, from the obligation of financially supporting the family. She can retain her own earnings from farm and wage employment as private wealth. In many cases, however, the wife's savings are used in family emergencies. More critically, her nest egg is insurance against destitution after divorce, when the ex-husband relinquishes responsibility for his former wife and children. Thus, in Malay-Islamic ideals, the moral authority of men over unmarried daughter, sister, and wife is rooted in male responsibility for the subsistence needs of the family. Male superiority is further enhanced by widespread beliefs in the spiritual vulnerability of women.

Cultural mechanisms for circumscribing female movement and power seldom constrain older women, especially those who have had many children and are past menopause. Whereas the blossoming young woman is bounded by various taboos, the middle-aged woman enjoys an increasing informal authority within the domestic domain and among her kin. *Adat* recognizes the mother-child bond as more fundamental than formal descent through the father. For instance, a woman's children by different husbands, legally of different descent, are considered *adik-beradik susu* — "milk siblings" who remain with their mother upon divorce. Relatives with whom one has greatest contact and mutual dependence are likely to be from the mother's side of the family. And as mentioned before, the migrant worker or student commonly elects to "squat" (*tumpang*) with a female relative, seldom a male one. This dependence on and social influence of the mature woman is reflected in her free movement within village circles and further afield. Middle-aged women frequently visit each other's houses, go marketing, or travel alone to the *kebun*. They gather in groups to prepare major feasts and, spicing their gossip with sexual innuendos and the occasional acid comment, direct younger relatives in various tasks. In their own houses, older women are not constrained by sexual modesty and may go about their housework barebreasted. The grandmother is widely considered the ultimate source of wisdom and comfort in many families.

Whereas the aging woman is respected and often cherished, the sexually fertile woman is both dominated and feared — threatened by divorce, while threatening in certain situations to wreak havoc upon the family. Such male fears are prefigured in the seductive form of the female *hantu*. Women who die in childbirth are transmogrified into the *langsuir* ravening after the blood of pregnant women and their newly born infants. Failing to give life in her human form, the female *hantu* takes life. Her stillborn daughter (*pontianak*) is changed into a beautiful apparition who tempts unsuspecting men into marriage. She represents the threats posed by a single but previously married woman (*janda:* widow or divorcée). Malays consider the *janda* a sexually experienced flirt who seeks to lure unmarried men into liaisons or entangle happily married men in her schemes. Widowed or divorced, the *janda* is unlike the virginal daughter, sister, or wife; she is not under the moral-legal authority of any male kin, and only answerable to the Islamic judge (*kadi*).

This cultural construction of family relations is rooted in the historically produced interactions between Islam and Malay *adat* in a peasant economy. Everyday relations of production are closely interwoven into a formal structure of male authority and cultural mech-

anisms for the graduated domination of womenfolk. Malay notions
of male prerogatives and values of male responsibility toward women
are most easily expressed in the control of young unmarried women,
referred to as *budak-budak* (children/virgins), while single, previously
married women are most able to challenge male authority. But *kampung* society is in the midst of changing social relationships which
both dissolve and reconstitute bonds between parents and children,
male and female. As girls enter mass education and prepare for off-
farm wage work, household pressures on their economic support have
given virgins the latent powers previously associated with the *janda*.

widows
divorcee

Boys and Girls: Schooling for Success

The progressive integration of Malay *kampung* communities into the
wider society — through the expanded bureaucracy, spread of mass
communications, near-universal education, and the generalization of
wage employment — is turning young people, the *pemuda* (youths)
more than the *pemudi* (young unmarried women), away from village
livelihood. In everyday life, the preparation of schoolchildren for blue-
and white-collar jobs, together with the selective pressures of the labor
market, have loosened the involvement of *kampung* children in
agriculture.

Prior to the 1970s, before the large-scale entry of rural Malay children
into secondary education, boys and girls in *mukim* Telok had participated on a daily or regular basis in work on the homestead. The life
histories of adults who grew up in the 1950s and 1960s show that most
children from all levels of village society ended primary schooling at
Standard Six.[3] Many girls were sent by their parents for special Islamic
instructions or did not attend school at all.[4] The expectation was that
the youngsters were part of the family economy, and they were in-
structed to become good farmers like their parents. Children from age
five onwards could distinguish between red (ripe) and green (unripe)
coffee and were sometimes helpful in picking the cherries from the
low-slung branches. Older children, especially those over twelve years
who had finished Standard Six, followed their parents in their daily
rounds of tapping rubber, digging ditches, gathering coffee, and mis-
cellaneous oddjobs. Around the house, little girls did cooking, wash-
ing, and took care of younger siblings. Children seldom dreamed of
a future different from their parents' way of life.

In Kampung Telok, the administrative seat of the *mukim*, the families of civil servants were already retaining their children longer in school to increase their chances of obtaining government jobs. However, it was not until the mid-1960s that the first boys from Sungai Jawa were sent off to English secondary education in Port Klang. Noraini's husband Nawab tells me that when their son Yacob prepared to attend an urban Christian mission school, his neighbours warned that the boy would be turned by English education against his own Islamic faith and *kampung* origin. Yacob did not disappoint his parents. After graduating from teachers' college, he returned to help his parents rebuild their house. He is teaching in a *sawah* village in Tanjong Karang. To village parents, Yacob has become a model for children to do well in school and qualify for salaried jobs.

From the early 1970s, as "development" programs and propaganda *program* began to pervade the countryside, *kampung* parents have become anx- *PROPAGANDA* ious to keep their children, especially boys, in school as long as they can pass examinations and win government scholarships. Within the *mukim*, there are four primary schools which provide secular education and five village schoolrooms for Islamic instruction. Whereas secular education at the primary level is free, Malay children who attend Arab Islamic schools pay a small fee. Boys and girls in the two educational streams are distinguished by their uniforms. In the secular schools, boys wear shorts and girls wear uniforms based on the Catholic schools' pinafore. In the Islamic schools, girls dress in white headscarves and blue sarongs (which have the odd effect of making them look like small nuns). Boys also wear *sarung* instead of trousers.

The primary school in Sungai Jawa is the largest in the subdistrict. In 1979, there were 550 girls and 556 boys, most of whom came from the village itself, the rest from surrounding Malay communities.[5] Girls have generally done better than boys. Even very young girls are socialized to be obedient and to comport themselves demurely. These qualities have given them a good start in primary education, compared with boys who are not ready to take school lessons seriously. In my repeated visits to the school, boys were observed to be more spontaneous in the classroom and on the school fields, for schooling has not yet curbed their spirit of exploration and playfulness. Girls are generally more restrained, presenting a cool and neat contrast as they watch from the shadows of trees and verandah the sweaty play of boys. In one class room, I observed the tendency of the male teacher

Village schoolgirls look up to their teacher.

to turn most of his attention to the boys' side of the room, thus eliciting most of the responses from there. Girls are usually bent over their desks in work and seldom volunteer answers to questions. A few girls are made leaders of classroom projects because of their responsibility in carrying out orders.

In recent years, girls have been catching up and perhaps overtaking boys in gaining government scholarships for secondary education. The headmaster tells me that girl pupils are "more clever, clean, obedient, and dedicated . . . and also more fearful of teachers" than boys. A male teacher[6] elaborates, "According to Malay custom, girls are expected to follow instructions." The girls are so obedient, the teacher continues, that the FTZ factories are glad to have them when they fail to pass Form Three or Form Five.

In 1972, about a year after the FTZ was established, a coeducational secondary school was opened in Kampung Telok, thus making it possible for a larger number of village children to proceed on to secondary education. Previously, the nearest secondary schools, many of them operated by Christian missionaries for non-Malay students, were over 12 miles away in towns or in K.L. The influx of rural children to the new secondary school in Kampung Telok is also prompted by government supplies of text books and other materials, in addition to scholarships for a number of children in secondary school. It is becoming routine for above-average Malay children to receive scholarships to national universities and even for further education abroad. Nevertheless, village parents complain that the government is increasingly concentrating educational benefits for Malays in the "less-developed" states on the East Coast, and one can no longer assume that local bright students will receive government scholarships through college. The immediate effect of state sponsorship of rural Malay education is that the percentage of children from the local primary school who go on to secondary education increased from under 70 percent before 1972 to over 95 percent after 1973. Most of them proceed to secular secondary schools in towns, and about one-quarter enroll in Islamic institutions (*Sekolah Arab*). Those who receive scholarships are sent to the best secondary schools (mainly Christian institutions) in the capital.

The cream of the Standard Six crop thus culled off, the Telok secondary school is left with local students who are gradually sloughed off through nationally certified exams held at the Form Three and Form Five levels. In 1979, only 53 percent of the students passed Form Three and 29 percent passed Form Five. Students sit for Form Three when they are 16 years old or thereabout, an age when they can be legally employed. Those who obtain a grade "A," mainly boys, are sent off to vocational and technical schools in preparation for industial employment.

Compared to their good performance in primary school, the widespread failure of girls in the Form Three examination is symptomatic of a larger social reality. A few girls did so exceptionally well in secondary school as to be nominated as top students in 1977 and 1978. In the past years, some female students have received grants to pursue Form Six or attend teachers' colleges elsewhere in the country. For most girls, however, Form Three is the end of their school career. Social recognition of this fact is manifested in the new custom of school trips to the local FTZ after students have sat for their Form Three exams. Conveniently enough, many girls work as temporary operators while waiting for the results; those who fail, as well as many who pass, stay on as factory hands. The factories take in as production workers female graduates of Standard Six, Form Three, and Form Five. One factory considers Standard Six graduates the best assembly workers, since Form Five graduates seem more discontented with work conditions and may persist in looking for better employment opportunities elsewhere.

Thus, although all village girls and boys enroll in school at age seven, they drop out of school at different stages during their childhood and adolescence. More girls than boys end school at age twelve because they are needed to help with household chores and childcare at home. This is particularly the case for girls from poor families, since their parents spend more time on the road seeking wage work. Frequently, girls who drop out after Standard Six are the eldest in the family, i.e., daughters who have been given greater domestic responsibilities, and at a younger age, than most village girls. Eldest daughters often continue in this role of taking over housework and caring for their younger siblings until they get married. It is the younger sisters who are allowed to continue longer in school and/or end up as factory workers.

Ever since the large-scale entry of boys and girls into secondary education, few *kampung* adolescents engage in farm work during their nonschool hours. Some parents try to enforce regular work contributions from their children, especially the boys, by taking them to the *kebun* on weekends and school holidays. Even then, boys and girls only work intermittently in the gardens. The majority of parents, thinking how important education is to their children's future, seldom insist on their children's help on the farm. Those children who demonstrate some promise in their schoolwork are exempt from farmwork altogether. But whereas schoolgirls are still required to perform housework, boys spend most of their free time in ball games, scouting, and other extracurricular school activities. Parents complain that schooling not only takes children away from *kampung* work but that its associated activities and trappings are an additional drain on family resources.

Pemuda who fail the Form Three or Form Five certificate examinations are usually left in village society, living in their parents' homes, working as plantation laborers, factory workers, or simply waiting around for work more commensurate with their education. For instance, Fol is a 20-year–old man who left school after Form Three. After a year's training in mechanics, Fol has had eight different jobs in different urban-based companies. He worked, in rapid succession, in an air-conditioning plant, plastics works, wood workshop, chocolate company (followed by one year of unemployment, when he occasionally helped his father on the farm), a biscuit factory, mechanics workshop, and boiler works. The length of his tenure in these jobs ranged from one day to three months. In most cases, his salary was M$150 to M$165 per month, a sum he found did not compensate for the night shifts and the daily two-hour bus commute. Despite his checkered job history, Fol is bright and ambitious, though frequently discouraged. He often consulted his friends about openings for office boys in government departments. Factory employment, he said, "is inadequate remuneration for one getting on in age, because of the threat of being thrown out by the factory." Only government employment makes sense because it "provides guarantee for the future . . . it is permanent employment. The government cannot throw us out." When I pointed out that he was overqualified to be a peon he said it was "no sweat" since his strategy was to first get a foot through the government door. During the interview, a friend piped in to say that he considered himself very lucky to be working as a gardener in a government institution, even though his salary was only M$190 a month. Friends already employed in the lower echelons of state agencies are critical connections for funnelling these school leavers out of factory jobs, and/or unemployment, into public industries. Nevertheless, access to the labor market for *pemuda* is in general less limited in scope and in opportunities than it is for *pemudi* who have received the same education.

Just as rural boys are getting serious about academic work in secondary school, girls, in a reversal from their former position in primary school, begin to slip in their academic performance. *Pemudi* in their early adolescence are expected to take on more work responsibilities at home and in maintaining interhousehold relations. Their gradually increasing participation in these socially reproductive activities interferes with their work in school. Girls of twelve and older, at an age when most begin secondary school, are expected to do the daily laundry, help prepare lunch and dinner, and take care of younger siblings, especially if there is no older sister at home. As the girls grow older, they often take over most domestic duties from their mothers, who gradually play a supplementary role in cooking, cleaning, and childcare. It is the expectation and practice for middle-aged women who have daughters, or daughters-in-law, to semiretire from household chores and become more directly involved in matters affecting the wider community. Young women also spend a considerable amount of time serving neighbors, friends, and relatives who constantly drop by in the informal way of *kampung* life.

Village families, especially those still firmly involved with cash cropping, are active participants in social networks built upon dyadic relations of reciprocity. The services of young women, graciously performed, are crucial in sustaining these interhousehold bonds, since they are activated primarily through sharing childcare, domestic tasks, and the constant exchange of cooked food. In the event of a wedding, for instance, the host family would request help from neighbors and friends (both female and male) in the preparation of different meals and general festival activities which can last for three consecutive days. Female help in housework and childcare is also transmitted in institutionalized form through child adoption. For instance, when Noraini took to bed with a severe gastric pain, she sent for two adopted daughters (actually her nieces) to take over the housework. One daughter had married out, two were employed in factory work, and the last one was too young to do housework on her own. The two adopted daughters were sisters sitting for their Form Three exams the following month, but they were not unhappy to be asked to help out for a couple of weeks. Never very keen on school, they did not expect to pass the coming examination. In general, young women between the ages of 16 and 24 carry the burden of daily housework and extradomestic obligations, so that they are more busy throughout the day than persons in other age groups.

Besides their increasing domestic responsibilities, adolescent girls growing into adult female roles begin to turn their thoughts to romance and marriage, thoughts prompted in part by magazines, television, and movies. *Pemudi* taking the bus to secondary school sometimes ride off in the direction of Port Klang, where they spend their time wandering around movie houses and shopping complexes imbibing "urban culture." Brighter girl students are not immune to the perceived attractions of early marriage and homemaking. For instance in 1977, the most promising student at Telok secondary school obtained a "C" grade in her Form Five certificate; she was then planning to get married. In a significant shift from past attitudes, village parents prefer their daughters not marry straight out of school now that there are factory jobs close to home and daughters can be induced to earn an extra source of income. However, there are parents who send their daughters for a brief spell in Arab schools, which are said to produce good wives and mothers. Whether their daughter is educated in secular or religious school, wage earning or just doing housework, parents find it difficult to turn down a marriage proposal if the suitor is well-off (see Chapter 6).

Some girls drop out of secondary school because they lack the right combination of subjects to pass the certificate examinations. In the vast majority of cases, three subjects offered — carpentry, agriculture, and domestic science — are not taken by girls because their parents consider the first two "masculine" subjects, while the third (introduced into the curriculum especially for female students) is considered unnecessary since village girls are already proficient in cooking and all aspects of housework and childcare, learnt at the mother's knee. Finally, but not least, the presence of the FTZ just down the road from the school exerts an indirect influence on the poor performance of female students in secondary education. Many girls, already weakened in their resolve to do well in school, see in the FTZ the answer to their immediate future outside the school gates. This is especially the case for girls from poor families, who feel obliged to leave school early and to help supplement the household budget.

Since the large-scale entry of teenage girls into secondary school and factory employment, the only reduction in their family responsibilities is in farm work. Young women working in the factories refuse to pick coffee altogether; their mothers or hired female laborers perform this *kampung* activity. Nevertheless, daughters engaged in factory work cannot escape their share of domestic chores. Young women returning home from the night shift, too overwrought to sleep, often do the laundry and cook the day's meal before retiring. In total, factory women exceed by 3.5 hours the daily labor time of ordinary village women not engaged in regular wage work. As we shall see below, the special pressures on these young women not only exact a toll but also undermine the structure of male authority within the family.

It can be seen that the divergent experiences of *pemuda* and *pemudi* in secondary education, their different responsibilities in the domestic domain, and the increasing market demand for their labor power channel them into alternate career paths. In particular, the market use

A factory woman doing the day's laundry before going to work.

Credit: International Development Research Centre, Ottawa

of *kampung* women as a primary source of labor for low-skilled, dead-end jobs reinforces their tendency not to complete secondary school. Parents, who normally depend on daughters to perform most domestic tasks, also begin to see in them a source of supplementary cash earnings. Daughters are urged to enter the industrial labor market as early as possible because once married, they can no longer be depended upon for financial contributions. The majority of village women stop factory work upon marriage and can rarely be expected to contribute to their family of origin. *Kampung* parents therefore pin their long-term hopes on academically inclined sons who may land a government job and from whom parents can rightly make claims of support whenever necessary. In practice, the movement into education, and villagers' differential expectations of their sons and daughters — shaped in part by the selective market use of male and female labor — bring about the realignment of parent-child relationships which weaken considerably parental power to make children conform to Malay-Islamic ideals.

In the changing social and market context, daughters, as supplementary income-earners *par excellence,* are placed under special pressures in relation to domestic strategy of mobility. At the very least,
as more reliable contributors to the family budget than their brothers,
they keep their families afloat in a situation of threatened downward
mobility. But these women are neither classic proletarians nor classic
victims; the rerooting of their labor power in capitalist structures poses an
unmistakable challenge to domestic male authority, a challenge negotiated and deflected through appeals to emotional bonds and sentiments.

Daughters and Sons: Cooperation and Conflict

> Following Islamic rules, women must under all circum-
> stances, be subordinated to men. . . . [However] in [Sungai
> Jawa] girls have much freedom to pursue higher education.
> Even before there were factories, women were already free
> to work in the *kebun.* Now, they have more freedom — walk-
> ing around at night, making friends by themselves, etc.
> Older folks oppose [such conduct] but the government en-
> joins us not to beat the children. Daughters are allowed to
> work in factories because this is the age of inflation. Parents
> want them to help support the family, develop the country,
> advance industry so that foreigners will want to invest capital
> [here]. . . . [Besides, daughters are permitted to work in fac-
> tories because] parents also want their children to have ex-
> periences. The modern outfits of the young women also con-
> tribute to this age of inflation.
>
> Father of factory daughters, and
a regular listener to radio broadcasts.
>
> Today there are many young men like [my son]. Maybe they
> no longer care for their parents like people did in the old
> days.   Mother of factory man

Talking about the meanings of money, its acquisition, pooling, and
expenditure in Sungai Jawa, one notices too an inflation of sexual images. The commoditization of family relationships within the village
household has linked female sexuality to strategies of mobility and
mediation of class values. Here, I present some case studies of domestic arrangements which in demonstrating the increasing importance of female wages to family budget also capture the ascendency
of mother-daughter relationships and the parallel decline of male
power over daughter and sister.

In Sungai Jawa, the entry of *pemuda* and *pemudi* into wage employment does not automatically result in their handing over all their earn-

ings to their parents, even when they continue to live at home and eat with the rest of the family. In the late 1930s, Rosemary Firth observed that among the Malay fisherfolk on the Kelantan coast, the predominance of small households belied the fact that separate eating and budgetting arrangements existed under one roof (1966: 17). The Malay expressions *makan suku* and *makan sekali* refer to separate budgetting in the first instance and to joint arrangement in the second. In *makan suku*, the staple rice was purchased separately, while there was limited pooling of other resources. Firth's examples of household budgetary arrangement indicate that members individually acquired income from diverse sources; e.g., a man derived income from fishing, his wife from making mats and nets, his mother from her *sawah* fields, and his son as a busdriver (ibid. 18–21). We may therefore argue, although Firth did not explicitly acknowledge this, that the retention of individually acquired income by household members' constituted resistance to the collectivization of resources not obtained from joint production activities organized by the household head.

Such is the emerging trend in contemporary Sungai Jawa households. Earlier, I mentioned the control of resources by the parents who deployed their children's labor power in the *kampung* economy. The only instance of economic individuation existed between husband and wife, the former using his command of family resources to provide for family needs, while the latter retained private savings either from wage work or her own property. However, as the majority of households come to depend on a multiplicity of incomes, economic individuation within the household has increased correspondingly: members variously engaged in wage work may volunteer, sometimes under duress, to pool their earnings for joint consumption. My cases of household budgetting reveal that patterns of giving and taking are increasingly divided along generational and gender lines.

Frequently, the contributions of unmarried sons and daughters hinge upon their perceptions of family needs — i.e., whether these were adequately met by farm income — and the presence of younger siblings at home. I present two examples of sibling solidarity, one in alliance with, the other against, the parents:

Case A. This nuclear family consisted of a middle-aged couple and their five unmarried children. The separate properties of husband and wife, which came to 2.5 acres, provided the main source (*pokok belanja*) for family expenses. The husband also brought in M$125 per month as a rubber tapper. The three older children were wage workers: the son a stevedore and the two daughters factory workers at the Telok FTZ and Shah Alam. The mother was very effective in obtaining a total of M$150 from the working children each month, as well as their contibution towards the purchase of expensive items. She explained:

> Children and parents must discuss together before making a purchase. We must cooperate so that whether it is a good or bad purchase, we share the responsibility equally. Whether light or heavy, we carry the burden together.

A few weeks after these words, her 20-year–old daughter (a worker at the local FTZ) was arrested together with a Tamil foreman in a motel and charged by the Islamic Department with ''illicit sexual intimacy'' (*khalwat*). Her mother paid the fine and gave the girl a thrashing, followed by an order to change her job to another factory. This scandal has not suspended practical sense, the daughter's employment status, nor her support of the family.

Case B. In this example, a second marriage by the mother put an end to support by her working children. Fauziah was a 43-year–old widow in Tanjong Karang who held in trust six acres of land, half in *sawah*, half in coconut-cocoa, for her five children. In her early widowhood, she worked the land with the help of laborers while her children attended school. When her elder daughter became a factory worker in Sungai Way, she rented out her plots to tenants, retaining only her one-acre *pesaka* (inherited property) on which the family house stood. Her oldest son soon started teaching primary school in Jalan Klang Lama, and both working brother and sister remitted money home each month to Fauziah and the three younger children, one girl and two boys.

Two years later, Fauziah married a 64-year–old widower in Sungai Jawa, about 30 miles from her village. She attempted to divide her time between the two communities, leaving her teenage children to care for the household in Tanjong Karang. Her new husband had no property of his own but was holding his late wife's small property in trust for their adopted daughter.[8] He was often short on cash and depended upon Fauziah to bring rice from her farm. She even bought a television set for his house, justifying this to her children on the grounds that their own house was not fitted with electrical lines. Meanwhile, her new husband complained that "going back and forth like newlyweds" was made more difficult because he did not feel comfortable in "the children's father's house."

Not surprisingly, the two older children decided to stop giving their mother money. Fauziah's older daughter said, rather pointedly, "Let father feed mother." She and her brother handed money over to their younger sister for schooling and kitchen expenses. In another bold departure from past norms, the factory woman brought her boyfriend, a smalltown school teacher, to spend the night in her mother's house when the older couple were visiting. Ultimately, it was discreet pressures brought by the village headman which compelled the young lovers to stop this practice and bring forward their wedding date. Such incidents prompted Fauziah's husband to settle his affairs in Sungai Jawa and buy a house in Tanjong Karang, where he was born and still had kinsmen. It is probable that the two households will remain separate even after the older couple have relocated permanently to Tanjong Karang.

These two cases show that even when unmarried children become wage workers, the father is still expected to provide for the bulk of his family's needs. In case A, the mother carefully managed relations with the children to ensure a steady cash flow. In case B, the working children resisted supporting the remarried mother and saw their main responsibility as toward younger siblings still in school. The following examples illustrate that sibling solidarity is not always present, especially when brothers feel that their employment situation does not permit them to share their earnings. It falls upon their working sisters to meet various claims from parents and other household members.

Case C. The divergent expectations of sons and daughters in this household show that where the family is well-endowed with land, the education of sons is encouraged and no claims are made on their earnings. During the course of their marriage, the industrious and frugal parents have acquired nine acres of land to add to the husband's one-acre *pesaka*. They had eight unmarried children ages ten to 24 years living at home. By *kampung* standards, the two elder sons earned substantial salaries, one as a teacher trainee (M$800 per month), the other a factory technician (M$500 per month). Neither brother contributed to the family budget, even though a third brother had been accepted as a scholarship candidate at the National University but required a monthly subsidy of M$100. In fact, the father had set up a bank account for the educational expenses of his sons; he expected that the two younger boys would also go on to higher education and qualify as civil servants. His expectations for his daughters were more modest; the two elder ones had ended school at Form Three and were soon married off (the second one to Yacob). The youngest girl was doing poorly in school.

The two working sons kept most of their own earnings. They had bought motorbikes on credit in order to commute to work. Together, they purchased a set of formica-topped furniture, a stereo system, and a television set. Occasionally, they bought candies and imported fruits for their younger siblings. The father justified his sons' retention of their earnings because in his view the young men needed to save for wedding expenses (*wang hantaran*) and their future houses, although neither man was at that time planning to get married soon. Noncontribution by working sons, almost unheard of among working daughters, was tolerated because of their white-collar jobs, which enhanced the privileged status of all young men in Malay families.

Case D. In this example, three generations participated variously to care for an 80-year-old widower, a member of the village committee in Sungai Jawa. Unlike his peers, this old man was poor, living on his late wife's half-acre plot with his youngest daughter, age 28 and unmarried, and two granddaughters (ages 20 and 13). Daughter and older granddaughter were factory workers who contributed some M$100 each month for kitchen goods which the old man purchased on credit (a privilege granted him as a JKK member) from the corner Malabari store. The fathers of both granddaughters had settled outside the village on FELDA land schemes. The father of the younger girl remitted M$80 per month for her support. In addition, the old man also received monthly sums of about M$30 from two other married sons living nearby in houses built on their mother's land. In 1957, the old man had bought his own two-acre *kebun* in another village, but he was not able to plant it with oil palm until the early 1970s, when his daughter started working in the factory. Her cash contributions and a son's labor on the land have finally produced a small income from the maturing tree crop.

Thus this old man received a total monthly income of M$240 from six different sources, most of which went to food expenses. He also managed to save about $30 each year to buy fertilizers at subsidized prices (as a JKK member, he had prior access to the limited supply) for his palm holding. But it was the daily physical and emotional care of his daughter and granddaughters which assured the old man a good, though spare, standard of living. The small contributions from his sons must be seen in the light of his developing property which would produce sizeable earnings as the palms mature fully. He had six sons but because of land poverty three had moved out of the village and the remaining three (all married men with children) work as laborers at Port Klang. When time approaches for the partition of their parents' property, it is not uncommon for sons who have left to give up their rightful shares to those who remained in the *kampung*. It seems likely, therefore, that the two sons who were making monetary gifts to the old man were also strengthening their future claims on his property; one of them was also a sharecropper on the land.

Case E. Other old folk are not so well-cared for, and sons do not necessarily contribute to their upkeep simply because they own property. An old woman had a half-acre plot from her late husband, while her second husband held a 1.25 acre *pesaka*. Sparsely covered with aging coffee bushes and coconut trees, their *kebun* produced very low yields. To supply her kitchen, the woman coaxed vegetables from a clayey soil. Nevertheless, the couple and their working son still needed to spend at least M$120 per month at the village store. They sometimes received cooked meals from her married son and daughter (by the first marriage), but the old woman was disappointed that the son living at home refused to make a regular cash contribution to family expenses. She commented that he was not unusual, adding perhaps that *kampung* children no longer cared for their parents as in the old days.

Indeed, the 24-year-old son was unlike *pemuda* of earlier generations. He had failed Form Three and started work at 18 in a saw mill. He used his savings to buy himself a radio and bed (most *kampung* Malays slept on mats). At the time of my interview, he was working at a shoe factory at Port Klang, making only M$150 a month. He had recently bought a motorbike for M$1,800 but had paid up only M$700. Occasionally, he slipped his mother M$10 bills, but when she asked for more, he asked, "Who pays for the motorbike?" He also refused to work on the land which would one day be his, complaining that he needed to rest on weekends. Instead, he "cruised" around on his motorbike.[9] Thus, the generation gap in this family has been accentuated by *kampung-bandar* (rural-urban) differences in cultural values. The parents expected that in their old age their son would help them on the land, as in the idealized but fairly accurate picture of the recent past. The young man, entering the labor market at the bottom of the ladder, experienced frustration at the growing distance between his meager earnings and his acquired needs as a *moden* ("modern") urban worker.

These three cases demonstrate that when young men are engaged in wage employment, they often resist making a regular contribution to the family budget because of their privileged status at home, adequate family income from the farm, and/or their perceived need for more personal expenses than their working sisters. The final examples reveal that young men discontented with their job prospects have greater opportunities to take their time looking for the "right" job because working sisters can easily be persuaded, by the mother, to provide a steady cash flow.

Case F. Noraini and Nawab's household provides a fine example of how increasing dependence on daughters' earnings strengthens daughter-mother bonds while the unemployed son, though tolerated, becomes a focus of grievances. Nawab had lost his *pesaka* in prewar business ventures and now earned his living as a fruit peddler. His profits paid for daily household expenses while income from Noraini's small *pesaka* she kept as savings against rainy days. The oldest son Yacob had bought a one-acre plot in Sungai Jawa which he let his father use for raising annual cash crops. He also contributed rice on his monthly visits home.

There were seven children living at home (from ages 11 to 25) of whom four were still in school. Two older daughters worked in electronics factories and every month handed over a portion of their paychecks to Noraini. The 20-year-old son has not held a job since he graduated from an English-medium secondary school. Although the family enjoyed an adequate level of living, there was constant pressure to get him to apply for a position at a government office. Proud of his command of English and participation in local politics, his parents and relatives believed that he would easily obtain employment as an official (*pegawai*), thereby "earning thousands and thousands of *ringgit*." The young man's ambition to write television dramas was considered a pipe dream, much as they admired the awards his poems had won in media-sponsored competitions. For the past three years, while he wrote songs and organized village pantomimes, his sister had been balancing factory employment with household chores. She complained:

> The males often do not want to listen to their parents' advice, and so parents do not have much hope in them. . . . Boys only know how to eat.

Her brother's stubborn resistance to the bureaucratic straitjacket prevailed even when he was offered a job at the District Office. Nursing his sense of freedom, he occasionally chose to pick up cash cleaning cargo ships. However, it gradually dawned on him that the *kampung* appeared to have no place for a Chekhov; after I left the village, he wrote to say that he had put on a tie to work for the National Electrical Board.

Case G. In this final example, the earnings of working daughters sustained daily family needs while the mother again handled the finances. The household consisted of a middle-aged couple, their two younger sons (18 years and older), and a daughter (by the man's previous marriage), 39 years old and never married. The couple together owned two acres of cash crops, while the wife controlled an additional plot which she held in trust for her four children by a previous marriage. The husband referred to his wife as "the bank," since she handled all incomes from the *kebun* and contributions from her stepdaughter and two daughters who had recently moved out after marriage. The stepdaughter had become a tailor after her own mother died in order to support her father. She still made a monthly contribution of M$200 and, together with her stepsisters, had purchased the formica furniture suite and television set, *de rigueur* for families with any pretentions of upward mobility. The parents did not chip in for these consumer items because, as the father explained, "They are the ones making money."

Meanwhile, neither brother, both out of school for a couple of years, was looking for a job because work in the *kampung* was not desired, while urban-based jobs would not be tolerable without their own means of transportation, which they had yet to acquire.[10] It appeared unlikely that the stepsister, who provided the lion's share of daily expenses, would ever marry and move out; her unmarried status was the basis for the continued well-being of the household, despite her brothers' unemployed idleness.

The cases of household arrangements reflect changing patterns of domestic relationships and pooling of resources as more families come to depend on incomes derived not from joint production effort on the land but from the wage employment of individual members. Although only a few cases have been selected for presentation here, they and participation-observation in the district over a period of time permit the delineation of a number of trends concerning the changing dynamic of domestic relations.

In the generalization of commodity relations, the *kampung* father loses control over the children's labor while the mother, through her domestic influence over daughters, gains some control over their earnings for household expenses. The above sets of examples illustrate, respectively, (1) sibling solidarity in the sharing of earnings, (2) sons can and often do resist sharing their earnings, and (3) sons may remain unemployed indefinitely while sisters become regular cash contributors. They all demonstrate, in varying degrees, the growing centrality of working daughters in sustaining daily relationships of reproduction and the consequent strengthening of mother-daughter ties vis-à-vis men in the family.

Whereas the special pressures on daughters to make cash contributions and perform house chores represent a new intensified kind of *realignment* physical and emotional draining, the new dependence on their earnings provides daughters/sisters with critical leverage to realign domestic power relations. This relative autonomy is strengthened because parents feel that they can, for the time being, rely less on sons kept longer in school (training for bureaucratic careers) or out of the labor market by opportunities not commensurate with their qualifications or aspirations. The changing content of daughter-parent, sister-brother relationships is displayed in refusal of money to parents who remarry, criticism of brothers, more daring enjoyment of premarital sex, power over younger siblings who ask for money, and decisions to hand earnings over to the mother. While the edifice of male authority is maintained, male honor is in a fundamental sense undermined as the father's farm income steadily declines, unemployed brothers accept doles from working sisters, and the household budget derives increasingly from female wages. In many cases, it is the mother who prods daughters to begin factory work, who extracts their regular contributions, punishes but tolerates their sexual adventures, and persuades them to delay marriage. In effect, the employment status of working daughters has loosened many from father-brother control, connecting them instead to male power institutionalized in bureaucratic systems external to the *keluarga* (see Part III).

The Fractured Day

> Haste is seen as a lack of decorum combined with diabolical ambition.
>
>   Pierre Bourdieu (1963: 72)
>
> Time is now currency; it is not passed but spent.
>
>   E.P. Thompson (1967: 61)

Before we take leave of the workaday domestic scene, it is appropriate to mention that the individuation of domestic activities has been accompanied by a new apprehension and experience of time. Up until recently, Malay notions of work and its integration into everyday life were rooted in a precapitalist time-sense geared to internal promptings and the cycle of social activities. When asked how long a certain activity will take, old men, drawing on their handrolled tobacco, may reply with nonchalance, "Ah, two, three (etc.) cigars' time." As the leisurely pace of *kampung* life ebbs and flows according to the dictates of capitalist relations of production, some villagers have responded more readily than others. However, on hot afternoons, the villager espied from shady verandahs cycling earnestly to his *kebun* may be mocked as "beaten by his familiar-ghost" (*dipukul toyol*) to "plant capital" (*tanam modal*) while others take their customary nap. Locally, time is still perceived as a social-ordered rhythm, and the transgression of implicit time codes is a transgression of social rules.

In Sungai Jawa, resistance to the new urgency of "development" is registered in the malicious pleasure friends and relatives take in the misfortunes of those driven by the clock. A fine example of the latter are Ahmad and Edah, an enterprising couple indefatigable in their pursuit of alternative earnings (besides cash cropping). Ahmad

Men cooperate in erecting the house of a newly-wed couple.

Women plan a kenduri *marking a boy's circumcision.*

worked as a marketing agent and barber, while Edah grew vegetables for sale. Through the years, they had somehow managed to accumulate capital to add four acres to his small *pesaka*. For a couple approaching middle age, they were also unusual in having only two school-age children; Ahmad is reported to have said that having more children "would cost money." Their steady acquisition of wealth excited more than envy, since time-thrift held both back from acts of sociability. Instead of pitching in at a house-construction event or the preparation of a *slametan* (ritual meal), the couple often arrived late clutching some store-bought item as their contribution. Frequently, their children were torn from games with their peers and sent home to attend to studies. Neighbors whispered that their obsession with time was the work of the familiar *toyol* they had secretly raised to filch money from neighbors. Turning tables on his masters, the mischevious *toyol* drove them even harder to produce more wealth. Besides, people pointed to the contrasting appearance of the couple as evidence of the *toyol*'s handiwork.[11] Edah looked weather-beaten, and her heavy figure was a contrast to Ahmad, who was fair, slim and always neatly-clad in batik shirts, like urban Malays.

Much to their satisfaction, neighbors were soon presented with an incident which confirmed their suspicions that something was amiss in the tight schedule of this couple. For some time, idle youths clustering at village junctions had noticed that after closing his barber shop for the day, Ahmad stopped at another house on his way home. One evening, led by the son of a JKK member, the youths burst in and caught Ahmad locked in an embrace with the mistress of the house. The youths sternly warned Ahmad to stop his trysts, and social pressure was reinforced by broadcasting the scandal. Inflicted by shame, Edah offered to choose a second wife for Ahmad, but he declined. Since the incident, Edah has spent less time in the *kebun* and more on her appearance. At Hari Raya, she attended a *slametan* at a kinswoman's home wearing makeup and freshly minted curls. Looking relaxed and proud, Ahmad pointed out to me that his wife had a "maxi" (dress) on. The unfortunate event shows that not only is the loose time-sense inextricably bound to the various claims of social obligation but that leisurely pace is a mark of decorum. The man in a hurry surely has something to hide, and many an outsider, from colonial officials to development officers, have complained of, and given in to, the *kampung* sense of leisurely time.

From the individual perspective, the cycle of the daily activities was up until recently framed and balanced by the symmetry of Islamic prayers, a cyclical time joined to inner compulsions. Personal promptings and the task-orientation of rural work, rather than external impositions, guided passage through the day. Critically, *kampung* folk expected to work at their own volition, and any joint project was carried out with a minimum of supervision or rigid schedule. Old and young men have often claimed that they prefered to remain cultivators or unemployed rather than laborers to be "bossed" around by someone else. This complaint is not unknown among young women who, among all age-gender categories, are usually the only ones supervised, if at all, in their daily chores.

Before the recent restructuring of domestic activities by school and factory clocks, chores on the farm and in the kitchen were woven into the flow of social life. Although women's work was more continual than the sporadic work of men, the former played an important and frequently decisive role in determining the what and when of their duties. Young girls developed a sense of self-worth from their daily chores, the fine performance of which was a desirable quality of human relations, not an economic transaction. Nubile women were individually identified by their preparation of the popular chilli-and-anchovies condiment, by their aesthetically pleasing and yet economical performance of chores, or by their special way with children. In their daily round of work activities, all but young girls were usually free of female supervision and almost never under male guidance. When women came together for child-minding or feast-preparation, individuals carried out their preferred activities, pounding chillies here, stirring the beef *rendang* there, with no prescribed role or task. Slow stretches of dull routine were lightened by songs and jokes, often at the expense of the absent males. Besides, the larger rhythm of endless hot days, varied only by the monsoon, was intermittently broken by unexpected visits, rainstorms, the cycle of *slametan* meals, religious celebrations, and the fasting month which precluded the mechanical patterning of work characteristic of industrialized societies.

But, almost imperceptibly, a new regularity has settled into the irregular flows of village life. Young women are at the frontlines in confronting capitalist time, at school, factory and in the home. Bureaucratic and school schedules have fractured the week into workdays and weekends, accommodating the Islamic calendar by making allowances for long lunch breaks and half-days on Friday. It is however the factory clock which bites more deeply into the textures of *kampung* life.

At the Telok FTZ, young female workers ages 16 to 24 are clocked-in daily for eight consecutive hours, rigidly varied by two 15-minute breaks and a half-hour lunch. Every fortnight, production workers are placed on a different work shift, which radically alters their accustomed experience of day, night, and month, as attested to by missed sleep and menstrual cycles. Placed under continual male supervision, the meaning of work is reduced to repetitive time-motion manipulations, and factory operators have little sense of the entire production process and how the microcomponents they assemble are fitted into the larger scheme of manufactured things and social relationships (see Part III). After a day of physical and emotional stress in the factory, the young women return to eat, sleep, and perform household chores out of step with others in the family. Industrial discipline now structures the rhythm of home life, fracturing daily experiences into "work" and "leisure." Many women talk about the time "lost to the factory" as they try to wrest "free time" from housework for "spending time" in lost sleep or in the diversions of the consumer market. Since these young women continue to attend to domestic and social demands for their help, their time-thrift is not commented upon nor criticized. Factory women not only learn to balance this dual burden but also grapple with the sense of lost autonomy in work. Six or more years of schooling have failed to dampen their spirits, and they confront pervasive regimentation in their work life as a continuing personal, domestic, and social crisis (see below).

In this chapter, I have considered the changing meanings of "household," gender, and proletarianization in Sungai Jawa by discussing the restructuring of domestic relationships before and after national penetration by national agencies and late capitalist enterprises. As the rural household becomes more integrated into bureaucratic structures and different labor markets, the form and content of domestic relations are reconstituted but in culturally specific ways. The general movement of boys and girls into mass education produces a labor reserve for modern enterprises, while for the upwardly mobile, schooling provides an internal channel to the state system. The selective pressures of labor markets and divergent expectations of children have made young single women the pivot of domestic strategies of mobility.

As female sexuality becomes linked to class formation, young women find in their wage-earning role this paradoxical dilemma: the labor power which enables them to challenge male authority at home is also the means whereby they are subjected to intense capitalist discipline. The daughter/sister as factory woman is a new cultural configuration conditioned by the cash nexus within and outside the rural family. As temporary wage workers harnessed to family aspirations, young women experience a new alienation from work as well as from their families. In many ways, they are working and marrying out of cycles with old and reassuring norms of conduct and maturation. These contradictions are multiplied as more come to experience a *janda*-like freedom but yet remain formally of junior status within their families (as daughters/virgins), the labor market (as semiskilled workers), and society at large. In the next chapter, we will see how some village women seek to reconcile their contradictory status in the customary option of marriage.

Chapter 6

Marriage Strategies: Negotiating the Future

> Some of [the men's] talk is mocking, because in their view, perhaps, our work here [in the factory] gives us too much freedom, as for instance, always going out at night, "dating" with "boyfriend" . . . Ah, maybe they like [factory women]. They only talk, but they pick factory women too. . . . For instance, in my family, my brother himself has never talked badly about me; now, he is marrying a woman who works at the factory too.
>
> An unmarried factory woman

Marriage and the departure of children represent the ruptures and uneasy reconciliations of family relations between generations. The ways courtship and marriage are effected, however, are intimately connected to other systems of exchange and alliance in the wider society. In this chapter, I intend to show that marriage strategies — values, interests, and practices dictating the choice of spouses — have evolved in relation to changing Malay society and political economy. While improvisation has marked marriage customs in Sungai Jawa from the early days, in the late 1970s young women and men exhibited a striking sense of self in their matrimonial choices and negotiations. Personal aspirations and acquired interests can be more various than social practice, and few parties to the matrimonial game are fully satisfied with the negotiated contract, even within an expanding marriage economy. Family conflict, broken betrothals, divorces and the unwedded condition are the loose ends and ragged edges of the *kampung* society in transition.

For too long, anthropologists have been beholden to the concept of "development cycle of the domestic group," a process which is assumed to unfold inevitably according to prescribed cultural norms.[1] In an elaboration of this view, Pierre Bourdieu maintains that marriage strategies are the "socio-logical" outcomes of preexisting structural principles (1977: 58-70). This essentially static model of social reproduction is curiously disguised by an analytical dependence on the explication of marital strategies and maneuvers within a maze of given rules. However, by exposing hidden mechanisms which adjust practice to social structure, Bourdieu allows the possibility for individual innovation and the varied implications capital — symbolic and economic, invested and intended — can have for marriage strategies.

In the following account of courtship and marriage in Sungai Jawa, I maintain that among Malay villagers, changing self-identity, as much as the desire to ensure or advance social position, conditions the form and goal of marriage strategies. Family relations are taken as a set of cultural practices, an open-ended process (not "a cycle") through which members attempt to resolve contradictions born of feelings, material interests, and contingencies in particular historical circumstances. By means of case studies on courtship and marriage, I hope to illuminate the mechanisms whereby cultural practices remediated class values in matrimonial arrangements as Sungai Jawa grew from a pioneer settlement into the now commercialized hinterland of industrial development. Over the course of sixty years, manpower and landed wealth have been superseded by varied forms of capital in determining the repertoire of choices in the marriage market. Furthermore, the changing perspectives of young working women and men reveal their contrasting images of sexuality and options of marrying and not marrying.

Marriage Strategies of Earlier Generations

Among early male immigrants in Sungai Jawa, the critical question was not whether to marry, but when. According to old informants, some time after the turn of the century, two Javanese brothers applied to the colonial land office for the right to clear a river junction for settlement by immigrants from Central Java. By 1910, one hundred Javanese families and two Chinese stores constituted the growing settlement. Chinese river traders departing from Port Klang wended through the swamps in small boats, buying village crops, selling provisions, and forwarding credit. As Javanese men arrived in the settlement, they were immediately recruited by relatives, friends, and contractors to clear the jungle and establish holdings of food and cash crops.

It was not until after 1920 that villagers were permitted by the land office to grow the lucrative crop, rubber. Even then, they were penalized by land taxes: M$12 on a rubber lot (five acres) compared to M$3 for a lot planted with *kampung* trees. The gradual spread of rubber cultivation both drew more Javanese immigrants and pulled the settlement out of the backwaters. A schoolroom had been set up almost from the start to provide boys with Islamic instruction. By 1927 sufficient people and cash had trickled in to support the construction of a mosque in the heart of the *kampung*. When Sungai Jawa was linked by a cart track to the main road a few years later, the settlement, now splintered into twelve hamlets, had gravitated away from the riverbank towards the interior rubber country of the colonial economy.

In the frontier conditions, the active recruitment of male relatives and friends produced a skewed sex ratio within the community. Marriage for most male immigrants was further delayed because upon arrival they had to work off debts incurred on the way over before applying for a land grant to make a *kebun* and build a house. Only then were they considered eligible suitors for the limited number of nubile girls among the settler families. Furthermore, bachelors thinking of marriage had to leave the village and earn wages in plantations, perhaps making 50 cents per day. According to customary practice, bridewealth was in two parts: payment for wedding expenses (*wang hantaran*) and a gift of cash or gold (*wang mas*) to the bride, as required by the Islamic marriage contract (*akad nikah*).[2] An engagement ring was left to the discretion of the suitor. Marriage for some men was further postponed because they pursued Islamic studies, locally or further afield, while supporting themselves as wage laborers. From the 1920s onwards, an Islamic boarding school (*madrasah*) set up by a *kijaji* in Sungai Jawa also attracted young Javanese immigrants from other parts of the Peninsula. According to a village elder, most men were not ready to marry until they had property in land and house: "How could they have provided for a family otherwise?"

In contrast, girls in their adolescence and even childhood were married off by their parents hoping to attract energetic young men into their network. For instance, the stepson of a village founder married a 15-year-old girl in 1921. He was 23, had property and connections, while she was already a divorcée. Forced into marriage with an older relative when she was ten, she was subsequently divorced for refusing to consumate the union. At her second wedding, the groom gave M$60 in *hantaran* and M$22 as a bridal gift. He had earned the money digging ditches in a British plantation. In the local cashpoor economy, no other items were exchanged between groom and bride. She received household items and perhaps new *batik* from her parents. In a few cases, however, families rich in *kebun* but not in sons made over their daughter's *pesaka* upon her marriage, thereby having the pick of eager suitors. Competition among immigrant men in the marriage market was further intensified when the colonial government gradually banned alienation of jungle land and restricted rubber cultivation among *kampung* folk.

The place of *pesaka* in the marriage contract sometimes set the tone of emotional life. In one case, a man married his late wife's widowed sister in order to keep the sisters' *pesaka* intact, thereby maximizing the land area at his disposal. His second wife accepted the proposition but refused to work on the holding after marriage, despite his chiding. The significance of property in structuring the conjugal bond is brought home in another example where the wife was not only the propertyholder but 30 years her husband's junior. After twenty years or more of married life, she said, "He is only squatting here." Cheated of his *pesaka* by a brother, her husband came into the marriage without property and fathered three children. A feeble man now in his seventies, he also considered himself a squatter on his wife's land, unable to contribute labor.

For many women then, early marriage, wide age difference between husband and wife, and ease of divorce often resulted in two or more successive unions and children by different husbands. Older men and women who had married more than once usually claim that divorce was precipitated when their spouses developed a strong attraction to someone else. In one example, the husband noted that since his wife was the culprit, he denied her her rightful half-share of their jointly acquired property. However, he later bequeathed that property to the son they had together. Although incidents of divorce, abandonment, or death in a woman's married life were not uncommon, early generations of women in Sungai Jawa had many children. In my sample of 37 women aged 55 years and older — i.e., who married and had children before the war — the average number of children was 6.5, spaced throughout the reproductive life. Gradually, natural increase and immigration contributed to population growth which, together with the operation of Islamic inheritance rules, progressively reduced the land-person ratio in each successive generation.

By the war years, sorcery accusations highlighted the intensified competition among men for scarce nubile girls and scarce land. Adolescent girls who were to receive *pesaka* at marriage became the targets of marriage proposals, frequently rejected by parents waiting to receive the "right" match. Thwarted in their marriage strategies, disappointed suitors were often suspected of employing *dukun* (sorcerers) to inflict madness on the hapless maiden. In what follows, Noraini's mother, Natajah, relates her family story. Framed by avowals of contemporary Islamic disbelief in spirits, her account tells us that black magic on the heels of disappointed love had to be undone by other sorcerers and other lovers, sometimes found in the same man.

In 1943, Natajah was a 34-year-old widow who controlled 13 acres of cash crops left by her late husband, himself a *dukun*. Her elder girls, Norma and Noraini, were beautiful adolescents, much sought after by young and middle-aged men. Norma had had four suitors by age thirteen, when she showed signs of being a victim of black magic. She urinated constantly and was physically weak. Natajah employed a *dukun* who dug under their house to recover an effigy bristling with pins, believed to have been planted by a rejected lover. The destruction of the doll apparently cured Norma who soon after married and was given her share of the *pesaka*. After the birth of her first child, her husband struck her on the temple for speaking to another man. Natajah took her to the *kadi* and demanded a divorce. Norma remarried and had three children by her second husband. Her health gradually worsened and she died, purportedly of the same illness inflicted by black magic many years previously.

Noraini herself became vulnerable to sorcery attacks after Natajah had turned down three proposals for her hand. One magic spell cast to induce madness misfired and struck her younger brother. Babbling incoherently, he took to scaling house posts and prancing on the roof. Natajah rehired the same *dukun* who had treated Norma to cure her son. Nawab, the *dukun*'s apprentice stepson, set eyes on Noraini, asked for her hand, and was accepted. As Natajah explains, ''He was clever at his work.''

While black magic was directed towards destroying another man's potency (through the desired wife), other Malays discovered in trade the more potent alchemy for investment to wealth. In the quickening postwar years, some marital unions were effected with an eye to the market system. Take, for instance, the case of a villager who had made money processing and selling coconut and coffee during the 1930s and 1940s. He had acquired 15 acres of prime coffee gardens. In 1950, he arranged the marriage of his only daughter to a student at the *madrasah*, handing over a portion of the *pesaka* and jewelry to the young couple. The young man, who later became Haji (henceforth, Hj.)[3] Amir, was recruited into his father-in-law's coffee business and eventually took over the enterprise. In another example, Hj. Hadith rose from selling scrap rubber to land speculation after a second marriage. In the early 1950s, he divorced his first wife to marry a Chinese woman, who also divorced her squatter husband and converted to Islam. As business partners, they operate the largest Malay rubber company and credit business in the *mukim*. They also own provision stores, boardinghouses for factory workers, and rural and urban real estate. He is always referred to as ''Rich Man (*Orang Kaya*) Hj. Hadith'' and is perhaps the wealthiest self-made Malay in the subdistrict (i.e., after some politicians).

✓ We see then that up until recently, matrimonial strategies were in the hands of bachelors and the parents of nubile daughters. In the pioneer community where manpower and land were key to the good life, marriage was potentially a strategy of upward mobility for poor immigrant men. To parents, a daughter's well-made marriage could strengthen their economic position and ensure the transmission of social status. The skewed distribution of single men to nubile girls, and as time went on, of available land resources to population, generated intense competition for wives. On the one hand, sorcery attacks directed at would-be brides represented a symbolic protest which both divided and unified laboring men in the difficult task of social reproduction; on the other hand, girls forced into marriage at an early age gradually gained the right of self-determination in arranging later marital unions. As we shall see below, in the expanding post-independence economy, young unmarried women came to enjoy greater opportunities not only to enter the marital game but also to bear the consequences on their own.

Marriage Strategies and the Commodity Logic

From the late 1970s onwards, the expanding rural economy has had ripple effects on the marriage circuits of young women and men born and bred in Sungai Jawa. In the new political economy where *bumiputra*-ism carries great weight in national life, decendants of Javanese immigrants have begun to occasionally wed not only Minangkabau, Mandailing, and Batak, but also indigenous Malays, although the preference remains spouses of Javanese ancestry. In public discourse, Sungai Jawa folk claim *bumiputra* status, but in private conversations, they insist on their ''Javanese'' difference from other ethnic Malays.[4] Widespread awareness of the political, social, and economic implications of the national *bumiputra* identity has also encouraged marital alliances which cut across urban-rural, salaried-farmer divisions. In the discussion below, marital strategies within the expanded arena raise the following questions:

a) Where are spaces for maneuver opening up?
b) What are the stakes for the contenders?
c) What kinds of tactics for negotiation and interruption come into play?
d) What are the varied cultural forms which ensue in the marriage market?

In addition, although customary institutions and family interests constitute structuring forces in matrimony matters, nubile women and men are increasingly individuated in their perceptions, emotions, and conduct in courtship and marriage. Bourdieu has demonstrated that human action is not just reflex of structure but can also be the source of change within structural principles (1977). Here, I prefer to treat personal achievements (acquired values and practices) not merely as the external inscriptions of received social order but also as the inventive tactics which challenge and sometimes outplay received structures of domination (see de Certeau 1984). The following cases of matrimony, listed according to the divergent strategies of different social categories, will illustrate how conflicting values and improvisations continually rework cultural forms in the making of a marriage.

The Upwardly Mobile: Alliances and Accidents

For the well-off folk in Sungai Jawa, marriage as a rite of passage and the precipitating event of family dispersal has become the occasion to establish social connections further into the widening political economy. The marriage of the eldest daughter in particular hinges upon the establishment of ties with upwardly mobile men who would consolidate the family social position even as it embarks on the phase of dissolution. Sequestered by family and education from uncouth village contact, daughters of the well-to-do are magnets to the regions' eligible men. Competition for rich girls' hands is further narrowed by demanding expensive bridewealth from ambitious but poor would-be suitors. What is perhaps more interesting is the degree of poise and level-headedness displayed by young women in their marriage affairs.

<u>Case A.</u> By their fifties, Hj. Amir and his wife had become one of the most well-to-do couples in Sungai Jawa. They were ''comfortable'' because they owned some of the best coffee gardens around. In 1971, they went on the hajj and upon their return were granted their desire to have a son. After that, Hj. Amir retired from farm supervision to devote himself to religious study. Their house was elegant, raised above a well-swept compound surrounded by spice trees and flowering bushes. The family, however, was rather disliked by villagers for holding themselves aloof from social intercourse with all but a few select families.

There were four daughters. The eldest, Salmah, spent a few months in factory work, but after her father pulled a few strings, she got a typing position in a UMNO branch office. It was said that his party loyalty also helped secure scholarships for two other daughters, one to attend an Islamic college, the other a secondary school in K.L. Salmah did not get married until she was almost twenty-six, a rather late age for village women, but it was not for want of suitors. Her first suitor was a Batak driving instructor from an ordinary village family. It took four attempts before Salmah's family agreed to the proposal. Soon after, the Batak man suddenly broke off the engagement in order to marry Hj. Hadith's eldest daughter.

The young man was enticed by Hj. Hadith's offer of capital to purchase 15 acres, which the young couple planned to plant with rubber and oil palm. Hj. Hadith's daughter received a two-acre *pesaka* as house-plot, as well as funds to build a suburban-type bungalow. In addition, they received a monthly subsidy of about M$1,000 in rents received from Hj. Hadith's 16 rooming houses in Klang. To set up the young man in business, Hj. Hadith extended capital for the purchase of a petrol pump station.

When Salmah's mother recalled her broken engagement, she itemized the Batak's newly acquired capital and said that it had been their loss. However, Salmah got to keep the engagement ring. Her second suitor was the son of the *kampung kijaji*, a Form Three graduate at the local school. Given his father's esteemed status, Hj. Amir and wife could not very well turn down this proposal. After the engagement, Salmah suggested that he join the police force. Upon hearing this, the *kijaji* was grieviously wounded, having hoped his son would become an Islamic teacher. Some time later, in a departure from customary practice, the suitor took Salmah for a drive and told her he intended to make a *hantaran* of M$700.[5] She replied that these days payments were normally in the thousands. The engagement was thus ended.

Salmah was the only village woman I knew who have had two broken engagements and yet continued to receive marriage offers. In early 1979, an ex-classmate who had since become a policeman proposed and was accepted. Her mother explained that although he was sunburned and less handsome than previous suitors, he would soon be promoted to police corporal; his father had also been in the police force.[6]

As marriage negotiations proceeded, Salmah's parents rather uncouthly, in the opinion of other villagers, asked for a bridewealth of M$1,500. It was rumored that the actual amount handed over might have been M$2,100. In contrast to prewar practices, the exchange of nuptial gifts has become a conspicuous custom in village weddings, but the scale of gift-giving in Salmah's case was exceptional. She received fifteen trays of expensive clothing and accessories for the engagement and five more sets of gifts at the marriage ceremony. A smaller stream of gifts was sent to the groom's house. In preparation for the wedding day, Hj. Amir renovated his kitchen and built a new outhouse to be fitted with urban facilities. On the morning of her wedding, Salmah insisted on going to a Chinese beauty parlor in Klang. Heavy traffic delayed her return for more than an hour while the groom and his party waited anxiously in a neighbour's house. Threats to break off the wedding had been voiced when Salmah finally arrived in a taxi. Her humiliated father wrenched open the car door and tore at her hair. Relatives quickly interceded, thereby ending spectators' enjoyment of this undignified display of passion. Wiping away tears, Salmah and her intended participated in the "sitting-in-state" wedding ceremony (*bersanding*) while a cloud of excited gossip swirled around them. The next day, the couple flew off to Singapore for a honeymoon, an uncustomary climax to a Malay wedding. After one month's stay with her parents, Salmah decided to rent a house in K.L., which was midpoint between her job and her husband's in two separate towns.

The marriages of Salmah and Hj. Hadith's daughter illustrate the careful strategies of rich parents whose daughters were expected to be won by enterprising young men who would one day be dominant in the local political and economic arenas. Seducton by capital, bickering over the bridewealth, and the inflation of gift exchanges reveal the extent to which marital contracts have become commodified. Salmah was actively involved in arranging her own marriage and, somehow unrestrained by customary practice, managed to express, in her tastes and goal, a new kind of sexuality.

Case B. This example provides an interesting contrast, because it is the village groom who gains an urban, more successful spouse. Kamal was a 28-year-old librarian in a secondary school. He frequently met with Sharifah, a 23-year-old trainee teacher from Klang, after her evening classes ended. One night they were spied upon by colleagues who threatened to beat them up for illicit sexual intimacy (*khalwat*) and turn them over to the state Islamic Department. After a long discussion, the two decided to make amends for their indiscretion by marrying quickly. Sharifah's brother agreed to have the wedding in his house in Klang, while a small party was held in Kamal's home on his birthday, which rather conveniently fell in the following month.

Rumors claimed that Sharifah was pregnant and that her parents had demanded M$2,100 in *hantaran* because she was a teacher.

Case C. Another way whereby a marriage may be brought forward is illustrated by the case of Hamzah and his wife who had seven daughters but no son. Between them they had three acres of coconut and rubber, and two heads of cattle. Hamzah was a guard in a Port Klang warehouse; in the peak coffee season, he also worked as a marketing agent. His eldest daughter had married a dockworker two years earlier. He complained to me that it was difficult to have a family of girls, since his wife had to care for the holding and animals without male help.

The second daughter, Mahani, had completed Form Five and spent three months working in a Klang furniture factory when she received her third offer of marriage. The suitor was an *ustaz* (Islamic teacher in government employment). Mahani's mother felt that Mahani was "still a child." However, by noting that the *ustaz* was already attracted to her daughter, she implied that she could not put up a resistance to the match. She declared that although the family benefitted from Mahani's wages, the job was really not suitable for her delicate health; perhaps marriage would be a good change for her. More to the point, Hamzah pressured Mahani to accept the *ustaz*'s offer, on the grounds that the man was a state employee and already the owner of a brick house in a nearby town.

At the engagement, the mother, less eager than her husband to lose her daughter, requested that they wait two years before marrying. Soon after the ceremony, however, the *ustaz* began sending wedding gifts, including materials for the trousseau. He also pressed for the date of the wedding. He then offered a *hantaran* of M$1,500 without any negotiation on the part of Mahani's parents — "It is not proper to ask; our child is not a commodity" — and it clinched the deal; the wedding took place a few months later. Soon after Mahani moved out, her younger sister failed her Form Three examination and started working in an FTZ factory. Without the expectation of this fortuitous mix of events, it was unlikely that Mahani would have married so soon after starting to work. Mahani's beauty attracted a "good" marriage offer which might otherwise not have been extended to an ordinary village family.

Case D. This last example highlights, among other themes, the threat upclassing marital strategies can pose to the joint property and income arrangements of families faced with the impending departure of a son or daughter. The story revolves around Susi, an attractive 24-year-old clerk at the Telok school who daily cycled past the general provision store operated by Mahmud, a 39-year-old bachelor (and Nawab's stepbrother). Mahmud lived with his mother, Nana, a younger brother, and a sister who had an infant son (her husband was a soldier stationed in another state). When Nana was widowed, her stepson Nawab raised the children, initiating the two teenage boys into the shopkeeping business. As young men, the brothers bought their own village stores. Over the years, profits from the business went into *kampung* land, so that the combined family property amounted to 20 acres of cash crops and two shops. In early 1979, Mahmud acquired a house which he rented to migrant factory workers, keeping the extra income for himself. He was ready to get married.

Mahmud had failed in three previous attempts at the matrimonial game. The opinion of his mother and younger sister was very influential in his marital attempts. With the passing years, Nawab and Noraini worried about his ever getting married and having heirs to his considerable assets. The family lived so modestly that perhaps few villagers realized the extent of their wealth. Then Mahmud approached Susi's parents and asked for her hand. Her family was landless, squatting on a Chinese holding where the father worked as a rubber trapper. Three unmarried daughters in their twenties brought in additional earnings. Susi's earnings formed the largest portion of household income. Her father offered instead his eldest daughter, a 29-year-old domestic help in Tanjong Karang.Mahmud demurred on account of her age and appearance. Offended, Susi's father was said to have complained to neighbors, ''Who is this Mahmud; does he have land, house, and property to ask for my daughter?'' From Mahmud, he demanded a detailed account of his assets. Seeing a potential threat to their joint family interests, Nana and her daughter persuaded Mahmud to retract his marriage offer.

Over the next year, Susi wrote to Mahmud but received no reply; he told a female cousin that he did not want to ''reopen old wounds.'' Word drifted in that on many afternoons, in the company of female friends, Susi would burst into crying fits. Not long after, a contingent of these sympathetic women came to Noraini to report Susi's distress.

Nawab and Noraini thereby felt Susi "had shown her true feelings," and if nothing was done about the situation, she could very well lose her mind. They sent for her and asked how much *hantaran* she would expect in marriage. Wisely, she did not reply. Convinced of her sincerity, Nawab and Noraini persuaded Nana and her daughter that Mahmud should ask for Susi's hand again, pointing out that she should not be blamed for her father's insolent demands. Susi's mother also dropped by the Nawab household; her husband, she said, was possessive of his daughters and had not kept up with modern times.

Gaining confidence from the momentum of events, Susi told her father that if he continued to oppose the match, she would "go sleep in Mahmud's house."[7] Meanwhile, Nawab cautioned that in order to squelch unpleasant rumors, the marriage should be arranged as soon as possible. He suggested Mahmud make a *hantaran* of M$1,200 to show the public that he was not getting married under duress. Thus, we see the convergence of two sets of strategies: Susi's use of female intermediaries and the threat of madness, and the Nawab-Noraini interest in getting Mahmud married to produce heirs for his property.

Nevertheless, the deep resentment and felt threat to Nana and her daughter lingered on, to break out on the wedding day itself. At the *bersanding* ceremony, Mahmud's sister went up to the seated couple ostensibly to *saalam* Susi, but instead she pushed her to the floor. In the fearful confusion that followed, Nawab grabbed the sister, Noraini comforted Susi while Mahmud's younger brother *saalam*ed her. The bridal party departed in haste and the remaining women cried in shame. The incident put the final stamp on the rift between Mahmud and his mother and sister. He moved with his bride into his new house, thereby initiating the economic separation they had feared.

Although I began by talking about daughters as prizes to be won in the marital game, these examples suggest that the opposite view can also be maintained. Women — the would-be bride, female relatives and friends — played active roles in figuring out the stakes in a particular match, maneuvered in spheres inaccessible to men, and, in the process, redefined the forms of marital strategies and arrangements. Who was choosing whom, one may ask? Obviously, the wage earning status of young women has been critical in the degree of self-possession they displayed vis-à-vis potential husbands and authori-

Factory workers sitting-in-state on their wedding day.

tarian fathers. The reader may protest that these are biased cases drawn from well-to-do families; however, the following examples of marriage strategies among poor village folk should balance out these accounts.

Marrying Your Own Kind: The Working Poor

For an increasing number of *kampung* families, the marital stakes are not professional credentials, property, or business, but wage earnings. In the interest of pooling incomes, parents may attempt to arrest the departure of working children by delaying their marriage. The fact that parents often fail in this endeavor is evidence of the changing status of young wage workers within the family and in the marriage market. In selecting a spouse, the emphasis is less on accumulation of assets than on pinning down a provider.

Case A. Adnan was twenty-nine years old, the eldest of seven children of a farm laborer. For the past five years, he had worked in a car assembly plant in Shah Alam, where he also found a job for a younger brother. Two sisters worked in the Telok FTZ. Their combined contributions permitted a more tolerable standard of livelihood than could otherwise be expected from the father's tiny farm.

Two years earlier, Adnan had met his intended, a factory worker in Kuala Selangor; they had since been saving for marriage. As it was a "love inspired" match, Adnan had proposed marriage before his parents were told to make formal contacts. On their own, the couple agreed on a bridewealth by calculating the cost of a bed and bureau. He remarked, "With the price of things today, what can you buy with M$500? I figure that whatever she wants to buy, I will be needing too." Adnan was equivocal about his wife's work after marriage. She had indicated an interest in continuing her work in a timber yard, at least until the first child arrived. He commented, "It's her own affair."

For the wedding feast, Adnan spent M$500, and his father contributed M$1,000 and slaughtered one of his bulls. The contributions of guests, in cash amounts of M$1 to M$20 (in addition to gifts of rice, firewood, and cooked and raw food), added up to M$2,120. If we subtract the estimated value of the cow (M$500), the "gain" of the feast-giving was M$620. This Adnan's father would use to repair the house and for miscellaneous household expenses.[8] In the absence of such interhousehold dependence, the replacement of obligations by commodities can make the wedding a daunting experience for parents, as we shall see in the next example.

Case B. Ramli was a 21-year-old laborer living with his married sister in Klang when he decided to marry another factory worker. His father, Anwar, encouraged him to return to Sungai Jawa for the wedding. A rubber-tapper, Anwar had married Muslimah from another village after Ramli's mother died. Muslimah brought in a one-acre *pesaka,* raised Ramli and his sister, and had eight children of her own. Neither Ramli nor his sister remitted money to the family, even though their siblings were still young dependents.

Ramli's urban residence and interests determined the form of his nuptial celebration. His father paid M$600 for expenses which included rented chairs, tent, and the fee for a hired singer. Anwar also slaughtered an old bull. After the wedding, Ramli and his bride returned to Klang, leaving the parents to clean up. It was a disappointing show; few neighbors and friends turned up to help, and guest contributions amounted to only M$1,100, which, if the parents figured in the value of the bull, just equalled their initial expenditure. When Muslimah started to complain, I pointed out that perhaps they had made a gain, since the bull was too old to sell. She retorted:

> If this wasn't so, what could have been done? *Kampung* people are not all rich. If we did not have our own bull, things would have been really difficult. When we spend on others and not on ourselves, everything gets used up. . . . and I did not even get to keep the gifts. Raising children, you simply accept the difficulties that come with it. What to do? Only Allah knows [my problems]!

Ramli had married earlier than she had hoped, extinguishing her hope that he would help his younger siblings through school. Muslimah had recruited neighbors to help with wedding preparations, but Ramli's friends from town had not pitched in, arriving merely to enjoy the festivity. Even worse, instead of making cash contributions to the parents who were giving the feast, these young people bought consumer items for the bridal couple, in the Western manner. Thus, Muslimah felt those gifts should have been handed over to her. This episode captures the form of cultural change associated with migrant wage work; not only do parents sometimes lose control over their children's labor and the timing of their marriage, but economic individuation also extends to the realm of resource mobilization, thereby concentrating resources more narrowly in the hands of the wage worker.

Case C. This story indicates that migrant work also enables young women to be less concerned about parental wishes. Safuah seemed an unlikely candidate for handling her own marital affairs. According to her elder sister, she was a normal child until her second year in primary school. One day, urinating at an ant hill, she was possessed by a male spirit. Ever since, her ''masculinity'' was expressed in conduct such as dislike of housework, boyish restlessness, rough talk, and lack of interest in ''female'' things. She sat in class with a blank expression and would walk through thick undergrowth on her way home. At the end of the year, she dropped out of school but was ''very clever'' at reading and writing on her own. When she was sixteen, she began corresponding with a male pen pal she picked from a magazine. In late 1979, her sister failed Form Three and had begun working in a sardine factory in Klang. Although her wage was only M$120 per month, the sister was able to spend some money on dresses, shopping, and the movies. Safuah told her parents that she too would like to have her own money, and in January she began work in the same factory. Apparently, neither sister gave her parents money, although they lived and ate at home.

Now eighteen, Safuah arranged to meet her pen pal outside her factory. He was a 30-year-old divorcé who worked as a barber in a store front. He rented a room with his brother, a laborer. Early in March, Safuah did not come home for four days, causing her parents great anxiety. When she returned, she said that her "boyfriend" had taken her to Tanjong Karang to meet his mother, who was led to believe that they were already man and wife. Safuah had used up her savings of M$50 on bus fares and on fruits for the old lady. She did not enjoy her stay because she feared the woman and did not have enough to eat. Her parents, considering her "one screw loose" ("three-cornered," in the local parlance), did not beat her, but her father warned her about getting pregnant. The next day, they arranged the Islamic marriage rite, inviting relatives and neighbors to witness the event.

The groom was deemed not an upstart and therefore acceptable. However, he was too poor to give *hantaran*, and the newlyweds simply moved into his bare, rented room. A few days later, they were arrested in a raid by officials of the Islamic Department. They were briefly apprehended for *khalwat* until a relative arrived with the marriage certificate. After all this excitement, Safuah's father said he had not opposed the match because the couple had already chosen each other and been intimate. If he had tried to stop them from seeing each other, they might have run away. The only thing to do was to legitimize the relationship immediately. "Young people these days, you know. . . ."

Remarrying: A Woman on Her Own

Since divorces and remarriages have always been as common as shotgun marriages in Sungai Jawa, it is appropriate to discuss the strategies of divorced women left fending for themselves and their children. Over the past decade, the noncontribution of maintenance (*nafkah*) by husbands has been cited by the district *kadi* as the major cause of divorces in the region (see Table 15). The increasing influence of this factor in marital breakups is attributed to the irregular employment or migrant work which are the sources of livelihood of so many men. Deprived of sufficient financial support, more women have petitioned for divorce through their guardians.[9] Upon divorce, the former wife receives cash support for three months (in order to secure paternity claims if she is found to be pregnant in that duration). After that period, aid from her former spouse is totally at his discretion. In the majority of cases, divorced women receive no further support, and they have to draw upon savings and depend on parental help to raise children, who usually remain with their mother after divorce. In attempting to attract partners who would help raise their children, divorced and widowed women are both helped and handicapped by their *janda* image of seduction.

Table 15

Causes of Malay Divorces by Percentage Each Year,
Kuala Langat, 1969–79

Year	1969	70	71	72	73	74	75	76	77	78	79
Number of divorces	46	51	56	53	62	51	78	72	59	91	76
Nonmaintenance by husband	40	35	30	45	45	25	43	44	45	40	45
Incompatibility	30	35	40	35	30	35	35	30	30	25	15
Interference by family	10	15	20	5	5	15	10	6	10	30	10
*Extramarital relations:**											
Husband	10	7	5	10	10	10	5	10	10	3	10
Wife	5	5	5	5	7	5	2	5	3	2	15
Other reasons**	5	3	—	—	3	10	5	5	2	—	5

Source: Adapted from Kadi Mohammad Shari b. Ismail, Pejabat Islam, Sungai Jawa.

*This category mainly included cases in which the party had developed a strong attraction to a person other than the spouse.

**Included impotence, sterility, nonconsumation of marriage, husband's desire to take another wife, husband's drug addition.

Case A. When Minah was thirty-one years old, her husband died, leaving her to raise two girls. The older daughter, Ju, was considered "dumb" (*bodoh*). Minah held in trust her late husband's one-acre plot, but as a Batak who had married into Sungai Jawa, she had to eke out a living practically alone. She not only had to contend with loneliness but also with slurs from women jealously guarding their husbands. Three years later she received a marriage proposal from a landless estate worker. Sukor was a few years younger and had never been married. Minah could not bring herself to accept his offer until he "promised to take care of the children." After marriage, Sukor moved into her late husband's house and took care of the property. The couple began to work as a team of rubber tappers and in five years had saved money to buy a small plot in another village. Meanwhile, Minah had two more girls.

When the palms on the new holding matured, Sukor forced Ju, who had turned twenty-one, to marry a 45-year-old divorcé from his home village. Sukor felt it was time for Ju to marry out, especially when her younger sister, a bright girl of thirteen (but whose school career was ended), could take over most of the housework and childcare. The *hantaran* of M$200 (it would have been less had she not been a virgin) was spent on a feast for ten, and Ju did not even receive a new *sarung*. After the *nikah*, she just followed her husband home, without any ceremony. The marriage lasted one month, following a series of fights, Ju took the bus home. Both Sukor and Minah seemed to have accepted this turn of events and Ju slipped back into her former role of housekeeping, intending never to marry again.

Case B. In this example, the young woman's marriage, divorce, and remarriage are also episodes in a story of wider cultural change and conflict. Hawa was seventeen when she decided to marry a Banjarese soldier and follow him to British bases in Singapore, where they lived for five years. When her husband was discharged and had found a job in a newspaper office in K.L., they returned to Sungai Jawa with their two young daughters. Every day, Hawa's husband commuted to work in his car, but he forbade her to leave the house or mix with neighborhood women. In her view, he had been influenced by British army life: he frequently wore white shorts like "white men" and expected her to be showered and dressed when he returned home. Gradually, she found out that he kept a mistress in the city. After a fight, he divorced her.

Hawa moved back with her parents, receiving a monthly allowance of M$30 from her former husband. He had married his mistress, but Hawa heard that he was seeing other women. She added that his sister was similarly inconstant; she had been married six times. Hawa felt that her husband had not behaved like a *kampung* man. Instead of caring for his family, he had tried to confine her to the house ("like white men do their wives") and cheated on her. After the divorce, he dropped by occasionally and ("showing that he still has some sense") has recently decided to raise the monthly allowance for the growing chidren.

After her divorce, Hawa worked in an iron pipe factory, where she met her current husband, Suib. She exaggerated the number of her children to test his affection. Undeterred, he visited Sungai Jawa and presented a ring to her parents ("as if I were marrying for the first time"). They were married within two months, with "no courtship, no going to the movies, love letters, or romance." Suib left his old job and sought a better-paying one. He was from Perak, where his divorced mother still lived, but did not want to uproot Hawa and her children from Sungai Jawa. He planned to work in the Trengganu oil fields, returning for monthly visits. After a son was born, Hawa joined a party of coffee pickers to bring in more cash. She also went on the pill. Hawa was contented with her new married life in the *kampung* and had no regrets about leaving the urban, more affuent life she had known with her first husband.

I turn now to the relatively new option of delayed marriages for young women and consider how that possibility is linked to their working status and sexuality.

Delayed Marriages and Sexual Images

For increasing numbers of young women, city lights, wage employment, and educational credentials suggest the options of delayed marriage, which for so long has been the privilege of men. Age at first marriage is steadily increasing for young women, whether employed in wage work or not, to an average of 22 years. By postponing marriage in order to serve family interests, working daughters also discover the means to evade male domination in kinship and marriage. As the examples above have shown, single working women can and have deflected pressures from their families and asserted their own individuality in consumer behavior and choice of spouse.

Young women's perceptions of self, and of men, are increasingly refracted through the prism of the cash register. Daughters from well-to-do families are clear-eyed about emotions and personal interests when marriage has become the key to *their* social mobility. Daughters of poor families also evince self-reflection in their handling of relationships with parents, lovers, and husbands. Competition for male attention is shifting over to the realm of commoditized images, and the marital contract itself is gradually symbolized by market exchange. As the commodity logic comes to dictate taste, structure conjugal expectations, and dissolve customary obligations, young women, as much as men, are agents in renegotiating their futures in marriage.

The slippage in male ability to conform daughter/sister to male expectations has introduced a dynamic ambivalence in male perceptions of women. An unemployed youth made the caustic observation that factory women dress up to disguise their *kampung*-origin, but the effect of their cosmetic efforts was to caricature their country ways. Nevertheless, the single working woman or female college student who has some urban experience is regarded with a mixture of fascination and hostility by young rural men. This ambivalence pivots on their contradictory expectations of wife and sister/girlfriend. In their wives, young men seek the customary ideal of the subservient woman, recently recast as the modern housewife in magazines, t.v. dramas, and the lifestyle of the bureaucratic elite. However, young rural men are simultaneously drawn to the new working women. Their freedom, as expressed in commoditized image and conduct, makes for exciting dating partners. At the same time, the economic autonomy and widening horizon of young women also threaten male power in the home, as many young men with working sisters know too well. Thus, a factory woman can tolerate male mockery, knowing that it disguises both fear and attraction; her own brother is marrying a factory worker like herself (see quote above).

The truly ambitious young woman, not factory operator or clerk, but bound for college, seldom feels such emotional ease about her marriageability. Natajah's granddaughter Katijah symbolizes the tensions engendered in young rural women caught up in developmental and cultural change. In her adolescence, Katijah was a very nervous girl who took to wandering around on her own. She quarreled constantly with her mother, a very unusual situation in *kampung* families. For two years, she was placed in the care of Noraini and Nawab (who still covertly practiced sorcery). Katijah was a bright student and her future was decided for her when she received a scholarship to an urban teachers' college. There her disorientation was resolved by immediately plunging into the *dakwah* movement. She wore a veil and robes even on her visits home, presenting a stark contrast to the *sarung* and semitransparent jackets of village women, and the dresses and "Wrangler" outfits of factory workers. When I asked Natajah the meaning of Katijah's shrouded appearance, she said that it was a sign of her status as an educated Muslim woman. Natajah had been convinced that her granddaughter's unusual temperament was a residual effect of the sorcery attack launched at, but deflected from, Noraini years ago; now, she maintains, Katijah has been cured by Islamic revivalism.

Katijah is in her early twenties and is attempting to reconcile her wishes for both a career and marriage. Her mother insists that she does cooking and cleaning on her visits from college, but Katijah seems doubtful whether this customary practice would attract a marriage proposal. Despite her veil, which she sometimes manipulates to display her nape, she has cultivated a joking, even flirtatious relationship with her male relatives. Unlike less academically qualified village women, Katijah's hand has never been asked for. She is versed in the Koran but occasionally reads Western "romance stories" to improve her English.

Every year, weddings are held during the school vacation. As village elders spend cash and energy on matrimonial ceremonies, they observe that there is more conspicuous consumption, less hands willing to help, more urban visitors, and new rites ("fashion show," "pop band") to accommodate. The bride who is demurely led through the various rituals has probably displayed self-determination in the selection of not only the groom but also of wedding outfits, household items, and postmarital residence. Parents intervene in the marriage of their children to secure wealth or social position, but the market has expanded young people's room for maneuver in their own interests. In particular, young women, alternately quiescent and assertive, manipulate symbolic and economic capitals to forward their personal agendas. Increasingly a labor reserve for the wider economy, *kampung* women play a bigger role in adjusting customary matrimonial practices to personal wishes and variations in individual life trajectories. We now turn to the experiences of these young women in transnational companies which, by employing their labor power, have reconstituted their very sense of self as women and as a nascent proletariat.

PART III

Neophyte Factory Women
in Late Capitalism

Chapter 7

The Modern Corporation: Manufacturing Gender Hierarchy

Why are Malay women periodically possessed by spirits on the shop-floor of transnational corporations? Both Western educated and Islamic fundamentalist Malays had expected the disappearance of spirit beliefs when peasants began streaming into "free trade zones" and city life. What do episodic spirit visitations to modern factories disclose about the experiences of young peasant women assembling microchips? Does the "fetishization of evil" in the form of satan represent a mode of critique of capitalist relations, as Taussig has argued in his study of Columbian plantation workers? Or do spirit posses-sions represent cultural protests against acts of dehumanization? Caught between noncapitalist morality and capitalist relations, do Malay factory women alternate between compliance, self-regulation, and daily acts of defiance on the shopfloor?

To answer these questions, I will first discuss the role of Malaysian state institutions in (1) promoting export-industrialization as the means for integrating rural Malays in the capitalist system, and (2) the introduction, via transnational companies, of labor-intensive man-ufacturing into Kuala Langat, thereby changing the form and mean-ing of work for rural Malays. Their felt experiences, interpretations, and changing sense of subjectivity in the context of industrial work relations will be discussed in Chapters 8 and 9.

141

Capitalist Discipline and Cultural Discourse

> Bureaucratic administration means fundamentally the exercise of control on the basis of knowledge. This is the feature of it which makes it specifically rational.
>
> Max Weber (1964: 339)

> We must cease once and for all to describe the effects of power in negative terms. . . . In fact power produces; it produces reality; it produces domains of objects and rituals of truth. The individual and the knowledge that may be gained of him belong to this production.
>
> Michel Foucault (1979: 194)

In the late twentieth century, capitalist discipline introduced into industrializing societies involves a combination of labor discipline and different modes of control based on schemes of discourse/practice which reconstitute the subjectivity and countertactics of the subjected.

For Marx, power in capitalist societies is ultimately wielded by capitalists over the laboring population. In daily relations of production, labor discipline is enforced by different organizational techniques which objectify the worker by separating intellectual and manual labor (1974: 327–424). Weber sees a threefold division of oppressive power in modern bureaucratic societies. Rational-legal techniques govern the deployment of power through the state, structures of legitimate authority, and large-scale bureaucratic organizations (1964: 337–341). In the late 1970s, Foucault directed our attention to productive (rather than repressive) power, not located in institutions but circulating through networks of social relationships. In his view, "disciplinary societies" are characterized by schemes of disciplinary techniques ("technologies of power") which act upon the body and reconstitute subjectivity through knowledge/power systems (1979, 1979a, 1980). His analysis thereby casts light on those grey zones of contested terrains and self-preserves in everyday life.

Foucauldian concepts are directly relevant in delineating the modes of domination within high-technology factories. By refusing to separate practice from discourse (cf. the Marxian divorce of action from ideology), Foucauldian analysis identifies and exposes the power effects of knowledge/power on individuals, their reconstitution, and self-management. In social systems mediated by technology, such as transnational corporations, coercion is enforced not only through labor relations but also through corporate discursive regulation of work performance, comportment within and outside the factory premises, and the workers' sense of self. When one rejects the notion that capital-labor relations have an overdetermining logic, it becomes necessary to discover how discourse/practice colonizes not only different domains of everyday life but also the scattered, fragmentary acts of rebellion by subjugated people.

The State, Export-Industrialization, and Cultural Models

The rapid expansion of light manufacturing industries in Peninsular Malaysia since 1970 has been the consequence of a deliberate government policy in response to growing rural discontent.[1] The postindependence coalition government, headed by the UMNO party and buttressed by a carefully balanced multiethnic ruling group, continued to manage the export-oriented plantation economy still dominated by foreign investors.

In May 1969, violent communal riotings in the cities brought to national attention the economic plight of rural Malays. Population growth, falling commodity prices, and land concentration by the emergent class of Malay civil servants in rural society have contributed to an increasing incidence of landlessness and general poverty. Government statistics showed that since 1957, rural Malays have progressively lost their village land at the rate of about 10,000 families each year.[2] As many rural Malays became poorer, wealth disparity increased within the Malay community itself. Rural discontent spilled over in the communal riotings which state officials astutely recognized as antigovernmental protests. Following suspension of Parliament, the UMNO government introduced the New Economic Policy (NEP) in 1971 as the basis for restructuring the political economy. The NEP is aimed at the

> progressive transformation of the country's racially compartmentalized economic system into one in which the composition of Malaysian society is visibly reflected in its countryside and towns, firms and factories, shops and offices (*Third Malaysia Plan*, 1976: 9).

The centerpiece of this *pembangunan* program was "export-oriented industrialization" as the combined solution to basic problems of landlessness, rural underemployment, and growing political disaffectation as outmigration by young Malays increased.[3] In the industrial belt

along the Klang Valley, migrant youths contributed to the urban unemployed and squatter population. Government training programs,
transportation, and heavy industries absorbed those who were scho-
lastically qualified. Many of the migrants had failed Form Three or
Five; nevertheless, the expectations raised by their education caused
migrants to take their time looking for jobs considered more commensurate with their qualifications (Blake 1975).

By the end of the decade, these migrants had added to the rapid
growth (at the rate of 4.5 percent per year) of Kuala Lumpur and the
estimated 40 percent of city households living below the poverty level.[4]
Joining the stagnant pool of the unemployed, many migrants lived

Table 16

Peninsular Malaysia:
Distribution of Total Labor Force by Industry, 1970–80

	1970	1975	1980
Total labor force	*3.3m*	*3.9m*	*5.4m*
Industry (by percent)			
Agriculture, forestry, fishing	53.5	49.3	40.6
Mining and quarrying	2.6	2.2	2.0
Manufacturing	8.7	10.1	16.0
Construction	2.7	2.9	5.2
Transportation, communications	4.0	4.6	*
Wholesale & retail trade	11.4	12.6	23.5
Banking, insurance, real estate	0.8	0.8	*
Public administration, education, health, defense	12.0	13.0	13.2
Other services	3.7	3.9	*
Totals	100	100	100

*Included in "Wholesale and retail trade."

Sources: *The Third Malaysia Plan 1975–80,* 1976: 140; *Far Eastern Economic Review,* Asia
1981 Yearbook: 194.

in crowded rooms. Some picked up cash in petty crimes and drug peddling. One report noted that it was "almost impossible to talk about the migration of youths from rural areas to the city without touching on the drug problem." Others sought incomes as self-appointed car attendants (*jaga kereta* boys) or food vendors, or worked at odd jobs. In 1979, the majority of those who registered with the Selangor job placement office were between 15 and 24 years old, most of whom had at least lower secondary education.[5]

Although local academics and policymakers called for greater rural development effort to stem the rural-urban migration,[6] the Malaysian Home Affairs Minister asserted that the "urban drift" was "a deliberate . . . societal engineering strategy" within the framework of the NEP. He pointed out that the countryside was the "only . . . major reservoir" of labor power left for "economic modernization." Since the goal of the NEP was to "reshuffle the racial composition of the rural sector," the outmigration of Malays was in keeping with government policy.[7]

Between 1970 and 1980, a decade during which the labor force in agriculture declined from 53 to 41 percent of the total working population, the government established 59 industrial estates throughout the Peninsula. Nine of these were "free trade zones" (FTZs) for the location of the manufacturing subsidiaries of transnational companies. These foreign-controlled factories came to generate the largest number of low wage manufacturing jobs, primarily for Malay women. Rural outmigration continued unabated, only now increasingly constituted by young peasant women. They contributed to the growth in the manufacturing labor force which doubled from 8 to 16 percent by the end of the decade (see Table 16).

Thus, the integration of Malaysian female labor into global production systems was facilitated by changing corporate strategies, especially after the "oil crisis" of the early 1970s. To escape mounting labor costs at home and gain market access abroad, transnational corporations headquartered in Japan, the United States, and Western Europe began to scatter labor-intensive production processes throughout the third world. As a favored locale for transnational companies, Malaysia has hundreds of foreign industries manufacturing garments, foodstuffs, and electronics components, facilitating the large-scale entry of *kampung* women into industrial employment. In 1970, there were no more than one thousand Malay female migrants in manufacturing industries; by the end of the decade, they constituted some 80,000 members of the industrial force, over one-half of whom were employed in electronics assembly factories (Jamilah Ariffin 1980). The most common image of the new working class Malay woman is in fact "Minah *letrik*" (the local equivalent of "hot stuff").

These female members of the nascent Malay proletariat represent a fairly well-educated labor reserve, often overqualified for the semiskilled manual jobs offered by the transnational firms. A 1977 survey of Malay women workers in 120 factories located throughout the Peninsula reveals that almost one-half had lower secondary education, and one-quarter had prematriculation qualifications. Many had aspired to become clerks, trainee nurses, and teachers, but having failed to gain entry into white-collar jobs, were absorbed, along with a few illiterates, into the expanded pool of semiskilled labor.[8]

Different organs of the state apparatus thus facilitate the integration of Malaysian economy and labor into the global operations of transnational capital. Export-oriented manufacturing subsidiaries of foreign companies were attracted by fine locations of physical facilities and infrastructural linkages to ports, as well as generous tax exemptions (up to ten years), minimum customs fees, and unhampered transfers of profits and capital. The main condition required of these large-scale industries was at least 40 percent *bumiputra* (Malay) representation in their work forces. Firms were urged to invite Malaysian shareholders, but this was not a binding requirement. In the domestic arena, other government institutions engaged in the political disciplining of the newly constituted Malay working class. Drawing upon cultural, political, and economic discourse/practices, different state agencies courted foreign interests while regulating the labor responses to industrial discipline. Thus, the 1976 investment brochure, *Malaysia: Your Profit Centre in Asia*, provided legal guarantees for labor quiescence:

> Adequate legislation in industrial relations ensures the maintenance of industrial peace and harmony, thereby guaranteeing the smooth operation of production without undue disruptions.[9]

In practice, this labor legislation, both by omission and by implementation, favored transnational factories over Malaysian workers in at least two ways:

1) by facilitating the "runaway" companies in their selective use of the local population as a labor reserve to be attracted and discharged according to world market conditions, and 2) through bureaucratic expansion, counter large-scale resistance from below.

Government labor laws, by not setting a legal minimum to the wage rate nor correcting the sexual imbalance in wage levels, created a situation in which transnational corporations could lower production costs by employing a female-dominated labor force. Wages paid to female operators in the electronics industry are further varied by urban/rural locations. In a rural district like Kuala Langat, wages offered by electronics companies were not significantly higher than those in agro-based industries (see Table 17). It was clear to many female operators that factory wages were in general smaller than those paid in the lower-echelon white-collar jobs for which they had the necessary qualifications.

Electronics companies also attempted to limit the employment tenure of their female workers to the short span of their life cycle when they were most capable of intensive labor. Most operators were young

Table 17

Average Wage Rates in Selected Industries for Manual Laborers in Selangor, 1976

Industry	Daily Rated Wages	
	Male	*Female*
Textiles	M$ 3.05	M$ 2.43
Rubber products	3.85	2.88
Plywood	4.20	3.87
Sawmill	4.26	4.30
Chemical products	4.20	3.87
Machinery & parts	4.67	3.64
Electronics assembly firms, Kuala Langat (starting wage)	3.50	3.10

Sources: *Selangor State Development Corporation*, 1976: 22; fieldnotes.

women ages 16 to 25 years, mainly single. In this connection, government legislation for the protection of pregnant workers has had the unintended effect of reinforcing corporate policy to discourage married women from applying. Workers who got married while on the job could remain; however, they were often given counseling on family planning.

The rapid exhaustion of the operators — owing to high production targets and work rates, three-shift cycles, frequent overtime, and continual surveillance (see below) — also causes most of them to leave of their own accord after three to four years. An increasing number of Malay female workers in urban-based factories, however, are choosing to remain on the job for longer durations. Since many can no longer adjust to *kampung* life, factory jobs have become one of the few means of cash earning for female migrants, especially divorcées with children to support. It is common practice for electronics workers aspiring to escape the dead-end employment to apply repeatedly for job openings in the state bureaucracy. A woman worker at the Sungai Way FTZ was reported to have said, "If I could get an office job I would 'split' from this place. There is no future here. There are thousands of us and only a few promotions."[10] This weak structural integration of women into the industrial labor market, a situation fostered by corporate strategy, is frequently cited by male supremacist and capitalist pronouncements to justify the low wages of female workers.

The high turnover of female operators in electronics firms (5–6 percent every month in some enterprises), operating in tandem with corporate pressures against long-term employment, disrupted attempts at union organization. Contrary to widespread belief, labor laws allowed union formation in the so-called "pioneer industries." However, in practice, this ruling has not produced unions of electronics workers because amendments to the labor code severely restricted labor organization. For instance, workers with less than three years of employment in their industry cannot participate in unions, and strikes to force management acceptance of unions were forbidden. Other "management functions" which deal with promotions, transfers, and layoffs are not subjected to collective bargaining. The most direct obstruction to the formation of a union by electronics workers is the refusal of the Registrar of Trade Unions to recognize their membership under the national Electrical Industry Workers Union.[11]

Even for the older, existing male-dominated unions (representing one-quarter of the country's work force), restrictions on organized activities have progressively worsened. Between 1963 and 1973, the number of work days taken in strikes declined from over 305,000 days to 40,000, even as workers involved in these strikes increased four-fold.[12] In late 1979, a job action of employees of the Malaysian Airline System (MAS) ended in the imprisonment of 23 unionists without trial, under the Internal Security Act. New rulings were introduced to restrict contacts with overseas and international labor organizations which had offered support in the labor dispute. The overall effect of the proliferation of labor regulations on the newly generated female industrial workers is to deliver them, with little legal defense within their work situation, to the disposal of international capital.

The need to supply foreign companies with a continuous flow of rural women and men entailed not only a tightening up of legal rights but also a reorganization of Malay workers' understanding of socio-cultural change. As a nascent Malay proletariat accumulated in the cities, the state public relations organ introduced the "Look East" policy. In 1982, the Prime Minister declared that Japan rather than the West should be the model for future Malaysian society:

> It is true [the Japanese] are not very religious, but their cultural values are akin to the kind of morals and ethics we have or would like to have in this country . . . in the philosophy they have . . . profit is not everything. The welfare of their employees is important.

This emphasis on cultural values rather than technological expertise presented a moral imagery to validate the new labor relations and win Malay-Muslim support for a program in which Japanese companies are a major presence. In the face of radical Islamic insistence on the priority of "spiritual" over industrial development,[13] government officials claimed that this cultural vision of development would ensure Malay racial success, while being acceptable to both Muslim and non-Muslim citizens. At an *ulama's* conference, an official from the Ministry of Education argued that the goal of the "Look East" policy was

> to urge Muslims to follow the attitude and work ethics of a successful race as long as it does not contravene Islamic ideals and principles . . . we have to show [the working people] the achievements made by others. In this context, the Japanese and the Koreans are the best examples.

He further charged that 26 years after independence, Malay workers' lack of "work commitments" had left them far behind non-Malays, especially in the economic field.[14] An official slogan, "Efficient, Clean, and Trustworthy," was coined to link desired labor habits with loyalty to enterprise and country. This ideological construction of labor relations and national development wove around areas of potential dissent, strategically integrating perceived shared values, now in Japanese culture, now in Islam, into a cultural configuration for the management of the nascent Malay working class. Instead of using technology as a neutral arbiter between capital and labor,[15] this cultural model is couched in the vocabulary of moral responsibility and the welfare needs of the laboring poor.

Thus, embedded in multiple foci of power, the Malaysian state simultaneously courts foreign investors while disciplining, compensating, and manipulating Malay factions in different classes to facilitate the process of industrial transformation. Contrary to perspectives which assume lower-class resistance to state policies in the transition to industrial capitalism (e.g., interpretations influenced by Thompson 1963), I maintain that the Malaysian state, like many third world governments, utilized various strategies, increasingly enhanced by electronic technology, to regulate the integration of the laboring poor into the changing political economy. This is not to discount the many forms of revolts from below; but they cannot be assumed to be directed at capitalism or the state structure. Furthermore, as UMNO machinations have shown, political disciplining of discontented elements often involves the recruitment of individual leaders from popular resistant movements into the state apparatus itself. We will now turn to the modes of discipline exercised within the modern factory system.

Japanese Corporations in Kuala Langat

As part of its "rural industrialization" program, the Selangor State Development Corporation (SSDC) in the early 1970s set up a 50-acre free trade zone just outside Telok township in Kuala Langat. The FTZ was shared by three Japanese companies, two semiconductor assembly plants, which I will call Electronics Japan Inc. (EJI) and Electronics Nippon Inc. (ENI, the smaller of the two), and a manufacturer of musical movement components (MUZ). Initially, it was hoped that the Telok FTZ, with its lower land rates, would attract subsidiaries of transnational corporations otherwise locating in the Klang Valley. However, after Shah Alam had been established as the Selangor state capital, officials channelled foreign investments to the new town. The local FTZ thus remained small-scale, employing a total of approximately 2,000 workers. Nevertheless, for the local *kampung*folk, it represented qualitative changes in their experience of work and its meanings for young women.

For the majority of workers, the transition from peasant women to factory hands entailed two basic changes: (a) a shift from a flexible work situation to the hierarchical structure of industrial production, and (b) transition from autonomy in the work process to the oppressive compulsion of labor discipline. The qualitative changes were experienced in relation to the self and to other workers, as well as to work within social relations organized by the factories, and between the industrial system and local communities.

Nimble Fingers, Slow Wit

The organization of modern industrial structures has been analyzed in terms of the systems' peculiar advantage to late-developing economies and as characteristic forms of historically produced development strategies.[16] Eschewing Marxist claims that capitalist relations of production are governed by an internal logic, the critical questions to be asked are: Why is *female* labor preferred? What are the implications of a global production system in which relations of gender and of race are critical for the expansion of economic and symbolic capital?

The three Japanese factories are similarly organized according to an extreme separation of mental and manual labor greatly facilitated by the deployment of electronics technology. An overwhelming majority of their employees — 85 percent — were female. Altogether, 80 percent were female operators drawn from surrounding villages and beyond. EJI had the largest work force (1,030 members). Among the 826 female operators, almost 70 percent were Malay; the remainder were equally divided between Chinese and Indians (see Table 18). The other electronics firm, ENI, had 530 operators, while MUZ employed 232 factory hands, again overwhelmingly female and predominantly *kampung* Malay. From the perspective of the local communities, Sungai Jawa had about 400 young women working in the FTZ; 60 percent of them were employed in EJI alone, constituting one-third of its semiskilled labor force. Young women and men from other villages in the district and beyond rented rooms in Sungai Jawa, or in Kampung Melur, which was located between the former and the FTZ. Since this pool of rural women, as low-skilled labor, was easily expanded, and expendable, the factories could keep their wages low and yet still be supplied with a continual flow of female school-leavers each year.

At the electronics and micromachinery plants, management's definition of semiskilled operations as biologically suited to "the oriental girl" in effect required Malay peasant women to adopt such "feminine" traits. A Malaysian investment brochure provided the blurb:

> Her hands are small and she works fast with extreme care. Who, therefore, could be better qualified by nature and inheritance to contribute to the efficiency of a bench assembly production line than the oriental girl? [emphasis added][17]

Corporate policies have been quick to embroider on this tale of nimble fingers and slow wit. In ENI, the Japanese engineer asserted that

> females [are] better to concentrate [on] routine work [which may be] compared to knitting, generally speaking. . . . young girls [are] preferable to do the fine job than older persons, that is because of eyesight.[18]

At EJI, the Malay personnel manager stated candidly:

> [The] assembly of components is a tedious job . . . [with] miniaturized components we feel that females are more dexterous and more patient than males.

Thus, fast fingers, fine eyesight, the passivity to withstand low-skilled, unstimulating work are said to be the biological attributes unique to "oriental" women. In MUZ, the micromachine factory which produced over a million microcomponents each month, a Chinese engineer extended the biological logic by linking purported gender differences to variations in efficiency by sex and age:

> You cannot expect a man to do very fine work for eight hours [at a stretch]. Our work is designed for females . . . if we employ men, within one or two months they'd run away . . . Girls [sic] under thirty are easier to train and easier to adapt to the job function.

The Japanese financial manager was closer to the bottom line:

> Each initial work is very simple . . . if we employ female workers
> [it is] enough. . . . Also cost of female labor [is] cheaper than
> male labor in Malaysia, not so in Japan.[19] . . . If we have male
> assembly workers, they cannot survive. . . . Fresh female labor,
> after some training, is highly efficient.

By seeking young *kampung* women, the factories benefited not only
from the low labor costs, but also from the fact that they could "improve" upon teenage girls already socialized and schooled to be
diligent and obedient.

Recruiting Rural Women

The recruitment of these women for industrial work was not a problem because of their relative oversupply and the eagerness of peasants, village elders, and local institutions to send otherwise non-cash-
earning village women to the FTZ. To employ skilled personnel, like
technicians and managers, the corporations generally relied on the
district and labor offices. For female factory hands, the firms depended
on local village committees to announce the factory recruitment
drives. Moreover, girls who had failed Form Three were urged by
parents to register their names at the factories, which consequently
always had a list of waiting applicants. Managers at the three factories
reported no problems in getting the labor they needed, even if an immediate intake of one to three hundred female operators was required.
The personnel manager at EJI noted that every year the Telok secondary school "churns out workers." His counterpart at ENI commented
that whenever he advertised for 20 operators, about one hundred
women would apply. As the factory intake gradually slowed down,
new recruits were obtained by internal notifications to existing workers
to bring in their friends and relatives. Unlike urban-based industrial
estates, which relied on agents sent to the rural districts to recruit
Malay women (Jamilah Ariffin 1980), the Telok factories had easy and
immediate access to low-grade female labor.

The steady supply of village women as factory hands enabled the
firms to be selective in their use of this labor pool. In their employment policies, the three factories shared similar requirements in their
demand for female labor: young single women between sixteen and
twenty-four years old who had at least primary education, were from

poor families, and lived within 20 miles of the FTZ. Besides cost considerations, young women were demanded because they represented fresh and diligent labor. In particular, their eyes could withstand intensive use of microscopes employed in the wiring, bonding, and mounting processes of electronics assemblywork.[20] At ENI, which tended to attract From Three graduates, the chief engineer cautioned that "the highly educated person is very hard to control." He noted that there were low resignation rates for Standard Six graduates — "they went to work for a long time . . . [and] are usually from poor families which need support." The MUZ personnel manager agreed with this assessment, pointing out that "richer operators can leave at any time. . . . (We also look for) good behavior."

Corporate policies preferred their female operators to be "fresh" and single. It was generally believed that married workers had family commitments which distracted from their factory work. EJI conducted an in-factory survey comparing the performance rate of young single women (ages 16 to 24) and married women (ages 25 to 28). It was found that the former could daily assemble an average of 1,400 more components than the latter in the most labor-intensive sections (bonding and mounting). The supervisor commented, "It was very clear that married ladies cannot handle microscope jobs." What was not explicitly mentioned was that married women required periodic pregnancy leave and pay, and were usually reluctant to work night shifts. Besides, married women, who had generally been in the job longer than single women, had accumulated more wage increments over the years, thereby adding to the cost of labor. Since little skill was acquired in assembly work, it was no loss to the factory to replace an "old" operator with a fresh one who could be trained in two weeks to assemble component parts or mind machines.

Finally, the companies required their female operators (but not other employees) to live near the FTZ so that they could be easily available for overtime work and within the social control of villagefolk, institutions, and factories. All three firms subsidized 30–50 percent of bus transportation for their workers. Those who lived too far away would require higher subsidies and the long commute reduced corporate flexibility in requiring workers to work overtime, usually at little advance notice. The firms also preferred the young women to reside with families rather than rent rooms on their own. The majority of operators in fact lived with their parents, but a minority who came from villages further away either boarded with kinsmen or rented rooms. Thus, the majority of operators came to reside in *kampung* houses on the outskirts of the FTZ.

Ethnic Hierarchy, Gender Inequality

Within the factories, control over the workers was effected through relations of production, Taylorist methods[21] and overlapping schemes of disciplinary techniques for producing docile bodies and modes of gender/ethnic domination.

Electronics technology itself facilitated the extreme separation of mental and physical tasks so characteristic of the division of labor within the electronics industry. Following from Marx, Burawoy (1979) argues that the labor process under capitalism has its own internal logic and that industrial behavior cannot be explained in terms of cultural attitudes or orientations. However, I intend to demonstrate that the subjugation of labor to capital in modern factories does not proceed according to a pre-determined logic. The organization of capitalist production is embedded in and transformed through cultural discourse/practices. Furthermore, relations of production cannot be self-determining when played out through multiple forms of power.

In their system of labor relations, the modern factories in *kampung* society incorporated modes of domination based on technical expertise, ethnicity, and gender. The organization of work in EJI, which was more extensive and complex than in the other two firms, will be analyzed in some detail as an example of how transnational institutions are locally mediated by preexisting cultural constructions of inequality.

EJI was the subsidiary of a major Japanese corporation which has distributed production and marketing agencies all over the world, including Malaysia. In the Telok FTZ, the local factory produced two semiconducting products — transistors and capacitors — widely used in communications systems. The internal organization of production was divided into five major occupational categories, defined by technical expertise and earnings, and given further rigidity by interpenetrating structures based on nationality, ethnicity, gender, and age (see Table 18). At the top, the managing director and "professional" managers (including five engineers) of vertical subdivisions — manufacturing (two systems), production planning, and finance/accounting — were Japanese. The other two subdivisions, administra-

Table 18
Distribution of EJI Employees by Ethnicity, Gender, and Earnings, 1979

Occupational Rank	Ethnicity*				Gender		Total Workers	Salary Scale
	J	M	C	I	Men	Women		
Management								
Professional	10	0	0	0	10	0	10	$1,500-4,000
Nonprofessional	0	2	2	1	5	0	5	$ 800-1,080
Technical and Supervisory								
Engineer, foreman, supervisor	0	14	32	6	50	2	52	$ 785-895
Clerical staff								
Clerk, typist	0	17	19	7	11	32	43	$ 345-480
Service worker								
Phone operator, driver, guard, gardener	0	15	0	3	16	2	18	$ 225-290
Factory workers								
Skilled—technician, chargehand	0	56	21	19	71	25	96	$ 275-400
Unskilled—operator (daily rates)	0	460	48	74	5	577	582	$3.75-4.80(M) $3.50-4.00(F)
Temporary operator	0	135	37	52	0	224	224	$3.10
Totals	10	699	159	162	168	862	1,030	—

*J: Japanese; M: Malay; C: Chinese; I: Indian

tion and equipment maintenance, were headed by two Malays in the former and two Chinese and one Indian in the latter (see also Diagram 1).

In the "Technical and Supervisory" category, the management was unable to allot employees according to the specific ethnic distribution, primarily because there were few Malay engineers in the country — and they, in any case, preferred government employment. In-

Diagram 1

Work Organization and Occupation Ranks in EJI,
Telok Free Trade Zone, 1979

Managing Director

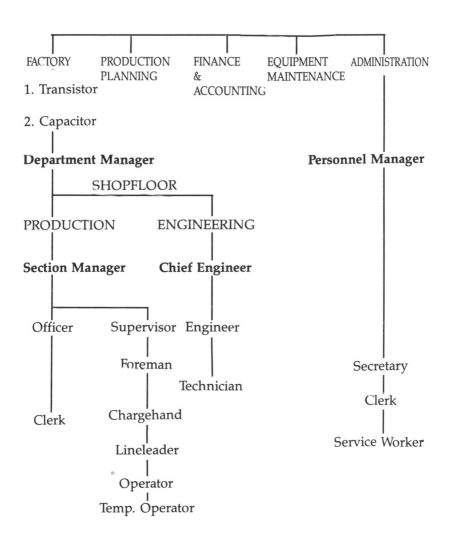

FACTORY   PRODUCTION   FINANCE   EQUIPMENT   ADMINISTRATION
PLANNING   &   MAINTENANCE

1. Transistor   ACCOUNTING

2. Capacitor

Department Manager   **Personnel Manager**

SHOPFLOOR

PRODUCTION   ENGINEERING

Section Manager   **Chief Engineer**

Officer   Supervisor   Engineer

Foreman

Technician   Secretary

Clerk   Chargehand   Clerk

Lineleader   Service Worker

Operator

Temp. Operator

stead, Japanese engineers supervised three Chinese assistants. The Japanese director of finance accounted for the ethnic composition at the upper corporate levels with the observation, "Japanese and Chinese are good for finance, the Malays for administration." Since the majority of employees were young Malay women in the bottom stratum of factory hierarchy, there seemed little choice but for the management to employ a Malay personnel manager and administrator to supervise the factory hands.

In 1976, disgruntled Malay (male) employees made allegation to the Malay paper *Suara Mederka* (Dec. 14, 1976) that no *bumiputra* were employed as foremen or supervisors in EJI; they also charged that salary differences were evident among members of different ethnic groups. EJI responded to the charges by pointing out that salary differences within the same occupational rank were due to the lower qualifications and probational status of Malay employees. To squelch the disturbing rumors, a Malay foreman was promptly promoted to assistant supervisor. The accusations of ethnic-color discriminations voiced by a few Malay men in lower technical ranks were supported by local politicians, who routinely urged the factories to give preference to local Malays in filling all levels of production and supervisory positions. However, the local school practice of transferring bright students for further training out of the district meant that few remaining students had qualifications for upper level positions. Those taken in and given on-the-job training felt frustration at lower wages and their subordination to supervisors of a different ethnic or national origin. Their poor grasp of English was an additional factor, since it was the lingua franca among the multiethnic, technical and managerial staff. Furthermore, Malay men found it unacceptable to work in semiskilled assembly work, since this category had been defined as "female." For instance, another immediate response of the EJI management to discontent was to promote three of the ten male operators to junior technician positions. Of the remaining, six promptly resigned, and only one continued as the factory hand performing "male" tasks such as packing and carrying crates.

Continual pressures for attaining maximum production levels often generated conflicts between subdivisions which, dominated by leaders of different ethnic origins, lent an ethnic tone to work disputes. In the transistor manufacturing section, conflicts often arose over the differing approaches of production managers versus engineers, i.e., between increasing productivity through labor relations and maximizing productivity through technical efficiency. Whenever machines broke down, engineers made technical adjustments which held up production, thus preventing shopfloor supervisors from attaining high output levels. For falling off production targets, the latter were penalized in their merit increments. Thus, whenever disputes developed between Chinese engineers and production supervisors, the more vocal of whom were Malay, Japanese managers stepped in. The management arbitrated tensions which, through its differential pressures on separate subdivisions, it had built into the industrial organization.

On the shopfloor, unrelenting pressures for high production rates also generated conflicts between supervisors and technicians. According to the Malay personnel manager, some Malay technicians

> misinterpret the work pressure by [non-Malay] supervisors as racial discrimination when it is really just the need to reach production targets.

It was his task to handle such misunderstandings at monthly meetings of the multiethnic supervisory and technical staff. A Malay technician told me about the possibility of separating work frustrations from perception of ethnic hostility:

> My supervisors are Chinese. I feel that their *relations* with Malays are good. Sometimes we Malays also treat them the same way, there is really nothing [problematic between us]. . . . Right now I have problems with the *material* . . . imported from Japan . . . but actually the *material* is not too good . . . This month we have had a lot more *defects*. Probably they [the management] are angry, but we pretend not to know . . . Sometimes they are always scolding us — foremen, supervisors, technicians — they berate everyone.[22]

Not unexpectedly, the demands for high production levels placed by the management on supervisors also shaped the labor relations among supervisors, foremen, and female operators. Diagram 2 represents the actual distribution of workers, by ethnicity and gender, in the microassembly lines of the EJI transistor division in 1979. Women workers, including chargehands and lineleaders, were massed below male supervisory/technical staff. On the shopfloor, the highest rank attainable by female workers was that of "chargehand" (assistant to foreman), but there were only 25 such positions for the 800 operators.

Diagram 2
*Ethnic and Gender Distribution in the Transistor Assembly
Section in EJI, Telok Free Trade Zone, 1979*

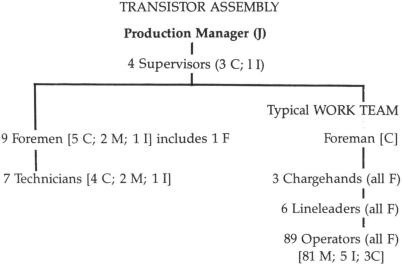

TRANSISTOR ASSEMBLY

Production Manager (J)
|
4 Supervisors (3 C; 1 I)

9 Foremen [5 C; 2 M; 1 I] includes 1 F

7 Technicians [4 C; 2 M; 1 I]

Typical WORK TEAM

Foreman [C]

3 Chargehands (all F)

6 Lineleaders (all F)

89 Operators (all F)
[81 M; 5 I; 3C]

Key: F: female; where gender not indicated, male personnel
J: Japanese; M: Malay; C: Chinese; I: Indian

One Malay woman had qualified for the post of technician, but she declined to accept it as the only female in that job category.

Within the electronics enterprises, a dual employment policy was commonly practiced to provide management with even greater flexibility in channelling, adding, or reducing semiskilled female labor.[23] Thus, at EJI, one-quarter of the total shopfloor labor force was made up of temporary factory hands on six-month contracts (see Table 18). Although these temporary workers, after the two week training period, were practically similar to regular operators, the imposed contracts enabled the management to pay them lower fixed wages and to release them at any time without benefit of the three-month wage packet paid to ordinary departing workers. Besides, temporary workers were often laid off before their three-month period was up, only to be rehired at the same daily rate whenever demands for electronics products increased again. In effect, they constituted the female labor reserve *par excellence* produced by modern industries competing in the highly volatile international market.[24]

Given the rapid transformation within the industry, the employment situation described above was itself undergoing change even as I was conducting research. Making long-range calculations, the EJI management decided to convert most of the production processes in both the manufacturing of transistors and capacitors to full automation. In April 1979, the labor-intensive sections — mounting, bonding, and molding — were gradually being automated so that the work force of 500 was reduced to 200. A number were transferred to the capacitor plant, while others, the temporary workers, were let go. The remaining workers were switched from intensive assembly work to tending two machines each and working three shifts instead of two, as they had previously. Productivity per worker was stepped up as the total output of transistors rose from nine to thirteen million components per month. The Japanese manager confided that in the future, there would be a slight increase in the recruitment of skilled male workers, while the number of female workers would be reduced through "natural attrition."

The finance director explained that automation was increasingly a saving even in Malaysia, where labor was cheap. He pointed out that when manpower was used, material wastage was high. For instance, machines were better at quality control than human beings, who also took more time and used more space. He expected that future factory hands would just tend machines. The stepped-up pace of work induced by automation was matched by a 90 percent increase in daily wage, but at the same time, previous production cash allowances were cut back, so that workers did not see a significant difference in their paychecks. The director concluded, "The time will come in Malaysia when we cannot rely on manual labor."

The production system at ENI was similar to that of EJI, but on a smaller scale and with less automated procedures. Thirteen Japanese expatriates dominated the management positions; on the shopfloor, three male supervisors and twelve foremen controlled 530 operators manufacturing semiconductors. This factory was the most controlled in terms of the spatial distribution of operators in a highly clinical setting, with supervisors watching them through glass partitions. Thus, besides Taylorist techniques which rigidly enforced control through the repetitive performance of decomposed tasks, surveillance as a modern form of power was pervasive within the electronics environment.

At MUZ, the hierarchical work structure was still heavily dependent upon female manual labor. There were two metalworking divisions, one for producing vibrating plates, the other for assembling micromusical movements. Operators working with vibrating plates were placed in individual booths, and their tuning of the plates produced eerie and piercing sounds in the otherwise silent workshop. For this additional stress, they were paid more (M$4.15 to M$7.50/day) than operators who assembled the movements (M$3.50/day). There were altogether 232 female workers, predominantly Malay, in both divisions. Having delineated the overlapping schemes of control in these corporations, we can now look at how labor relations, machine pacing, and surveillance were experienced by the neophyte factory workers.

Power Relations on the Shopfloor

I maintain that in modern industrial institutions circulating discourse/practices produce and reproduce, in daily conditions, cultural concepts of male domination and female subordination which are infused into and became the "common sense" of power relations.[25] The work organization situated and utilized operators for optimal technical efficiency and surveillance. Taylorist methods set the pace and governed repeated, mechanical actions, but it fell on foremen to ensure compliance with the ultimate rule: attainment of the highest production targets by individual operators within each eight-hour shift. Such control did not go unchallenged.

Corporate managements in the Telok FTZ report that levels attained by Malaysian factory women consistently compared favorably to those of Japanese workers. The locale for the lowest production costs of musical movements in the world, a MUZ official reported, was Malaysia. Because of the high costs of machines, as compared to labor, the director said that there were no plans in the immediate future for automation at MUZ. Labor-intensive production in Malaysia, for instance, was more profitable than the fully-automated plant in Japan. Productivity at MUZ was measured by a controlling chart based on standard time and special targets of 100 percent efficiency for the units produced. Lost time, including visits to the locker room, was also calculated into the standard time allotted for specific tasks. Workers were sometimes rotated, as in musical chairs, to discover which job best suited their ability to achieve high production goals. Similarly, soon after ENI began operation, the Japanese director was pleasantly surprised when Malay operators who had been on the job for only two and a half months were tested:

> [T]he running rate of skillfulness of ENI Malaysia is higher than that of Japan; [this is] beyond our expectations (factory document, 1977).

Thus, the Malaysian subsidiary was more profitable than the parent plant in Japan, aided by the fact that Malaysian-manufactured components gained easier entry into American and European markets than Japanese goods. A Japanese engineer in the firm provided a further cultural explanation for higher labor productivity in Japanese firms abroad. In recent years, he said, Japanese workers had become scarce and were ''not so good'' as their predecessors. They were ''too American in culture, ideas, way of life . . . some of them did not want to stick to one company.'' Nevertheless, despite the high production rates in Malaysian subsidiaries, Japanese corporate managers felt that in order to compete successfully with American enterprises they had to continually upgrade the production targets of Malaysian workers. Using the family analogy, another manager commented:

> Parents do not say that they are satisfied with their children; every time parents hope for more from their children.

It fell to the foremen to enforce such endless expectations on female operators. In all three companies, each foreman was placed in charge of ten to forty operators in each production section. In explaining his function to me, the director of ENI described the foreman as ''the head of . . . family members.'' A glance back at Diagram 2 shows that the foreman led a pyramidal distribution of female workers, the chain of command passing from him to the chargehand, lineleader, and rows of operators at the bottom. Foremen were also in charge of two to seven male technicians, depending on particular production sections. The work team in fact suggested the Japanese peasant household — *ie* — a thick nexus of claims and obligations, a miniature gender hierarchy, and coordination of group interests.[26] To implement production goals, foremen relied heavily on their chargehands to deal directly with operators. Noraini's daughter, who was a lineleader at EJI, described her role:

I hate it if I get ordered to do this, do that; I don't like it. The foremen, they give this job, that job, and even before my task is done they say do that, do this, and before that is ready, they say do some other work. At times I tell the operators and they get angry too because of the repeated orders. . . . It's like *pass order.* [The foremen] instruct the chargehand, the chargehand tells us lineleaders, after that the lineleaders inform the operators. My friends [the operators] sometimes get angry because of the endless orders to work fast. . . . Sometimes . . . I try not to [give instructions] immediately, but in *slow motion,* while I am talking to them; this way, it is not *direct.*

After EJI had begun to automate some of its production processes, the pace of work increased greatly, as did the responsibility of individual workers. One overtaxed factory hand complained:

With automation, our *production* target is increased further and we feel even worse than before; more tired, more exhausted . . . more attention is required for watching the *machine.* Previously, [I worked with] one *machine* but now that I am a *checker,* ah, I watch over five *machine.* For the operators there are now two *machine* for each to tend; in the past, one *machine,* one person.

Not only were female workers under increasing work pressures, but they resisted the extreme discipline it would require of them and their co-workers. Thus at EJI, a Malay woman had been trained for the position of foreman, but she was said by the supervisor to lack the necessary "leadership qualities," such as the ability to give and stick by decisions, to be authoritative so that male technicians would comply, and to have a "fierce" demeanor so that the operators would take their instructions seriously. Lurking in this male supremacist description was the implicit acknowledgement of Malay women's reluctance, if not refusal, to be employed as the vehicle for submitting others to factory discipline. When female workers in different ranks were friends or relatives who had grown up together, it became doubly stressful for higher-rank female workers to articulate power relations vis-à-vis their "sisters." Many operators who had qualified for the jobs of chargehand or lineleader turned down promotion for this very reason, despite the higher wages offered. They preferred to work as operators doing overtime to earn the wage difference.

Male authority and power were seen as necessary qualities in supervising female workers. Although most Malay factory women were "very obedient and hardworking types," it was considered necessary in all three factories for foremen to be very strict with them. At MUZ, the engineer assistant and head of the in-house union described the female operators whose interests he supposedly represented:

> Obedience covers all; [it makes them] easier to control. But they are emotional — they cry when errors are pointed out — the threat [is felt] there. Some [however] yell at you.

At ENI, a female office worker noted that when foremen scolded the operators, the latter were not allowed to respond, but had to be "very polite." She had observed an incident in which an operator had forgotten to punch her time card and stood there for half an hour explaining to her foreman why she forgot. Besides the fear they felt for certain foremen, operators were also reluctant to voice their grievances because of the threat of further penalization, such as being fired. Crying sometimes seemed the only way to seek relief from being reprimanded and to obtain pardon.

The foremen, who were not uniformly strict and harsh with operators, were themselves under continual pressures to implement high production goals, depending on market conditions. One EJI foreman told me that even after the introduction of automation, it was possible to

> still improve productivity in certain processes . . . [I will] try to set a target calculated up to a maximum capability of [the] machinery. Sometimes [I] have to push workers beyond maximum when demand is good — directive from [the] top.

The felt oppression is expressed by one operator as a form of trickery:

> What do the workers want? We don't want to be shackled as if we were forced to work. If we are being tricked then we must do the work, but if we are not, then don't force us. Sometimes they *pressurize* us if *production* falls. [We are] forced to go beyond the *target*. It is the management that forces us . . .

Nevertheless, it was in the daily exercise of power relations between female workers and foremen which, because emotion-laden and infused with ambivalence, was key to enforcing work discipline. Central to the foremen's domination was the authority to determine which individual workers qualified for special rewards or micropunishments on a daily basis. In all three firms, the low wages operated as a powerful stimulant on the operators to produce above average output and take on more unpleasant tasks, for which they were given cash allowances. When asked why she worked overtime, the lineleader quoted above explained that she felt "cheated" (*rugi*) if she did not work on Sundays, when wages were 50 percent more than regular daily payments, in addition to her six-day work week. Special "incentive allowances" were given at both EJI and ENI to workers whenever they took the night shift (an additional M$1.50 to a daily average of M$3.50 to M$4 in 1979). "Efficiency allowances" were awarded to those operators whose production output went beyond the calculated average. These allowances were allotted on the basis of daily production charts kept on individual workers either by themselves or by a lineleader, and then adjusted by foremen after consultation with chargehands. These cash awards, finely graded into increments of a few cents per day, were given to operators who might almost double the average daily output. In EJI, for example, before automation was introduced, some operators in the bonding section could assemble 6,000 components per shift, compared to the average of 3,200. Thus, the "efficiency" allowances greatly increased the productivity of the workers, who were then awarded with minimal wage increases of M$1 to M$40 per month.

Cash rewards were also paid for particularly stressful tasks, such as the use of microscopes in the electronics factories and the tuning of plates in the micromachine plant. For production processes involving microscope use, fresh recruits were routinely used so that by the time their eyesight had deteriorated in a couple of years, they would be replaced by new operators. A few might continue at the same tasks, wearing prescription glasses, or be transferred to other tasks; others resigned because their physical capacity for the work had been literally used up. At EJI, out of the original batch of 300 microscope workers recruited in 1975, only 30 were still thus employed after four years. Foremen and supervisors not only determined the meting of allowances on a daily basis, but they also made recommendatons for "merit" and "attendance" awards given at the end of the year.

Such relations based on daily interactions and meeting "common" goals induced a sense of family feeling. The operator cited above felt conflict between resisting management pressures and implementing foremen's orders. She obeyed foremen because "they knew our problems," not like "people who sit in the office." Furthermore, there was a sense that their relationship with the foremen could be negotiated:

> Sometimes we let the foremen know that we do not like to be forced, we have empathy, we know our duty. We must perform our duty well, if everything is fine, but if the machine is not good how can we work properly? We have been gathered here in the same place so let us all be considered the same way — one *company*. We in one section consider ourselves as one family . . . because we are more closely connected to [our foreman].

By citing "family" (*keluarga*), "empathic feeling" (*timbang rasa*), and their own sense of duty (*tugas*), women workers appealed to the foreman's humanitarian values as a means of softening his control.[27]

Often, appeals to family sentiments were ineffective against continual monitoring of work schedules, work time, and work records. Factory hands in EJI and ENI could be dismissed for being absent for more than two consecutive days. Few operators had ever lost their jobs this way, although during the festival season, there was a greater incidence of one-day absenteesim. A description of the operators' work schedule imparts the stress they felt in riding the industrial treadmill. At ENI, workers in the bonding and mounting sections alternated between two shifts: from 6:30 A.M. to 2:30 P.M. and from 2:30 P.M. to 10:30 P.M. Those in other production sections had to work three shifts every two weeks, taking the night shift from 10:30 P.M. to 6:30 A.M. In the latter case, even after the Sunday rest, workers did not have enough time to adjust their bodies and eating pattern properly for the next (morning) shift. They had to wake up at 4:30 A.M. and catch the bus at some distance from the *kampung*. If they missed the factory bus, they had to wait for public transportation which brought them to work an hour late, a situation that earned a scolding and loss in daily wage. Women workers who asked for medical leave could be rudely questioned by some foremen making humiliating innuendos about their social activities.

Besides continual work pressure, the most stressful daily experiences for operators were to be watched over and monitored by a few overzealous foremen. During the night shift, for instance, some operators might sneak away to the locker room to take naps and thus earn a reprimand from foremen. Beyond such clear breaking of rules, however, some foremen were anxious to confine operators to the workbench by carefully screening requests for permission to go to the toilet, the factory clinic, or to the prayer room (*surau*).[28] Government regulations gave Muslim workers the right to break for prayers (at five intervals distributed throughout the working day), but most operators limited themselves to one obeisance at sundown, taking about 15 minutes between work shifts. Others might decide to ask permission to leave the workbench more frequently — right in the middle of production — to pray. This loss of time the factory management had to tolerate.

In addition to time transgressions, operators chafed at factory regulations requiring special overalls and footwear. One of them saw restrictions on movement and clothing as yet another form of control.

> It would be nice working here if the *foremen, managers,* all the staff members and clerks understand that the workers are not under their *control.* Hm, there is a great deal of *control.* . . . Once my friend, she wanted to go and pray, she was wearing her house slippers, [but the foreman] would not allow that, she had to wear [regulation] shoes there too. This is called *"control"* too, isn't it?

Another operator complained that the factory overalls were too tight, but they were not allowed to unbutton a little even though they had Malay clothing underneath. Furthermore, they had to change their shoes before entering the workshop. She considered such dress regulations as part of the general "tight discipline" in the factory and said that the workers needed more "liberal" rules.

This change from village social contexts, in which women were seldom monitored by someone in their work but enjoyed self-determination in setting the pace of their daily activities, was traumatic. Since the Malay *baju kurong* was a loose and flowing tunic and *sarung,* usually worn with sandals or Chinese clogs, the tight factory overalls and heavy rubber shoes both extended and represented the workers' sense of being controlled in body and movement.

Factory discipline, when strictly enforced, also suppressed the spontaneous friendliness of Malay women who, though initially shy, were quick to display affectionate interest in friends and co-workers. Thus, one immediate influence on the tenor of their daily lives was whether their foremen treated them warmly and kindly or were too distant. Very few operators confessed to disliking their foreman on the basis of his (non-Malay) ethnicity; they based their judgements on his humanitarian treatment of female workers, which they opposed to heavy-handed control. One woman described her Malay foreman as follows:

[He] *controls* more than others. He does not wish to be friendly even with us operators. That is really his attitude. Yes, he *controls* more [than other foremen]; for instance, whatever operators do, it angers him. . . . If, for instance, we become tired during the night shift, other foremen will just let us be as long as the operators have done their work. He isn't like this, he really watches us. If we gossip, he glares. Sometimes, if he is standing behind us . . . he will not let us get up even once . . . He does not talk with operators, he is not like other foremen.

However, daily interactions with foremen also engendered romantic interests in the young women workers lacking previous exposures to nonkin male company. Attraction usually developed because they felt that certain foremen, sometimes Chinese or Indian, wère kindly towards them. The supervisor claimed that he told foremen to treat all female workers "equally, but a few fall in love." Such favoritism was strongly discouraged by operators (other than the smitten ones) who argued that "dating" behavior was not "proper," especially between Muslim women and non-Muslim men. Some years earlier, a Chinese foreman had converted to Islam to marry a Malay operator, but it was one rare exception to the tendency for such romances to be terminated because of strong social pressures exerted by coworkers. Although they criticized such liaisons in terms of Malay-Islamic practices, operators were in fact also resisting unequal treatment on the shopfloor.

Other forms of *kampung* mechanisms reconstituted in the factory included the customary prestige of male status and female deference to male authority. At EJI, for instance, two female foremen chosen for their technical qualifications were ineffective because male technicians had little confidence in their authority. Male instructions, even when given by unreasonable foremen, were obeyed, although not without covert resentment. While Malay women were conscientious and docile in their work, they disliked being overtly controlled, scolded, or threatened. Thus, kindly foremen who played their role more akin to "father" or "brother" could win the workers' compliance and loyalty, and foster a comfortable "family" atmosphere in the midst of rigid control. A Chinese supervisor told me that in his dealings with operators

force [is] not so important as understanding of subordination . . . Mutual understanding and respect [are] very important for

[the] leader's control.

He added that it was important to encourage the workers daily and to compliment them on their handiwork.

The Family Way: Managing Maidens and Morality

Corporate management of female workers went beyond the reworking of authoritarian moral habits into daily work routines. In its general treatment of the female labor force, the Japanese company in *mukim* Telok was careful to insert its organization into the local social matrix, taking into consideration the network of relationships workers maintained in *kampung* society. The male-dominated industrial system overlapped, to an important extent, the structure of unequal relations in local communities. "Traditional authority"[29] in the rural Malay system was vested in Islamic or political leaders over ordinary folk (whose loyalty they engaged); in parents over children; in elders over juniors; and in men over women. As mentioned above, the deference village women showed men was more an ideal than a fact of everyday life. However, the junior status of young nubile women (commonly referred to as *budak budak*, the term for "maidens" as well as "children") made them more susceptible to male authority. Thus, corporate pronouncements about the factory as "one big family" concerned for the "welfare" of the workers were directed as much at their village elders. The manipulation of emotions by appeals to morality was an important dimension of corporate coercion.

In MUZ, large framed posters proclaimed the "company philosophy":

to create one big family,
to train workers,
to increase loyalty to company,
country and fellow workers.

At EJI, the "one happy family" working together was not stirred by calls for loyalty to country but by rules spelled out in a little book referred to, rather inappropriately, as "The Bible."

It was the ENI personnel manager who tapped local cultural sentiments and family norms with particular *savoir-faire*. A smooth Kelantanese with the air of an enlightened bureaucrat, he explained that his firm was "more Eastern in nature" than the other companies. There were no social gatherings or parties held on factory premises which might encourage the mixing of male and female workers. The company was located in a "*kampung* area where the outlook of the people [was] too religious, old-fashioned." He admitted, though, that his factory had no time for social functions. Citing press reports about factory women being "too free" and the few cases of prostitution reported in urban-based FTZs elsewhere in the country, he spelled out his firm's policy:

> We do not want to go against Malay culture, *and* Japanese culture too . . . We are entrusted by the parents to give the girls good employment, not otherwise. This is a family system; we are responsible for the girls inside and outside the factory. If the girls get sick, for example, we send them home by private cars. . . . Of course the workers are not too happy — "too much control," they complain. But we say the big "Yes" here. Parents are very happy and we never receive any phone calls or letters from parents calling for their daughters' resignation — like other companies [do].

Indeed, this social control was so effective that the monthly turnover was no more than two percent, compared to four percent at MUZ and six percent at EJI.

The companies' attempts to adhere closely to local norms and mores not only reassured parents but also acted as a mode of social conformity which, calculated to "make everyone happy," distracted them from their work conditions. Thus, corporate policies toward workers' "welfare" and "benefits" (such as production allowances) should be discussed in relation to the ways workers' grievances were dealt with. In MUZ, soon after production began in 1976, a Chinese supervisor who supported work action to demand higher wages was dismissed. A small multiethnic group of female workers went on strike to protest his dismissal. They also attempted to prevent other workers — the majority of whom did not understand the action or know the issues — from working. The strike dragged on for a couple of weeks, until the MUZ management prevailed upon the *ketua kampung* of Sungai Jawa and the *penghulu* to talk to the workers. These community leaders warned the workers that if they continued striking, they would lose their jobs and the factory would have to close down. The strike was thus ended, without reinstating the supervisor.

By 1979, MUZ had a union which was recognized by the state registrar because it could be affiliated to the federation of Metal Industries Employees Union. However, the Japanese director commented that the "connection [was] not so effective." In fact, he explained, the MUZ union operated like company unions in Japan, which settled their problems through internal consultation with corporate managers. The Malay personnel manager said candidly:

> We recognize the union in order to make them [the workers] happy . . . [we] increase efforts on welfare, benefits. We bring them to a point away from the wage focus — otherwise, heaven will be the only limit to wage demands . . . we create a happy family environment.

The union leader, who was also an assistant engineer, agreed. His job at the factory was to design "controlling processes" (using Taylorist methods) directed at increasing the productivity of the workers. The role of the union, in his view, was to

> look after the welfare of the workers,
> work hand-in-hand with the recreation club,
> promote relations with the management —
> we swim or sink together
> [with an embarassed laugh].

He said that the management considered basic facilities like a canteen as "welfare" services. The "recreation club" had been set up for workers to participate in sports, parlor games, and singing. There was a "pop" band supplied with electric organ, guitars, drums, and saxophone by the firm. Perhaps, not unexpectedly,

> the workers are not so outspoken; [there is only] a bit of opinion, no counter-proposal to what the management decides [about recreational activities].

This was the situation in a union with ten elected representatives, two of whom were females representing women workers who constituted 80 percent of the labor force. It could be because Malay women workers were seldom interested in the so-called "recreational activities" (which appealed almost exclusively to urban-bred and male employees) but were more concerned with improving their low wages. The major part of the operators' complaints dealt with poor wages, and, in early 1979, when the management decided to consider a new wage scale, there were fewer complaints at union meetings. Nevertheless, the union leader reiterated that the role of the union was "as an intermediary between workers and the management . . . as a watchdog, for both sides."

In the other two firms, electronics workers had not yet succeeded in forming unions, nor had they really been shown how to do so. In addition to the registrar's refusal to recognize unions set up by electronics workers, the latter had to contend with corporate tactics. In 1978, workers at EJI demonstrated for company recognition of their union. The strike went on for a few weeks but ended without obtaining its goal. Striking workers were not sacked but forfeited their wages for missing work. They were, however, given a feast at the annual year-end party for raising production levels. A technician told me of his attempts to get outside support:

> Concerning the union, I had spoken with —— and was straightforward and clear with her at the time when she was the Minister of Culture . . . but I myself still do not understand [what unionization involves]. But if I already knew, then I would surely set one up, whichever way . . . I feel a union is like a 'social group,' we can take one action against the management. I feel that this is a right.

Instead of even an in-house union, the company itself had set up a "Joint Consultative Committee" (JCC) in 1976, made up of eleven "elected" employees (i.e., heads of work sections) and three managers. The JCC managed to meet once every three to four months and fell into disuse after one year. The personnel manager said that this was because workers had no confidence in their leaders. A different view was given by a foreman: the JCC was "like a puppet" which did not have any of its requests fulfilled. It "died" when the management did not call for reelections the next year.

The firm came up with yet another "better" alternative, the personnel manager pointed out. Each work section was to have its own "employees' monthly meeting" and then send an elected emissary to meet with the management. Operator representatives were to meet with the personnel manager separately from foremen and supervisors, who had their own meetings. Such meetings operated in effect as a "grievance procedure system" to pass all complaints to the top management. In response, the managing director circulated memos which were also pinned up on notice boards. Group leaders were required to poll their workers for reactions to plans and report back to the management. The final decision was taken at the top and implemented by the section leaders.[30] An operator who represented her section said that most shopfloor leaders reported that workers wanted higher wages, but this vote was "overruled" at the meetings. They also requested two pairs of regulation shoes and overalls, but the personnel manager made vague promises contingent upon further increases in production output. These monthly meetings thus basically operated as a surveillance vehicle through which discontent could be turned into account, workers "normalized" and spurred on to greater effort.

Corporate strategies regulating operators' emotions and conduct importantly involved social relations with the *kampung* communities from which they hailed. Rather than encouraging individuating attitudes among the first-time workers, as some Western firms have done,[31] the local Japanese factories sought to uphold social obligations which still bound the workers to their rural households. This reworking of local communal values not only helped to reinforce the discipline of workers on the shopfloor but also to preserve the conditions in which rural parents continue to send their daughters to the factories for cash earnings. Although the three companies in Telok were in competition with each other, there was "unofficial coordination in the field of public relations." Managers in the different firms checked with each other over donations to local events like school sportsday, the Boy Scouts Movement, Prophet Mohammad's birthday celebrations, Farmers' Fair, and the like. One factory contributed over M$1,000 each year to events at the village, *mukim*, and district levels. A corporate official noted that this was a "social obligation" because "our people being from the *kampung* are not well-off." The firms had tried to deflect fund appeals from outside the district, urging the *penghulu* to call off some of the pressure.

What did such attention to rural society produce in terms of symbolic capital? As the following will demonstrate, the social standing of corporate managers was enhanced in the eyes of village elders, whose moral support could be depended on for the social control of their working daughters. The ENI personnel manager, an ex-army officer in his early fifties, presented himself as "foster father" (*bapa angkat*) to the operators whom he referred to as *"budak budak"* (children/maidens). In place of a union, monthly invitations were sent to parents of thirty operators to spend an afternoon at the company. Usually, half the parents came, sometimes after travelling a long distance. These parents' assemblies were intended, he told me, to acquaint the parents with the working hours, the factory procedure of overtime . . . so that parents will know when to expect their daughters to return from work . . . [and] to educate the parents who do not know this is a mass specialized production system.

A common parental complaint had been the mandatory night shift, which meant that their daughters had to walk to and wait at the bus stop in the dark before and after work. Some parents requested that factory buses pick the women up from their village homes. Another worry was the amount of time working daughters spent in activities outside home, under the pretext of working "overtime." The manager patiently explained that if operators were retained because of overtime, those in the morning shift would be delayed for two hours, while workers in the afternoon schedule (which let out at 10:30 P.M.) would be asked to arrive for work two hours *earlier*. Bus drivers were ordered to take female workers home within the hour of release, and parents could check their daughters' overtime forms. This "cooperation" the management extended to parents in monitoring their daughters' movements between home and factory reassured village folk that ENI managers were indeed *bapa angkat* concerned about the moral protection of their "wards."

Parents' meetings had perhaps more critical uses for the management. At one meeting I attended, the rural folk arrived, dazed after a hot trip, and were ushered into the cool conference room where they fell into an awed silence. The personnel manager handed out colorful pamphlets on his company (in both English and Malay), while delivering a public relations pitch. After explaining the factory work and bus schedules, he said he hoped their "discussion" (it had been a monologue) would be a "dialogue." This was received in baffled silence since villagers were not accustomed to bureaucratic Malay liberally sprinkled with American clichés. He wanted to know whether the workers had any problems at home, whether they complained about problems at work but were too "bashful" (*malu*) to let factory personnel know. He reassured the parents that their "female children" (*budak budak perumpuan*) cried easily and would surely confess problems to their mothers and fathers. However, he was practically their *bapa angkat*, so if the parents would "cooperate," let them tell him the complaints of the children. The sole response was a father from Banting who wanted to know about medical care for workers.

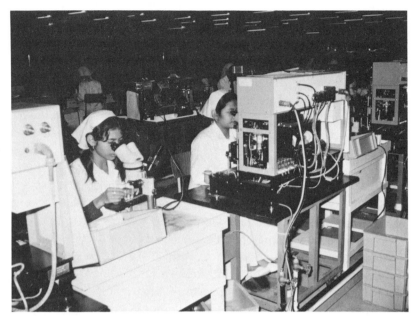

"Through a glass darkly"

Credit: International Development Research Centre, Social Sciences Division, Ottawa

There were no further questions, and the manager asserted that opportunities for promotion at his factory were better than in government service, that the operators had more allowances than even clerks (failing to mention that the former's wages were much lower and that miniscule allowances required additional labor input). The parents were then shown a film on the international operations of the corporation.

In the final half hour, they were taken for a view of the shopfloor, which they observed from behind glass panels. Here, the parents asked many questions concerning the work their daughters did. They were finally ushered back to the meeting room and served curried puffs, potato chips, and soda water. It was clear that the visit had been a success, for the parents were suitably impressed by the factory and by the fact that a high-ranking Malay official had put himself at their ''service.'' Seduced by an in-factory view most rural folk would never have, the parents unwittingly played a part in the surveillance scheme, thereby adding their own moral weight to these controlling processes based on knowledge.

Corporate disciplinary techniques involved not only the surveillance but also the encoding of Malay female sexuality, in work, movement, and residence. ENI tried to group outstation workers in the same cluster of rooming houses (mainly in Kampung Melur). The personnel manager said he felt responsibility for the young women from distant villages: "since they are exposed to dangers, we have to look after them." Operators employed at the other two firms also rented rooms, but usually it was their landladies who acted as self-appointed custodians, mediating between the workers and the *kampung* residents. Most of the boarders were from villages in the southern half of the district. They commonly sent from M$30 to M$50 home each month. Sometimes, these migrant workers had to borrow money from their supervisors to pay the rent. Four to six boarders would share a single-bedroom house for about M$40 a month. Others took two-room houses for twice as much rent. Since, in addition to remittances, they had to purchase their own food, migrant workers were seldom able to save. Operators living with their parents displayed envy and even hostility toward the outstation workers who were said to have more "free time" (from housework) and to escape from customary family control. However, these migrant workers were sometimes visited by parents who had failed to receive the monthly check. So even workers "living on their own" were subjected to some of the constraints of *kampung* and family life, a situation which the factories were comfortable with. This partial incorporation of female migrants into the local villages checked public opinion quick to comment on their "immoral" conduct and the "disorganizing" effects of rural industrialization. While corporate managements might have been genuinely concerned about the welfare of migrant workers, these social arrangements enhanced corporate regulation of its female labor force beyond the factory gates.

The modern corporation in Kuala Langat thus introduced a whole network of power relations which operate in different local situations: state agencies, unions, corporate structures, industrial workshops, factory meetings, *kampung* groups, and village households. Whereas other studies of the labor process in late capitalism focus on the subjugation of labor to capital, stressing the centrality of Taylorist techniques and the divorce between mental and physical labor (e.g., Braverman 1974), I have looked at the multiplicity of overlapping disciplinary techniques which produce biological objects, docile bodies, and sexualized subjects in in transnational companies. In the industrialization of the Malaysian economy, relations of domination and subordination based on gender, more than ethnicity, became consistently salient in different spheres of daily activity. With government backing at the national level, and by their delicate reconstitution of *kampung* institutions and values locally, Japanese corporate managements effectively curtailed the workers' potential for organized action. We must therefore question notions about an inherent logic in capitalist relations and labor resistance, as well as assumptions about class "self-making" (Thompson 1963). My reservations about reification will be made clear as we finally turn to the contradictory images, spirit visitations, and sporadic tactics of resistance as Malay peasant women were constituted as the first generation of an industrial labor force.

Chapter 8

Neophyte Factory Women and the Negative Image

> The ceremony of innocence is drowned.
> William Butler Yeats
> *The Second Coming*

A visitor to large Malaysian towns will be struck by scenes of factory women not common even ten years ago. Streams of uniformly clad young women, looking rather like schoolgirls, can be observed eddying around bus stops, food vendors, or outside FTZ gates. In the evening, dressed in more colorful Malay or Western clothes, these neophyte factory workers may be seen on their way home to squatter lodgings, shopping at marketplaces, or wandering around downtown. A running commentary often follows in their wake. Shop assistants, passers-by, and street urchins may cheerfully greet them with "minah *karan*" ("high voltage Minah," a variation of "Minah *letrik*"), "*kaki* enjoy" ("pleasure-seekers"), and, sometimes, more insultingly, "*perumpuan jahat*" ("bad women/prostitutes"). Not only people in the streets but the Malaysian press, politicians, administrators, educators, and Islamic groups have all raised key moral issues in a cacophony of critical commentaries about women of the nascent Malay working class. I maintain that this explosion of sexual discourses, counterpointed by the voices of factory women, are produced out of conflicting modes of control exercised by dominant groups deeply ambivalent about social change in Malay society.

179

Other descriptions of the Malay female industrial force in Malaysia have focused on the issue of exploitation in transnational industries (Linda Lim 1978; Grossman 1979; Munster 1980), the problems of migration (Jamilah Ariffin 1980), and the role of spirit possession episodes in the industrial setting (Ackerman 1979; Ackerman and Lee 1981). This chapter brings some coherence to these apparently divergent themes by discussing how Malay factory women in coastal Selangor and Penang experienced, interpreted, and reacted to capitalist relations which constrained them at work while promising social emancipation.

To discover the changing sense of subjectivity in the proletarian situation, the Marxist notion of false consciousness no longer suffices. James Scott has pointed out that resistance by subjugated populations often has its basis not in class interests but rather in a "moral economy" under siege (1976). My concern here is not to give greater weight to one view or the other, but in fact to demonstrate the power effects of discursive practices which encode and construct power relations in shifting domains of everyday life. As Foucault's works have shown, cultural concepts are not the mere epiphenomena of class power or cultural values but are constituting knowledge/power systems producing the "truths" whereby we live our lives. Feminist analysis often errs in merely showing up the male bias of "ideological" constructs without attending to the daily production and reproduction of relationships according to "given" male-supremacist principles.[1] In other words, authoritative languages and the ideas they construct do not merely "reflect" material relationships but constitute our very experience of reality. Thus, Raymond Williams urges Marxists to consider hegemonic language as "practical consciousness," "constitutive activity" involved in the material production of "Truth" (1977).

Taking an oblique stance to this metadebate, my intention here is to discuss the social experiences of Malay factory women in terms of the cultural constitution of a specific "class sexuality"[2] and the kinds of "truth" asserted by different groups in the political arena. I will begin by explicating how Malaysian industrialization has been accompanied by a variety of discursive practices about the individual and the population which increasingly shape and give intelligibility to different domains of social life. The process of subjectivization induced by these sexual discourses will be considered in terms of self-regulation and resistance tactics, as factory women attempt to construct a new configuration of morality and identity in their own terms.

Sexual Metaphors and Social Control

Since 1970, the media, radio, and *Televeshen Malaysia*, which are controlled by the state, have played an increasing role in focusing attention on young Malay women and have provided the frame of reference for public discussion of their new status. Newspaper articles popularized familiarity with appellations coined in the streets, describing the apparent proclivities of Malay working women for activities such as *jolli kaki* (seeking fun) and *jolli duit* (having fun with money). Women who seek Western-type recreation in bars and nightclubs were referred to as "*kaki* disco." In particular, the emphasis on "electric" (a triple pun on the women's industrial product, their imputed personality, and the bright city lights they supposedly seek) and "feet" (*kaki*) implied the unhampered (*bebas*) freedom associated with footloose behavior and more than a suggestion of "streetwalker" (*kaki* also implies the sidewalk — "five-foot-way": *kaki lima*). By reiterating such negative images and playing on "jolly" and "enjoy," the media and public developed the image of Malay factory women as pleasure-seekers and spendthrifts pursuing Western modes of consumer culture.

Indeed, many factory women, especially those working in urban-based FTZs, acquired eye-catching outfits and spent their off-hours shopping and going to the movies. However, conspicuous consumption and participation in a Western youth culture were most prevalent among young middle-class professionals and university students, but the press has chosen to highlight such activities among working class Malay women. An operator from Sungai Jawa commented with some bitterness that the public considered factory women on the same low level as streetwalkers. She pointed out that office workers were also known to be "immoral" (*tak ada moral-lah*), but the public "raised itself above those who work in factories because they did not have [high academic] qualifications." By riveting public attention on the female workers' consumption, the press trivialized women's work and helped divert discontent over their weak market position into the manageable channels of a "youth culture."

The mass circulating press, radio, and t.v. talk shows also operated as a vehicle for public officials and politicians to make pronouncements on Malay working class women, amplifying events which tarnished their reputation. From 1976 onwards, newspaper reports intermittently carried stories about factory women in the Penang Island Bayan Lepas FTZ, said to service soldiers and tourists, under such headlines as "Factory Girls in Sex Racket."[3] In early 1979, *The Star* proclaimed in its front page "It is not fair to associate *all* factory girls with immorality."[4] Factory women featured in the story were from maintained peasant villages working in the FTZ. They rented rooms in local *kampung* and were watched over by the village elders so that they would not "fall prey to any city playboy." As the oldest and largest FTZ in the country (twenty transnational firms employed some 18,000 workers), the Bayan Lepas FTZ has developed a reputation for sexually permissive *female* workers. Factory women were dubbed factory-specific nicknames such as "micro-*syaitan*" ("micro-devils") for operators at Microsystems, and "night-sales" or "*nasi sejok*" ("cold rice": "cold" goods) for those working at National Semiconductors. Malay women in other FTZs were also described as "preyed upon" and "tricked" into prostitution. An Ipoh industrial estate has earned the label of "the Malaysian Haadyai," after the famous Thai red-light border town frequented by Malaysian men.[5]

The alarm raised over the perceived threat of Malay factory women asserting social independence, thus casting doubts on official Islamic culture, has prompted state officials to call for greater control of women in the growing Malay working class. In 1980, the then deputy prime minister noted that rural women who worked in factories were said to become "less religious and have loose morals." As a champion of the export-industrialization program, he advised that the solution to the problems was not to blame the factories but for people to guide the "young girls" to "the right path."[6] The public association between Malay factory women and "immorality" had become such a national issue that further state action was required to quell the fears of Malay parents back in the *kampung*. In the next year, the Welfare Minister called for orientation programs to be set up by *kampung* youth associations to prepare village women for urban life so that they would not fall into the "trap" and "discard their traditional values" in town.[7]

The academic community stepped in to define the problem of "immorality" among Malay factory women as the outcome of "rural-urban migration" and Westernized urban culture rather than industrial employment. This *"sarung-*to-jean movement," the vice chancellor of Universiti Malaya argued, resulted in problems of urban living which could be alleviated by providing counseling, recreational, and educational facilities. "Lack of recreation," he says, "leads to untoward patterns of behavior."[8] He headed a huge foreign-funded project to study the social welfare needs (dormitories, transportation, and mosques) of Malay factory women in cities (non-Malay working women were not part of the target population). Thus, through the expansion of what Foucault called "bio-power," new administrative and regulatory mechanisms, in addition to social discourses, came to problematize the sexuality of Malay working women: their relative economic freedom was linked with the irresponsible use of that freedom to indulge in an orgy of pleasure-seeking activities. Greater public control came to be exerted over their "leisure" time (which in actuality was very limited), while simultaneously diverting attention from the harsh realities of their "working" time.

Islamic groups aligned with and against the state have joined the debate over the changing status of young Malay women. State Islamic offices, like other governmental agencies, tended to direct attention towards the perceived misuse of "free time" by industrial women, whereas Islamic revivalists (*dakwah*) movements were more concerned with questions of defining appropriate spiritual and social boundaries. Since the early 1970s, the NEP has brought thousands of young rural Malays into urban factories and educational institutions, feeding and increasing the rate of cultural change. Malays educated abroad returned with a new commitment to fundamentalist interpretations of Islam and its centrality in defining not only the political economy but also gender roles in Malaysia. This new Malay intelligentsia, fired with religious fervor over official corruptions and the goals of *pembangunan*, increased the vigilance of state Islamic institutions in monitoring the deportment of young Muslim women.

To the young Malay women, the subject of all this scrutiny, official Islam, as represented by state religious offices, was experienced as a legal system which dealt with marriage, divorce, inheritance, and religious offenses. Since the "moral" status of Malay working women had become suspect, there was a tightening of religious surveillance of sexual conduct. More frequent raids were reported in the poor lodgings and cheap hotels inhabited by workers and the semiemployed. As the examples of some women from Sungai Jawa had shown, under current official reading of Islamic offenses, Muslims may be arrested for *khalwat*, or "close proximity" between a man and a woman who were neither immediate relatives nor married to each other. Offenders caught in situations suggestive of sexual intimacy (but not in *flagrante delicto*) were fined or jailed for a few months; the sentences varied from state to state. Muslims could also be arrested for *zinah*, i.e., illicit sexual intercourse, which was more severely punished.

Although theoretically there was general surveillance of the entire Malay population, the understaffed religious offices seemed to have turned their attention to areas where Malay factory women were concentrated. Factory women seen walking around at night were sometimes threated with arrest for *khalwat* by men who were not members of Islamic offices.[9] Both parties arrested in an incident were punished, but sometimes the female partner was given the heavier sentence. When the culprits were too poor to pay both fines (M$1,000 or more each), the payment was sometimes made jointly to release the male offender so that he could return to work while the female offender served the jail sentence.[10] The religious authority became one of the more critical agencies disciplining the social conduct of working Malays, subjecting women to greater sanctions than men.

Malays in the *dakwah* movement — "a politically informed resurgence" (Kessler 1980) — were mainly disaffected students and intellectuals more concerned with the inculcation of Islamic-Malay ascetic values than punishing those who deviated from principles of moral behavior. For many of the educated younger generations, especially members of the dominant *dakwah* group ABIM (*Angkatan Belia Islam Malaysia:* Malaysian Islamic Youth Movement),[11] Islamic revitalization provided a means for reaffirming *kampung* values (Kessler 1980) and of "striving (*perjuangan*) for religious truth" (Nagata 1981: 414) in the alienating Western urban environment. Others joined Islamic sects like Darul Arqam and Jamaat Tabligh, which offered alternative versions of an Islamic society they would like to see installed in Malaysia.[12] Different *dakwah* groups demanded, among other things, a new model of Malay womanhood.

The modern, religiously-enlightened Malay woman was defined in opposition to what was considered capitalist and derivative of Western individualist and materialist culture. Through a radical reinterpretation of the Koran and Sunah, the revivalists called upon Muslims, but especially Muslim women, to abstain from Western forms of behavior like drinking alcohol, driving cars, and watching television and movies (regarded as the major vehicles for transmitting undesirable foreign values). Instead, women were encouraged to veil themselves modestly, observe the segregation of the sexes, undertake community services, and engage in serious Koranic studies. Although few, if any, of the Malay factory women (as compared to office workers) donned Arabic robes in voluntary *purdah*, the *dakwah* movement has struck a responsive chord in many young women who wished to be recognized as morally upright Muslims engaged in honest hard work (*kerja halal*). They saw in Islamic resurgence an assertion of pride in Malay-Muslim culture and an affirmation of its fundamental values in opposition to foreign consumer culture. For instance, the widespread influence of foreign advertising and the promotion of beauty contests in American electronics companies have promoted Western images of feminine passivity and consumption (see Grossman 1979). The Consumer Association in Penang found in a recent survey that factory women appeared to spend more money on clothes and cosmetics than on nutritious food (Gay 1983). Assailed by contradictory, unflattering representations of themselves, factory women often sought in Islam guidance self-regulation to comply with work discipline and to inculcate an ascetic attitude towards life. An operator in EJI revealed the anguish caused by bad publicity, and her innocent complicity in greater social control:

> I feel that society views us with contempt because we are factory workers. Factory women sometimes associate in an unrestrained (*bebas*) manner, as when men and women talk among themselves, hmm, outside [the home] and released from the custody of the parents (*kongkongan ibubapa*). . . . Society only knows how to criticize (*caci*) but does not know the significance of our work in the factory. . . . What ought to be done is to set up religious classes . . . to give warning (*bimbangan*) to factory workers, and then to set up rules against unrestrained interaction (*kebebasan*) among workers within and without the factories. This is in order to increase *discipline*. Most of us read the newspapers. [Let them] explain the problems of us factory workers to the public.

As might be expected, Malay working class youths were less easily cowed. Radical criticisms of transnational corporations by intellectual leaders of ABIM have provided worker-members the elements of a political idiom to articulate their experience of *"exploitasi"* in the production process. A Malay technician at EJI, who had joined ABIM when he was at a vocational school in Kuala Lumpur, saw through the management strategy of giving annual dinners to workers as a means to "ease their hearts" and make them "forget" basic issues like wages and work conditions. He claimed that as a member of ABIM he was not "blinded" (*buta*), like *kampung* folk, by the disguised intentions of corporate management.

> I know my own feelings [of being manipulated], I know the feeling of other [workers]. . . . Therefore, I am sort of in *revolt* behind their [i.e., management's] back.

He argued that there was no "one road" to solving the problems faced by Malay factory women who were badly underpaid and "stamped" with a degrading image. He rejected the university chancellor's proposal to build dormitories near FTZs. "I feel that to tie them up like this . . . is not the *democratic* road. We cannot tie them up . . . it is not practical." Such statements by working class Malay women and men reflected attempts to formulate social arrangements which would link Islamic ideals of chaste, honest work, and relative gender equality with democratic notions, based on an alternative subjectivity.

The *Kampung* and the World

> The young coconut is bored by a squirrel. [*Nyiur ditebuk tupai*]
> Malay proverb

In rural Selangor, Malay women employed in the Telok FTZ, together with their parents, rejected the commoditized image of factory women as illegitimate and an affront to Muslim womanhood. The image of "factory girls [as] synonymous with good time girls"[13] assailed *kampung* morality and expectations of female loyalty to family interests. Village factory women struggled with simultaneous efforts to be true to family claims on the one hand, and to claim new rights as workers on the other. Such conflicting claims were not usually resolved in favor of individualism as a crucial part of their self-image.

Factory employment gave the young rural women a measure of economic independence from personal subordination at home but simultaneously intensified their contractual dependence on men in the industrial hierarchy. Thus, many factory women felt their unfreedom *more* at the threshold of economic emancipation. Even as they became integrated within a rigidly unequal system of work relationships never before encountered in Malay peasant society, their nonwork activities increasingly came under the surveillance of a censuring public.

In fact, local Japanese corporations, by reworking indigenous institutions of familial and village cooperation into production relations, have socialized rural Malay women as an industrial labor force in ways which won the approval and implicit cooperation of rural society. Furthermore, the induced docility of factory women sprang from a practical assessment of their insecure position within the labor market and their powerlessness to change it. Eric Hobsbawm's description of the induction of European peasants into industrial capitalism in the mid-nineteenth century will find an echo in the *kampung:*

> (T)he workers themselves provided their employers with a solution to the problem of labour management; by and large they liked to work, and their expectations were remarkably modest . . . [they] came from an environment where hard labour was the criterion of a person's worth and wives were chosen not for their looks but for their work-potential. . . . In brief, though naturally not insensitive to the difference between lower and higher wages, they were engaged in human life rather than in an economic transaction (1977: 260–61).

Malaysian novelist Shahnon Ahmad, perhaps a stranger to Marxist writings, wrote of weather-beaten young women in Malay rice villages, "Men did not look for beauty when they asked for a wife" (1972: 71). In *mukim* Telok, factory women were still very much bound by their noncapitalist sense of work relations and obligations to family claims.

The overlap between family and factory interests in keeping young working women in a socially subordinate position impressed on the factory women a hierarchical image of society. Moreover, the ever-present charge of non*kampung* and "unIslamic" behaviour operated as a powerful sanction against activities which could be construed as violations of local norms of male-female, child-parent relations. Islamic resurgence among the Malay intelligentsia, and general public surveillance, made factory women "increasingly aware of their duty to guard and uplift their public image," as a social welfare officer urged.[14]

Thus, Engel's assertion that the first condition for the liberation of women was their entry into public industry (1972: 137–38) notwithstanding, there was less individuation among factory women in Sungai Jawa and surrounding villages than one might expect. The majority conformed to *kampung* norms of male authority, female modesty, and maintenance of obligations to one's family and community. In their daily lives, as previous chapters have shown, factory women adhered to what constituted "proper behavior" in *kampung* and Malay-Muslim terms. They voiced approval of "punishment" for those who deviated from the norm. Within the factories, operators themselves were a force for cultural conformity, bringing pressures to bear on those women seen to flout Malay-Muslim norms. To their more conservative sisters, workers unrestrained (*bebas*) in their handling of money and social intercourse were seen as responsible for tarnishing the collective image of Malay factory women, bringing shame (*malu*) to their community and disgrace to Islamic womanhood. It bears repeating that such self-regulation sprang as much from private resentment as imposed conformity; in certain situations, peer pressure also constituted tactics of resistance to unequal treatment on the shopfloor.

All the operators I asked agreed that they considered themselves members of a single family at their workbenches; all were ready to help each other out. People often stopped their own work (at some cost to their wages) to help neophytes who had trouble assembling microchips or understanding orders. As one explained:

> Those of us who work in this factory, if we are in the same section, we are like brothers and sisters. Ah, we get along together, no problem.

Another said she considered her foreman to be like a parent (*orang tua saya*), even though he was Chinese, because he took the place of her father at work, and she respected him. As mentioned earlier this sense of family was responsible for work teams attaining high production levels, even when workers felt resentment at management demands.

Family-like relations went beyond cooperation in work; the operators felt a collective responsibility to criticize co-workers perceived to deviate from common group interests while pursuing their own individualistic interests. When asked what values operators might or might not share in common, a worker replied:

(T)here are those who like a *sosial* life, and those who do not. [Those who are] *bebas* like to do their work in their own way. Some of the workers are like this. There are others who, following our elders, do not like to be *sosial*, do not like to mix freely with men. Sometimes, those who are *sosial* do not do their work correctly. They play at work because what they really want is to be free to move around. Yes, they can be cooperative [at work] but outside the *kampung* they just want to go places, near and far. In the factory, they follow others; outside, they do not.

The term "*sosial*" had entered Malay parlance to refer to young unmarried women and men who freely mix with each other, quite contrary to *kampung adat*, which expected informal segregation between single members of different sexes. Thus, the word was a slang term not applied to villagers of other age groups, who were usually quite sociable, as required by custom. Factory women who were *sosial* (i.e., unhampered by convention or *bebas*) were seen to be less hardworking, careless about their work, seeking self-gratification, and unrestrained by parental guidance. Another operator elaborated:

(O)ur values and theirs are entirely different . . . they want *bebas* values, do not want to be tied down. They do not want to be shackled (*berkongkong kongkong*) so that they can go out and be *bebaslah*. The wages they receive they keep for themselves, only occasionally do they contribute to their families. It would be better if their earnings are for their families, that way, they will not bring disaster to their families, do something that will bring them shame.

Factory women were particularly vigilant in regulating relations among men and women who met in the workplace. "Dating," a Western practice in which a man selected out a woman to spend time alone together, was particularly censured when it involved a Malay operator and non-Malay foreman. A developing romance inevitably produced a *krisis* situation as gossip flew through the ranks. Not only did such *sosial* association tax *kampung* notions of sex segregation, it was a violation of Islamic injunctions against liaisons with non-Muslims.

In 1979, a Chinese foreman at EJI took a Malay operator out for Chinese New Year. After spending the night in Malacca, they returned to her village and he was threatened by local youths. Her parents told them to leave him alone. The next evening, four to five youths attacked him outside the factory gates. In the words of the Malay supervisor, he was "left half-dead and [was] unconscious for three days." He required some stitches on his forehead but intended to return to work after a few days. When she heard the news, the operator cried and visited him in the hospital. She believed that the attackers were not from her village, otherwise her *kumpung* folk would know their identities. She insisted that they had gone to Malacca with her parents' permission. According to rumors, all villagers, except her parents, were angry about the dating because (1) the man was Chinese and not a Muslim, (2) they did not know if the couple intended to get married, and (3) they went outstation together without having been married to each other. The supervisor commented that if her parents had announced that the couple were engaged the attack would not have taken place.

The anxiety this incident produced among co-workers is revealed in the following statement:

> When such an unfortunate incident occurs, we all help . . . the other workers scold the *operator.* They reprimand her for making this mistake. If she wanted just to be friendly, then she shouldn't have allowed it to develop into a conflict involving someone of a different race. [This is because] if she goes out with a non-Malay people will not look kindly upon it. This was why they beat him up. If she had dated her own people, it would have been alright, but she should not do it too often, because if she does it frequently, it is not nice, is it? [Going out] with non-Malays, once, twice is alright but if one does it regularly, say four, five times, then people will say doesn't she know how to conduct herself? [We operators] have only scolded her and told her not to do this again.

Another factory woman said that co-workers usually advised interethnic couples to forget their romantic interest in each other. It was not a matter of feelings, she emphasized, but of social relations. Since *kampung* elders would oppose marriage to "outsiders" (*orang asing*), it would be difficult to maintain such relationships.

Special attention from foremen also generated competition, however covert, among operators. Their moralistic tones and censuring statements were fraught with the effort of upholding noncapitalist values and yet poisoned with secretly nurtured envy of the *bebas* women. Women from other villages who rented rooms near the FTZ were considered to be the most *sosial.* They were perceived to have too much free time from housework and had no one to control their movements. A worker from Sungai Jawa remarked:

I think that the workers who are *bebas*, I believe most of them live in rented rooms, not with their families. It is possible that this is one reason why they are not guided or restrained by their families. Because of this, they feel *bebas*. Most of the [local] workers do not want to be *bebaslah*, they are true Malays who have been properly brought up by their parents.

Generally, migrant female workers were viewed by others as ''not wanting to follow *kampung* ways,'' their general conduct frequently described as ''not Malay'' (*bukan Melayu*).

Social independence displayed by some factory women was perceived by the majority not only as a violation of local norms but the road to personal disaster. Those women who want too much *kebebasan* (unseeming liberty), who wanted to do things their own way, it was thought, would inevitably fall victim to unscrupulous men. Such women, it was remarked, were ''so free that they had no thought for their families.'' They followed ''whatever their hearts desired'' and ended up ''damaging themselves'' (*merosakkan diri sendiri*), i.e., pregnant and abandoned. To most factory women, the charge of being ''too *bebas*'' or ''too *sosial*,'' when they only sought freedom of movement outside the *kampung*, was loaded with the implicit meaning of looking for illicit sexual activities. Gossip became such a powerful mode of social control that the women themselves, by criticizing others perceived to be more *bebas* while idealizing chastity, enforced their own lack of emancipation, despite their ability to earn money of their own.

Not surprisingly, positive attempts at constructing their own gender identity depended on a cult of purity and self-sacrifice. Many neophyte factory women in Sungai Jawa identified with an intensified Islamic asceticism (advocated by *dakwah* members) which not only incorporated *kampung* emphasis on daughters' loyalty and moral virtue but also a new kind of sexual repression not inherent in earlier generations. Since the women's new self-esteem was based on their wage contributions as unmarried daughters, many postponed marriage to fulfill such familial expectations, thus prolonging their junior status to their parents and to male authority. In Sungai Jawa, the average age at first marriage for women increased from 19 to 22 years between 1976 and 1980, when many village women began working in the FTZ.

Postponement of marriage introduced new problems of controlling adult daughters and guarding their virtue. Malays acknowledge sexual drives and provide cultural means for their adequate satisfaction in daily life. Up until recently, parents arranged early marriages for sons and daughters for (among other things) the legitimate management of sexual needs (see Banks 1982: 88–90). When marriage was delayed for women, their sexuality became more susceptible to individual control; greater social discipline was considered necessary to reduce this threat to male authority. Thus, the self-esteem and self-image of rural factory women became inextricably tied to prolonged junior status, increased Islamic chastity, and the rejection of social emancipation promised by wage employment. Many working women continued to share the *kampung* and Malay vision of society which was Islam-informed, dominated by men, and in which women could not seek social autonomy. When asked about the distribution of authority within her factory, an operator replied:

> I think all [authority positions are filled by] men, only the *chargehands* and *lineleaders* are female. I feel that this [arrangement] is just normal. . . . This I feel is really because we are women and so must follow the orders of a man. In the house, this depends on persons concerned, but outside the house, in the factory, then we better obey [men's] orders, whatever they say. Because they are men and also their [work] rank is higher than ours. We are only ordinary *operators*. If we have female *foremen* or female *supervisors*, we will also have to follow their orders.

Another worker did not see any flexibility in male-female power balance within the family, although she too saw the possibility of women gaining authority positions in the industrial system.

> In Malay society, men ought to be at the top. Father has more authority (*kuasa*) than mother because he is male. This is as it should be. It is not surprising that at the workplace/factory all the persons in authority are men. If women get promoted along with men in the factory, then it is fine. In the house, it is not possible that women have authority, because really men are the ones with power. . . . In the home, whenever there are problems, women are inadequate, they cannot think deeply, like men. Women are always hasty, they cry. Men try to think, to rise above the problem. Thus, in other families, things are also like this. Women today may have the same experiences as men but in the home men ought to have more authority, because this is an Islamic law.

Drawing on Islamic notions of women being more endowed with passion and men with rationality, this young woman's perceptions were constituted by *dakwah* views on domestic power arrangements, at a point when Islamic and social authorities were insisting on paternalistic control just as working women threatened to undermine it within the family rather than in society at large.

Almost all factory women I interviewed felt that the Malaysian public denigrated them. Pointing to the link between their "immoral" image and weak market position, another worker protested:

> (T)he chances for employment in this country are still limited. In our country, we Malaysian women need greater security in our livelihood so that there will be no occasion . . . to work like street-walkers (*macam pelacur*). Such opportunities can be greatly broadened since right now [our chances for work] are limited. The jobs available are still limited compared to those available to men. Also currently women who are employed are very few and so they tend give priority to housework because employment with the government [greatly desired by women] is still restricted.

This statement, made by a Form Five graduate in the Telok FTZ, more accurately pinpointed the problems of Malay working women than the sensationalist coverage in the media.

It did not occur to any factory woman to question the overall male-dominated systems in the household, factory, religion, and wider society. They wished for an improvement in their economic position but not a social emancipation in which they would share power with men in general. However, the absence of an alternative view of society did not mean that women workers were not engaged in constituting their own subjectivity or in occational acts of defiance in different fields of power relations. These did not constitute "class consciousness." The next chapter will consider their tactics of resistance, a new vocabulary of protest and self-consciousness which sporadically disrupted the surface of daily social conformity.

Chapter 9

Spirits of Resistance

We now turn to the off-stage voices of factory women, the self-perceptions which have emerged, partly in reaction to the external caricatures of their status, but mainly out of their own felt experiences as wage workers in changing Malay society. I have argued that in a society undergoing capitalist transformation, it is necessary not only to decipher the dominant gender motifs which have become the symbols of relations of domination and subordination, but also to discover, in everyday choices and practices, how ordinary women and men live and refashion their own images and culture. Disparate statements, new gestures, and untypical episodes will be used to demonstrate how concepts of gender and sexuality became transmuted through the new experiences of the emergent Malay working class.

The contradictory experiences of Malay factory women indicate that we need to reformulate the relationships among class, resistance, and consciousness. Frederick Engels rather hastily asserted that the first condition for the liberation of women from their oppressed status was to bring the whole female sex into public industry (1972: 137–38). As the previous chapter has shown, the first condition of women's induction into industry was subjection to increased external control. This is not to deny that wage employment has also had gradual, corrosive effects on the extraeconomic relationships which continued to bind workers to their families and community. In Telok, it was the particular insertion of Japanese industrial organization into the *kampung* milieu which has preserved female compliance with male authority and slowed individuation from the fabric of rural society.

Ronald Dore has remarked elsewhere that the Japanese factory system "enhances enterprise consciousness; it also . . . does less to develop individualism" (1973: 215). Of course, extrafactory influences can undo corporate restraints of self-expression.

For the village adolescent girl working in a Japanese factory, her meager earnings became a means to venture further afield, to explore and acquire a shifting, partial view of the widening social universe. New relationships, ideas, and images imparted a fresh self-consciousness and promptings to greater individual determination in thought and behavior. Assertion of individual versus family interests has its source in a new subjectivity constituted as much by educational practice, state agencies, and the media as by the labor process. In the factories, consciousness of mistreatment *as human beings* (*manusia*) by particular foremen or the management (*majikan*) was partial and discontinuous; there was no coherent articulation of exploitation in class or even feminist terms. At the most, one may say that the following instances of individualistic conduct, acts of defiance, and violent incidents were scattered tactics to define and protect one's moral status; as such they confronted the dehumanizing aspects embedded within capitalist relations of production. At issue is not a conscious attack on commodity relations but rather the self-constitution of a new identity rooted in human dignity.

A New Subjectivity

In Sungai Jawa, the most acceptable form of self-assertion among factory women was their control of savings, i.e., after family contributions had been deducted from their wages. Out of the 35 workers I interviewed at length, two-thirds came from families with five to nine siblings still at home. By routinely contributing half or more of their monthly wage packet, these working daughters gained a measure of self-esteem which made the low wages somewhat more tolerable. One young woman gave a practical assessment of her economic situation.

> Factory workers regard the work they hold not to be of high rank. But although factory work is low status, they help their families if they can. So they feel a little satisfaction — but not much.

Another woman worked out the family budget in which she and her brother paid for vegetables and other foodstuffs while their father bought the rice. She said that such an arrangement could be "considered fair" (*jadi kira adillah juga*).

Yet another operator chafed at her low wages and complained that her co-workers did not have the proper perspective with which to compare their earnings or situation with conditions in urban-based factories. She commented:

> (T)he workers, they cannot differentiate between the section in which they work and other divisions. Thus, the party above [i.e., the management] likes their ignorance and they work as if they are imprisoned (*kena kongkong*). As we Malays say, "like a frog beneath the coconut shell," they don't know about other things.

A few factory women were concerned not with looking for better conditions in factory work but viewed their wages as a means to improve their technical qualifications in order to compete for better jobs. Seventy percent of the interviewed workers had Form Three to Form Six certificates; one-third were using a portion of their factory earnings to pay for typing or academic classes which they attended after the factory shift. These classes were based in urban institutions, usually in Klang, and the commuting involved additional expenses. Most of the operators aspired to permanent careers in government service, stating that they would not stop work even if they got married and had children, because civil employment was well-paid and secure. Some factory workers had voiced interest in becoming policewomen, and one, in becoming a nightclub singer or firefighter.

For most adolescent girls in the *kampung*, looking for a steady job has become the rule once they left or dropped out of school. Earlier generations of young women had fewer years of schooling, married in their teens, and only worked intermittently for wages in village smallholdings or estates. With the introduction of mass education, better communications, and establishment of the factories, village girls wanted to seek their own employment and earn their own income of their own accord and not just under family pressure. For instance, an 18-year-old woman from the rice district of Sabak Bernam had left a large family of girls to stay with her married sister in Sungai Jawa in order to work in the FTZ. When asked why the public looked askance at outstation factory women, she answered:

> Maybe village people regard female workers as less than sweet (*kurang manis*) because a nice woman in their view stays in the

house. But because in this era women and men are of the same status (*sama taraf*) then we also want to seek experiences like men, in earning a living, looking for a job. . . .

Seeking work for their own economic interest also meant facing the uncertainty of their market situation, compared to the relative security of peasant families who could make a living off their own land. When asked whether her economic situation could be considered better than her parents', a factory woman replied:

> I feel that [comparing] myself with my parents, their work situation is better. Since I work in the private sector, the management at whatever time . . . can throw me out (*bolih membuangkan saya*) . . . but in their work, my parents are self-employed and there is no one who can prevent them [from working].

Another woman noted, however, that it was nevertheless preferable that there was factory employment for women, since it was increasingly difficult for men to find work in the *kampung*. Although rural women sought in factory employment a source of independent wealth, in practice, their low wages, the unavoidable claims of their families, and insecurity of employment did not provide a sufficient basis for economic independence.

For the majority of factory women then, their modest savings were employed as a means of compensation for hard work, low wages, and family support. Shopping expeditions after payday, when *kampung* women to go into town, were consumption activities to make up for long hours lost to the factory. "Leisure" became detached from "work" as the rhythm of their lives changed. A village woman described her joyful splurge in town.

> After getting my wage I straight away go to Klang to *jolli jolli*. I go to the movies and walk around. I buy knickknacks for the house, and sometimes I buy clothes.

"Making jolly with money" (*jolli duit*) was also part of the overall attempt by some rural women to change their status from ascribed (*kampung*) to attributional. In their excursions into towns and farther places, young village women were exposed to an alternative status system based on the attributes of an urban-based, Westernized culture. Some working women demonstrated this alternative status largely defined by consumption and "presentation of self" (Goffman 1959). They went into town in their Malay *baju kurong* and returned in mini-skirts or tight T-shirts and jeans. Whereas in the recent past the painted face was a mark of prostitution, regular visits by "Avon ladies" to even remote villages have increased *kampung* cosmetic sales fourfold in two years.[1] Village women were said to be willing to spend a great deal to achieve the "Electric Look." Such a code of dressing may be construed as simply consumerism, an attempt to ape urban "youth culture." However, it was also a deliberate mechanism to distance themselves from the *kampung* community and seek acceptance in the urban milieu. For some women, such inventive presentation of self also challenged *kampung* definition of male and female sexuality. A village woman observed with some hostility:

> (I)t is not nice the way [some factory women] attempt to imitate male *style*. Like, they want to be *rugged*. For instance, men wear *"Wrangler,"* they want to follow suite . . . some of them straight away take on the attributes of men in their clothing, they forget their sex. If they are already very *bebas* they forget that they themselves are women.

Indeed, *kampung* women increasingly sought rights previously limited to men. Almost all factory women chose their potential spouses either directly, through correspondence, or by accepting a suitor's overtures. This autonomy was directly based on their earning power, since increasingly, village women were expected to save and contribute towards their own wedding expenses and bridal furnishings. Most village parents have given up arranging marital unions for their children, although "go-betweens" were still hired to formalize matches privately initiated by the couple itself. In a few cases, especially when the family had no male head, the young women simply announced to their mothers that they were getting engaged. Some mothers were even unaware of their daughters' courtship and simply went along with their personal arrangements for marriage. A village mother told me that young women could meet potential husbands all over the place — in the factories, in towns, on their way to work — and there was no possible way, nor inclination, on the part of the parents to monitor their daughters' social contacts with men. Most young women I interviewed would not let their parents pick their future spouses, the usual retort being "What if I don't like him?"

Such self-determination and ability to resist parental authority increased young women's awareness of control over a personal life separate from that of the family. One heard numerous cases of young

working women running away from home to escape intolerable domestic situations. For instance, a 21-year-old operator from Banting
was ordered by her mother to marry a well-off man in his forties. She
told me that she rejected the match and planned to resign from ENI
and go stay with her married sister in Kuala Lumpur. A 19-year-old
woman confided to the factory nurse that she had been involved in
an incestuous relationship with her widowed father for three years.
The negative result of her pregnancy test was a source of relief to the
factory medical staff since they were uncertain about what to do with
the case. Subsequently, the woman took her own decision and sought
refuge with her maternal grandmother in town. Even with limited
economic independence, village women demonstrated an emerging
sense of personal responsibility in dealing with the consequences of
their action, thereby challenging *kampung* notions about the helpless-
ness of *budak budak*.

As Chapter 6 has shown, individuation in economic matters, attitudes, and conduct has led a small but growing number of rural
women to bypass *kampung* conventions and cross different social
boundaries on their own. While "illicit" love between single people
or persons not married to each other has always been part of village
society, we may say with some confidence that "dating" practices
have become more common with the large-scale participation of
young women and men in wage employment. What has changed is
that affairs between single persons, which in former times usually
culminated in marriage, now have less certain outcomes as village
elders lose their ability to enforce social norms over an increasingly
mobile and dispersed population. Since the opening of the FTZ, four
cases of abortions have been reported among unmarried factory
women in the area. A woman from Sungai Jawa had her illegitimate
child in the home of a married sister and then gave the infant up for
adoption in another village. Other unwed factory women who became
pregnant had abortions outside the *mukim,* and thereafter sought
employment in other villages and towns. Female relatives provided
sympathy and material support to help these women begin life
anew.[2]

In venturing beyond the socially confined circumstances of *kampung*
life, factory women also came into increasing daily contact with other
Malaysians. Talking about her workplace, an operator disclosed her
widening social horizon:

(T)here I have friends from Pahang, Trengganu all from far away.
. . . For instance, if they come from Negri Sembilan, I come to
know their customs and traditions . . . the way of life in their
state.

Other young women began to associate, for the first time in their lives,
with non-Malays as co-workers and friends.

(W)e get to mix widely with peoples other than Malays — Indians, Chinese and other who are not Malaysians. My thinking has already changed little by little as I get to know their man-
nerisms, their ways. Previously, before we had experience, when
we were not yet *bebas*, we did not get to know their ways, but
now little by little we are learning about other races.

The proletarianization of rural Malays and increasing daily association with workers of other ethnic identities do not inevitably lead to
a political movement which would replace ethnic hostility with class
consciousness, as some scholars have claimed (Zawawi and Shahril
1983). The structuring of social relations and class interests along
ethnic lines by industry, state agencies, and groups founded on communal interests would continue to constitute the "reality" whereby
ordinary people conducted their lives and achieved practical consciousness. In the Telok industrial system, which by economic calculation and political expediency was a miniature replica of the wider
ethnic and gender divided society, conflicts produced by unequal relations of production often took on ethnic tones.

Unleased Spirits: The World Decentered

> The basis [of capitalist society] is that a relation between
> people takes on the character of a thing and thus acquires
> a "phantom objectivity," an autonomy so strictly rational
> and all-embracing as to conceal every trace of its fundamental
> nature: the relation between people.
>
> Lukács (1982: 83)

As capitalist development reworks the basis of social relations, the
changing sense of personhood and of things is most intensively experienced in the realm of production. However, consciousness of in-
justice and being treated "like things" among neophyte factory
women was partial, discontinuous, and seldom articulated. Sporadic
forms of protest, both overt and covert, were not so much informed

by a specific class consciousness as by the felt violation of one's fundamental humanity.

As elsewhere in the Peninsula, the self-definition of Malay peasants in Telok was still overlaid with noncapitalist native status categories, primarily extraeconomic, which still prevailed in contexts increasingly defined by capitalist relations.[3] Self-definition among rural Malays was at once localized and universal: *orang kampung* versus *orang asing* (villagefolk versus outsiders); *orang Islam* and the legal term *bumiputra* vis-à-vis *orang asing* (in the sense of persons outside the Islamic-Malay community). This social consciousness, as Hobsbawm has commented about noncapitalist cultures, was simultaneously lilliputian and global; it often went beyond any consciousness of "classness" among agrarian peoples (1971: 10). As I have argued in preceding chapters, peasant adherence to noncapitalist worldview has been used to advantage by capitalist enterprises both to enhance control and disguise commodity relations. However, the noncapitalist universe can also furnish rural people with a moral critique of the dehumanizing aspects of market relations.[4] In Telok, culturally-specific forms of protest and retaliation in the corporate arena were directed ultimately not at "capital" but at the transgression of local boundaries governing proper human relations and moral justice. A young woman from Sungai Jawa disclosed her sense of having been tricked into working under unjust conditions by the management:

> For instance, . . . sometimes . . . they want us to raise *production*. This is what we sometimes contest (*bantahlah*). The workers want just treatment (*keadilan*), as for instance, in relation to wages and other matters. We feel that in this situation there are many [issues] to dispute (*bertengkar*) over with the management — because we have to work three shifts and when the *midnight shift* arrives we feel sort of drowsy and yet have to use the *microscope*, and with our wages so low we feel as though we have been tricked or forced (*seolah macam dipaksa*).
>
> This is why we ask for justice because we have to use the *microscope*. . . . Justice because sometimes they exhaust us very much as if they do not think that we too are human beings (*manusia*) . . . so that from time to time we must protest, that they should not rap (*menutuk*) us too much.

Most factory operators, less outspoken, nevertheless felt the same sense of having been taken. They resorted to indirect resistance which was culturally consistent with their subordinate female status. Capitalizing on beliefs in their emotional instability and susceptibility to male power, factory women reacted in expected ways to intolerable demands. Crying was a common response to verbal abuse which could deflect disciplinary action. Some operators who could not keep up with repeated orders to attain high production targets deliberately slowed down their normal pace of work, became careless in the assembly of components, or simply lost their temper. In their resistance to being treated like things, mounting work pressures (*tekanan*), and harsh (*keras*) foremen, workers often cultivated an unconcerned, uncomprehending (*tidak apa*) attitude towards orders and the technical details of production. A common tactic was to make excuses to leave the shopfloor by citing ''female problems'' which had to be attended to in the locker room. Alternately, they sought release to adjourn to the prayer room, confronting foremen who tried to limit prayer time. Thus, cultural conformity and covert resistance fed on each other as factory women in daily life fought for and held on to a residual space for the preservation of human dignity. However, the locker room and prayer room, as refuge from work discipline and surveillance, were also the places in which operators were seized upon by vengeful spirits.

The rural Malay universe is still inhabited by spirits which move easily between human and nonhuman domains. Thus, familiar spirits such as *toyol* help their masters reap wealth out of thin air, while the *pontianak* birth demon threatens the life of newly born infants. Another group consists of possessing spirits which are associated with special places marking the boundary between human and natural worlds. These include (1) aboriginal (Negrito) and animal spirits inhabiting old burial grounds, strangely shaped rocks, hills, or trees; (2) holy men or well-known ancestors (*datuk*) dwelling in sacred abodes (*kramat*), such as grave sites and natural objects; and (3) *syaitan* (evil spirits) of Islamic origin. Malays believe that women lacking in spiritual vigilance become possessed by angry spirits (*kena hantu*) when the victims wander unsuspectingly onto the sacred dwelling places of spirits. In his study of spirit seances in Kelantan villages, Clive Kessler observes that middle-aged women were particularly susceptible to spirit affliction, possibly because of their vulnerable social status at this phase of their life cycle (1977). Susan Ackerman maintains that in rural Malacca threats of spirit possession operate as a sanction against self-assertion on the part of young Malay women engaged in industrial work (1979: 13). Over the past decade, spirit possession episodes have proliferated among the young Malay women who flock in the thousands to urban institutions. Newspaper reports of the sudden spate of "mass hysteria" among young Malay women in boarding schools and modern factories have interpreted their causes in terms of "examination tension," "the stresses of urban living," "superstitious beliefs," and, less frequently, "mounting pressures" which induced "worries" (*keciwa*) among female operators.[5]

The Management View of "Mass Hysteria"

The late 1970s produced a flurry of newspaper reports on "mass hysteria" in free trade zones.[6] In 1975, forty Malay operators were seized by spirits in a large American electronics plant based in Sungai Way. A second large-scale incident in 1978 involved some 120 operators in the microscope sections. The factory had to be shut down for three days and a spirit-healer (*bomoh*) was hired to slaughter a goat on the premises. The American director wondered how he was to explain to corporate headquarters that "8,000 hours of production were lost because someone saw a ghost."[7] In late 1978, a Penang-based American microelectronics factory was disrupted for three consecutive days when fifteen women became afflicted by spirit possession. A factory personnel officer told reporters.

> Some girls started sobbing and screaming hysterically and when it seemed like spreading, the other workers in the production line were immediately ushered out. . . . It is a common belief among workers that the factory is "dirty" and supposed to be haunted by a *datuk*.[8]

The victims were given injectable sedatives while hundreds of other female workers were sent home. A *bomoh* was called to ritually cleanse the factory premises, but workers' demands for a feast (*kenduri*) elicited no response. A few days after the incident, I interviewed some workers about "filth" (*kotor*) in the factory. They pointed out that the production floor and canteen areas were "very clean," but factory toilets were "filthy" in two senses: pollution by soiled sanitary napkins and by evil spirits. In recounting the incident, a worker remembered that a piercing scream from one corner of the shopfloor was quickly followed by cries from other benches as women struggled against spirits trying to possess them. They would struggle so hard that sometimes ten supervisors could not control one afflicted worker who would shout "Go away!" Most spirit incidents were also linked to the appearance of *datuk* apparitions, sometimes headless, gesticulating angrily at the operators. A third example occurred in 1980 when spirits afflicted 21 women workers in a Japanese factory based in Pontian, Kelantan. As they were being taken to ambulances, some victims screamed, "I will kill you, let me go!"[9]

In Kuala Langat, spirit possession incidents among Malay factory women reiterated themes of filth, angry spirits, fierce struggles, and rites of exorcism. Interviews with factory managers and workers reveal contrasting interpretations of the episodes: biomedical causes versus pollution-violation imagery. At ENI, the personnel manager said that the first spirit affliction occurred five months after the factory began operation in 1976. Thereafter,

> we had our counter-measure. I think this is a method of how you give initial education to the workers, how you take care of the medical welfare of the workers. The worker who is weak, comes in without breakfast, lacking sleep, then she will see ghosts!

Those who have had two previous experiences of affliction were dismissed for "security reasons." Village elders protested, claiming that ghosts in the factory were responsible for the women's condition. The manager agreed but pointed out that these "hysterical, mental types" may hurt themselves when they flailed against the machines, risking electrocution. In his view, "hysteria" is a symptom of the women's rural-urban transition. "They move from home idleness to factory discipline. The ghosts disturb only the new girls." In contrast to managers in other firms who operated on the "basis of feelings," he used a "psychological approach" to deal with recurrent spirit visitations:

> You cannot dispel *kampung* beliefs. Now and then we call the *bomoh* to come, every six months or so, to [waving his hand vaguely] pray, walk around. Then we take pictures of the *bomoh* in the factory and hang up the pictures. Somehow, the workers seeing these pictures feel safe, [seeing] that the place has been exorcised.

Similarly, whenever a new section of the factory has been constructed, the *bomoh* is sent for to sprinkle holy water, thereby assuring workers that the place is rid of ghosts. Furthermore, the factory nurse periodically toured the shopfloor to encourage female workers to talk over their problems with the "industrial relations assistant." Complaints of "pain in the chest" (*sakit dada*) meant that the workers were emotionally upset and should be allowed to go to the clinic. The nurse also recommended that spirit possession victims be sent home for a day or two on medical leave. However, neither she nor the industrial relations assistant was consulted about the policy to sack workers after their third affliction. She noted:

> It is an experience working with a Japanese company; they do not consult women. To tell you the truth, they don't care about the problem except that it should go away.

EJI also commenced operations in a spate of spirit possession incidents. The production supervisor told me that in the following year, a well-known *bomoh* and his retinue were invited to the factory *surau* where they read the *yasin* prayer over a basin of "pure water." Those who have been visited by the devil drank from it and washed their faces, a healing ritual which made them immune to future spirit attacks. A *kenduri* of saffron rice and curry chicken was served to managers and officers, but not a single operator (or victim) was invited. A month after the ritual, spirit attacks resumed, but involving smaller numbers (one or two) of women in each incident. The *bomoh* claimed that the *hantu* controlling the factory site was "very kind"; he merely showed himself but did not disturb people. Now spirit attacks occurred only once a month. Last year, the supervisor sent home a possessed woman who was all rigid, with eyes turned inwards. She had put up a terrific struggle. Since the nurse could not do anything to help, the victim was given special leave of up to a week, to be healed by the *bomoh* in her home village. The supervisor admitted, "I think that hysteria is related to the job in some cases." He explained that workers in the microscope sections were usually the ones to *kena hantu*, and maybe they should not begin work doing those tasks. However, he quickly offered other possible interpretations. There was one victim whose broken engagement had incurred her mother's wrath; at work she cired and talked to herself, saying "I am not to be blamed, not me!" Another worker, seized by possession, screamed, "Send me home, send me home!" Apparently, her mother had taken all her earnings. What do the spirit attacks really mean to factory workers themselves?

troublesome approach...

presumption of a distinct of protest

In Their Own Voices

I wish to discover, in the vocabulary of spirit possession, the unconscious beginnings of an idiom of protest against labor discipline and male control in the modern industrial situation. Spirit visitations to both foreign and local factories with sizeable numbers of young Malay female workers engender devil images which dramatically reveal the contradictions between Malay and capitalist ways of apprehending the human condition. I.M. Lewis has suggested that women's spirit possession episodes are "thinly disguised protest . . . against the dominant sex." By "capitalizing on their distress," the victims of spirit possession called public attention to their subordinate position and sought to alleviate it (1971: 31, 85). In the following cases, spirit imageries reveal not only a mode of unconscious retaliation against male authority but fundamentally a sense of dislocation in human relations and a need for greater spiritual vigilance in domains reconstituted by capitalist relations of production.

An ENI operator described one incident which occurred in May 1979:

> It was the afternoon shift, at about nine o'clock. All was quiet. Suddenly, [the victim] started sobbing, laughed and then shrieked. She flailed at the machine . . . she was violent, she fought as the foreman and technician pulled her away. Altogether, three operators were afflicted. . . . The supervisor and foremen took them to the clinic and told the driver to send them home. . . .

> She did not know what happened . . . she saw a *hantu,* a weretiger. Only she saw it, and she started screaming. . . . The foremen would not let us talk with her for fear of recurrence. She was possessed, maybe because she was spiritually weak. She was not spiritually vigilant so that when she saw the *hantu* she was instantly afraid and screamed. Usually, the *hantu* likes people who are spiritually weak, yes. People say that the workplace is haunted by the *hantu* who dwells below . . . well, this used to be all jungle, it was a burial ground before the factory was built. The devil disturbs those who have weak constitution . . . [therefore] one should guard against being easily startled, or afraid.

In a separate interview, another female worker told me what happened after the "*penyakit histeria*" (hysteria affliction) broke out:

> The work section was not shut down, we had to continue working. Whenever it happened, the other workers felt fright-

A bomoh *divining the cause of a young woman's affliction.*

ened. They were not allowed to look because [the management] feared contagion. They would not permit us to leave. When an incident breaks out, we have to move away. . . . At ten o'clock they called the *bomoh* to come . . . because he knew that the *hantu* had already entered the woman's body. He came in and scattered flour all over area where the incident broke out. He recited prayers over [holy] water. He sprinkled water on places touched by the *hantu*. . . . The *bomoh* chanted incantations (*jampi jampi*) chasing the *hantu* away. He then gave some medicine to the afflicted . . . He also entered the clinic, *jampi jampi*.

[After their recovery, the victims] never talk about [their affliction] because they don't remember . . . like insane people, they don't remember their experiences. Maybe the *hantu* is still working on their madness, maybe because their experiences have not been stilled, or maybe yet their souls are now disturbed (*jiwa terganggu*).

Other interviews elicited the same images: the erection of the FTZ on the burial grounds of aboriginal groups; disturbed earth and grave spirits swarming through the factory premises, weretigers roaming the shopfloor. Women not spiritually vigilant were possessed by the *hantu*. The *bomoh* was hastily summoned to perform exorcist rites. Recovering victims suffered from amnesia, their souls not properly healed. A woman told me about her aunt's fright in the EJI prayer room.

> She was in the middle of praying when she fainted because she said . . . her head suddenly spun and something pounced on her from behind.

Furthermore:

> Workers saw "things" appear when they went to the toilet. Once, when a woman entered the toilet she saw a tall figure in the midst of licking sanitary towels ["*Modess*" supplied in the cabinet]. It had a long tongue, and those sanitary towels . . . cannot be used anymore.

These vivid images of harassment by spirits on the factory floor and places of "refuge" like the prayer room and toilets are symbolic configurations of the violation, chaos, and draining of one's essence. Pervasive threats of possession induced the need for vigilance, looking behind one's back and over the shoulder to guard one's body and soul against violation. The *bomoh* has become a fixture of transnational production operations in Malaysia; however, his slaughter of chickens or goats on factory premises has been insufficient to placate the unleashed, avenging spirits of a world torn asunder.

A medical model is increasingly replacing native interpretations of spirit attacks. Using terms like *penyakit histeria*, some operators have come to accept scientific explanations of these events, as offered by the management. Thus, one operator mused:

> They say they saw *hantu*, but I don't know. . . . I believe that maybe they . . . when they come to work, they did not fill their stomachs, they were not full so that they felt hungry. But they were not brave enough to say so.

The male technician gave an even more alien reading of the women's afflictions, as much to convince the anthropologist as himself.

> I think that this [is caused by] a feeling of *complex*, that maybe *inferiority complex* is pressing them down, their spirit, so that this can be called an illness of the spirit (*penyakit jiwa*), conflict *jiwa, emotional conflict*. Sometimes, they see an old

man, in black shrouds, they say, in their microscopes, they say.
. . . I myself don't know how. They see *hantu* in different places.
. . . Some time ago an *emergency* incident like this occurred
in a boarding school. The victim fainted. Then she became very
strong like *a strongman or a strong girl*. It required ten or twenty
persons to handle her. . . .

If indeed spirit possession episodes provided female workers the
guise to launch attacks on male staff members, they certainly never
came close to challenging male authority on the factory floor or elsewhere. In effect, the enactment of "ritualised rebellion" (Gluckman
1958) by Malay women in modern factories did not directly confront
the real cause of their distress, and instead, by operating as a safety
valve, tended to reinforce existing unequal relations which are further
legitimized by scientific notions of female maladjustment. A woman
in ENI talked sadly about her friend, dual victim of spirits and industrial discrimination:

> At the time the management wanted to throw her out, to end
> her work, she cried. She did ask to be reinstated, but she has
> had three [episodes] already . . . I think that whether it was right
> or not [to expel her] depends [on the circumstances], because
> she has already worked here for a long time; now that she has
> been thrown out she does not know what she can do, you know.

In circumstances calling for the denial of oppressive conditions,
some operators slipped into the vacuous state induced by popular
music. Malay, Hindustani, and Chinese tunes, adjusted to a sooth-
ing level, alternating by the hour, were piped into the shopfloor. It
helped them forget their bodily aches or the work they were doing
because they were borne along in daydreams. Others cultivated a
spiritual vigilance through performing more prayers, to shield themselves against attacks by malevolent spirits.

More direct tactics have emerged for silent renegotiations of rules
on the shopfloor. Some operators, without the guise of spirit possession, have undertaken deliberate but surreptitious attacks on factory
equipment. Such machine wrecking is to be differentiated from the
preunion tradition of early English labor movements which by
publicly attacking factory property, engaged in "collective bargaining
by riot" (Hobsbawm 1964: 6-7).[10] In the Telok FTZ, the subversive
acts were spontaneous, carried out by individual workers

independently of each other. When production targets seemed unbearable, or a foreman had been especially harsh, operators registered their private vengeance by damaging the very components that they had painstakingly assembled. Others stalled the machines and thus interrupted production. The cumulative effect of countless subversive acts, as evidenced in thousands of defective components at the end of the month, constituted an anonymous protest against mounting work pressures rather than a collective action with specific demands on the management. The Malay technician quoted above explained this subterranean resistance.

> There is certainly a lot of *discipline* . . . but when there is too much *discipline,* . . . it is not good. Because of this the operators, with their small wages, will always contest. They often break the *machines* in ways that are not apparent. . . . Sometimes they damage the *products* . . . This is something entirely up to the *individual operator,* [an action taken] on their own. I feel that it is indeed proper that they do this because their wages are small and we cannot *blame* them. *Blaming operator is nothing* [sic] because . . . if they have problems they are not about to tell anyone. Because others will not listen to their complaints . . . Because they do not have a union. I cannot [propose wage increases on their behalf] because if you value yourself you want to get *promotion* if you can, and so we can't talk about this [to the management]. Thus, all that I do is behind the scenes. Because if one cares about one's future, one's *career,* then one is forced to keep quiet. Thus, even if one sympathizes with the operator (*simpati dengan operator*), one is not brave enough to speak up.

In the absence of a union, covert revolts sometimes developed into acts of retaliation against factory men, the intimate supervisors as well as tormentors of operators in daily life. Factory women on occasion manipulated their kinsmen's sense of honor by gossiping and crying about mistreatment in the FTZ. In 1976, an Indian foreman was set upon, "beaten and badly hurt on the face and stomach by an unknown gang," according to EJI records. A Malay assistant foreman coming to his aid was also beaten up. According to an informal questioning of workers, the foreman deserved punishment because he refused workers their 15 minute breaks, insulted them about personal matters, followed women into the locker room, and threatened to terminate their employment whenever he felt necessary. He became blacklisted among village youths. In spite of the incident, the foreman was retained and told to modify his conduct. Of the operators he had terrorized, only one resigned in protest. I have already mentioned the Chinese foreman who was beaten up for dating an operator. Another Chinese foreman said that this was only part of the story. All male supervisors in the factory, he claimed, had been privately warned by Malay youths that reports of their mistreatment of women workers would invite physical retaliation. Operators pointed fingers at foremen who were said to restrict their rights to pray, to move about on the shopfloor, or who pressed them too hard to attain high production targets. *Kampung* youths, in the tradition of enforcing rough justice and settling scores, were ready to make covert attacks on the blacklisted factory men. Possibly, in the case of the Chinese foreman, his romance with a Malay worker marked him out as a scapegoat to be used as warning to all male factory staff. There had been at least two other incidents of nocturnal attacks on male workers — none of local origin — outside the FTZ gates. Rural youths not only empathized with the women's harassment in the workplace, they were also resentful of these outsiders, both non-Malays and Malays, placed in daily contact with nubile Malay women.

The policing of rural society by young men focused on deviant social behavior, particularly when "outsiders" were involved. *Kampung* elders gave tacit approval to such activities, including attacks on outside men who were perceived to be infringing on local territory and young women. Any untoward behavior, such as frequent visits to the home of an unmarried woman, could be considered as "dishonoring" her reputation. Such an intrusion was to be redressed by youths waving staves to warn off the culprit, ripping up his bicycle/motorcycle tires, or giving him a thrashing. This *kampung* mode of enforcing social norms has come to constitute the shadowy side of rural relations with "strangers" at the FTZ. The two *mukim* policemen usually feigned igornance of such violent incidents since they were regarded as within the province of *kampung* leaders. Factory managers too avoided direct confrontation over the incidents, preferring to negotiate privately with local headmen and policemen over possible measures to reduce attacks against factory men. For their part, the "protection" village youths extended to working women compensated for their reduced sense of "honor," intangible values in effect purchased by female earnings which helped sustain rural livelihood.

The lamentations of possession victims decry the dislocations experienced by peasants in an industrializing world. The issue is not one of ''false consciousness'' or everyday forms of resistance which may culminate in large-scale rebellion. In the factories set up by transnational corporations, the constitution of new subjectivities unavoidably calls forth countertactics which proceed against neither capitalism nor the state. The spirit imageries of filth and violation speak out against male oppression as well as a deep sense of moral decentering, insisting on an ancient equality rooted in common (ungendered) humanity. Where self-regulation failed, the inscription of microprotests on damaged microchips constituted an anonymous resistance against the relentless demands of the industrial system. These nomadic tactics, operating in diverse fields of power, speak not of class revolt but only of the local situation.

The *syaitan* hovers over the passage of Malay peasants from a moral economy to an economy of commodities. Inducted into production systems where principles of assembly, disassembly, and reassembly are the cybernetics of control, Malay women have emigrated to the state of twentieth century homelessness. In constructing substitute homes and new identities, Malay working classes may recreate a collective consciousness which will transcend particularistic, *kampung* bonds.

Chapter 10

Conclusion

As I made ready to leave the field, my ears registered something odd in the *kampung* lingo which had become overly familiar. The daily talk of young women and men, who had learned to read and write but not how to speak English, was liberally sprinkled with "I" and "you" in place of "*aku*" and "*kau*" or "*kamu*." These could be read as linguistic signs of complicity by rural Malays in their own domination by an English-speaking world. Indeed, rural folk noted that English was spoken by the *guru*, and *pegawai*, even the sultan; it was the medium of a new prestige which had finally come within the reach of the *kampung* born and bred. And yet, their "I"s and "you"s embedded in Malay speech bespoke a concentrated self-consciousness, an assertion of individuality within the modulated and self-effacing discourse of villagers. Whereas some village women only found in spirit possession a preconscious vocabulary denied them in everyday life, other rural women and men discovered in phrases of American English the means to fashion new linguistic forms which altered their relations with each other and with the world.

In this cultural drama enacted in a corner of the Malay Peninsula, I have drawn on the archives and participated in fieldwork, using my ears as much as my eyes, to capture some of the disruptions and contradictory forces at work in Kuala Langat and beyond. I eschewed explanations of cultural change determined by an overriding logic others have sought in "modernization" or "the capitalist mode of production." I also refrained from making coherent "the native's point of view," since there are many different kinds of "natives" and I had con-

215

tact with only a few hundred. These presented a diversity of opinions and views, all historically constituted and varying by ethnicity, class, gender, and exposure to alien cultural elements. In capturing some of the discontinuities of experience in cultural change, and the multifoci of contestation in an industrializing society, I aimed to break with conventional ethnographic practice and to produce a partial picture of changes within a segment of Malay society, not to claim to have represented the "Truth." It is incomplete, fraught with ambiguity and shifting perceptions, the way life is experienced by people who live outside ethnographic texts.

My aim has been to place human interest at the center of the ethnographic endeavor. Specifically, I sought to learn how some rural women and men have struggled to understand their experiences of changing relations of domination and subordination in the Malay Peninsula from British intervention onwards. I began by looking at the incorporation of Malay cultivators into a world capitalist system, but came to question whether changing relations of production constitute a privileged category in our understanding of cultural change and people's sense of themselves in a particular society. As my writing unfolded, it became clear that I was looking at the complex and shifting series of power relations which have come to shape everyday existence, both for the informants *and* the anthropologist, in the late twentieth century. We are enmeshed in different but overlapping fields of power, using different cultural strategies in interpreting local conditions and our places in the world. Can anthropologists and other social scientists continue to hide behind apparently "scientific" or "naive" claims to "objective" representations? The microrelations of departments, in controlling the content of journals, conferences, and other academic institutions, continue to reproduce "anthropology" according to established frameworks (from functionalism to political economy), while screening out "illegitimate" forms of ethnographic descriptions which question their authorized representation logic. June Nash's *We Eat the Mines and the Mines Eat Us* and Michael Taussig's *The Devil and Commodity Fetishism in South America* are rare ethnographic attempts to explore cultural change generated in encounters between local and global conditions (Rabinow 1985: 12). My task in this book has been to hew closely to the views of a subjected people, which both incorporate and challenge imposed Western categories of rationality.

It has become fashionable in recent years to handle power in terms of given unities and oppositions: monopoly of power versus the powerless, domination versus resistance, exploitation versus protest. Anthropologists have yet to find descriptive forms, beyond "naive" functionalism or imputed "false consciousness," to consider people's complicity in, and transformation of, their own domination. This has been a study of how rural Malays engaged in cultural constructions and reconstructions within the capitalist transformation of their society. Their tactics of resistance, retaliation, and negotiation shifted according to the institution of successive modes of discipline in production systems and other areas of life. Their ideological understanding of changes in local society centered around a making and remaking of self and of social conditions at different phases of integration within the world system.

In Chapter 2, I discussed how British colonial administration involved not only the introduction of new relations of production and exchange but also novel constructions of Malay identity in relation to subsistence agriculture, land, and the wider society. My gleanings of archival records revealed that rural Malays in coastal Selangor resisted agrarian policies which discouraged cash cropping on village lands. Malay village households made the transition to commodity production, evolving multi-occupational strategies to cope with the vicissitudes of the world market system within which they were now embedded. Except for a small group of civil servants, few were able to accumulate wealth to increase social differentiation within village society.

In Part II, the critical role of the post-independence state in the reconstructions of social life provided the context for my discussion of changing agrarian relations and the emergence of a Malay proletariat in Kuala Langat. Chapter 3 mapped out the contours of a new tropical economy based on smallholdings, plantations, and the "free trade zone," served by a fine communications network, which variously embodied contemporary forms of domination by capital and the state. The expanded structures of administrative offices and political parties not only sustained and reproduced new relations of control but also reformulated local expectations about Malay culture, social mobility, ethnic and gender identities. Political discourse on Malay *pembangunan*, together with bureaucratic mechanisms for selective individual upward mobility, provided cultural justification of the social order.

Thus, ideological domination operated not necessarily as a coherent system of statements issued from above, but rather through a complex series of mechanisms whereby meaning was coded and mobilized in the daily activities of *kampung* folk: in development projects, school programs, welfare services, party politicking, and religious practice. The dominated were generally in complicity with the appropriation of the fruits of their labor; there was no inevitable resistance from below, informed by an apparent logic of struggle against capitalism or the state. For the nascent Malay proletariat, problems of land hunger, official corruption, and unequal distribution of the spoils of "development" did not undercut state legitimacy, and demands for justice were couched in personalized terms, within the field of local power relations. Through varied policies deployed in the name of "development," the meanings of female sexuality were defined and redefined in terms of discipline of the body in the factory and social control of the body politic.

Under conditions of new linkages to the state bureaucracy, expanded labor markets, population growth, and mass education, rural households increasingly sought in cash farming *and* wage labor the necessary means of survival. In Chapter 4, I discussed why old forms of household strategizing — through the deployment of family labor in agriculture — were no longer salient in a wage labor economy. Statistical measures of household land access, composition, and time budget were selectively used as approximations of a fluid social situation. For instance, large households which might have been taken as evidence of use of child labor revealed divergent patterns of resource sharing upon closer investigation, with children as often as not economic dependents rather than contributors to the household budget. Quantitative data on households captured a process of land dispossession among village Malays who allocated increasing amounts of time to wage employment. Data on occupational distribution indicated the significance of bureaucratic structures and political party organization as institutional channels for maneuvering within a situation of class differentiation. The new rural middle class — officials, teachers, and professionals — were now tied more closely to national, political, economic, and social circles than to village society. As rural society became firmly woven into the circuit of capital production, more *kampung kebun* were reduced to housing lots for a migratory labor force fanning across the country and overseas.

The changing structure of family life and new sexual images as illuminated by family relations and romances formed the subject of Chapters 5 and 6. The introduction of mass education for village children and the selective demands of wage labor markets came to condition parental expectations for their sons and daughters. As the rhythm of *kampung* life became regulated by the school bell and factory clock, teenage girls were increasingly pressured to drop out of secondary school to earn factory wages for their households. In contrast, adolescent boys were encouraged to pursue their academic careers in the hope of landing jobs in the white-collar professions. This divergence in roles between boys and girls affected domestic relations of consumption and increased economic individuation within as well as among households. Social differentiation fed envy of economically successful villagers who were seen as going against the cooperative ethos of *kampung* life, now irretrievably fractured into ''work'' and ''leisure.''

This decentering of rural Malay society was manifested in the marked emphasis on individual interests and the acquisition of symbolic capital by the young in matrimonial negotiations. Marriage strategies became increasingly conditioned by the wage earning capacity of a potential spouse, acquired tastes, and an expanded marriage circle. For what was negotiated were not merely relations among villagers but social relationships in a wider field which could facilitate upward mobility. In many cases, the changing roles of young village women made delayed marriages a new option, and their images as factory women, exciting dates, and old maids were generated out of their changing position in the labor market and a break with the customary life cycles of village women. For their families, and village men, these young women displayed an uncomfortable degree of poise in negotiating their own future; their sexuality came to be perceived as a threat to social norms at home and within *kampung* society.

In Part III, this theme of the making, breaking, and remaking of cultural images and practices was pursued within spheres *kampung* women were drawn into as members of a nascent industrial force. In Chapter 7, I described how the Malaysian state operated as a coordinator of different structures of power: foreign corporate investments were linked to the state apparatuses for the ideological domination and political disciplining of the new Malay working classes. Drawing on Foucault's insights, I discussed novel power configurations in domains such as the family, factory, *kampung*, and state institutions which reconstructed the meanings of Malay female gender and sexuality. In Japanese factories, the experiences of Malay women workers could be understood in terms of their use as "instruments of labor," as well as reconstitution by discursive practices as sexualized subjects. Discipline was exercised not only through work relations but also through surveillance and the cooperation of village elders in managing the maidens and their morality. Assailed by public doubts over their virtue, village-based factory women internalized these disparate disciplinary schemes, engaging in self- and other-monitoring on the shopfloor, in *kampung* society, and within the wider society.

Through a discussion of the conflicting gender images and discourses generated in the wake of Malay proletarianization, I illuminated in Chapter 8 the processes whereby factory women, subjected both to factory surveillance and the public gaze, were controlled by "invisible" power relations. While different groups fought for hegemonic domination in terms of cultural authenticity, Malay factory women were consistently delegitimized as falling off from "traditional" standards of conduct and morality. One response among factory women to this "symbolic violence" was their call for greater social vigilance and "moral purity." The painted countenances of other working women represented assertions of individuality as well as concealed the "hidden injuries" of class.

The eruptions of spirit possession episodes in transnational companies disclosed the anguish, resistance, and cultural struggle of some neophyte female workers. In Chapter 9, I traced the dialectic between their spirits of resistance and the enforced discipline of a working class in the making. Caught up in the problematics of labor and the problematics of self, resistance within the institutional constraints of capitalist production called forth images of social dislocation, draining of their essence, and violation of their humanity. Their sexuality has been mapped out as an arena of contestation; it could, alternatively, become the means of gender domination, the basis of a self-defining identity, and a challenge to male domination in different social domains. The *hantu* symbolism, shifting in and out of their consciousness, spoke not of an ideology of class struggle but of the right to be treated *as human beings*. Spirit attacks were indirect retaliations against coercion and demands for justice in personal terms within the industrial milieu. My ethnographic descriptions attest to the deconstructions and reconstructions of gender in the shifting webs of agency and domination within the family, the labor system, Islam, and the wider society. Malay factory women were in the process of reformulating a class sexuality. Their struggles to pose new questions and redefine the meaning of morality represented a quest for self-determination against agencies of power and capital which treat human beings like raw resources, disposable instruments, and fractured sensibilities.

An anthropology for the late twentieth century would attend to such human struggles for morality in their own terms and in the constitution of their own subjectivities. In our quest to illuminate human engagements with the problems of modern life, we cannot ignore the negotiated realities of third world peoples caught up in international flows of practices and meanings (Hannerz 1985). Their marginal voices and cultural inventiveness are not so much an index of an increasing repertoire of choices as a skepticism of inherited thought, a laboring with morality. Women are engaged in daily battles within relations between the powerful and the weak, a structural contestation which has often, but not inevitably, been culturally constructed as a gender dichotomy. In the modern age, new forms of domination are increasingly embodied in the social relations of science and technology which organize knowledge and production systems. The divergent voices and innovative practices of subjected peoples disrupt such cultural reconstructions of non-Western societies. By listening to polyphonic tones challenging dominant themes, and attending to lives conducted in shadowy recesses as well as under the spotlight, anthropologists can disclose myriad aspects of our modern condition.

Notes

Preface

1. "Malay" refers to persons of Malay-Muslim identity in Peninsular Malaysia, including immigrants from other parts of the Malay-Indonesian archipelago who have been assimilated into the dominant indigenous group. Malay identity is defined in the Federal Constitution of Malaysia. Since the late 1960s, the term *"bumiputra"* ("sons-of-the-soil") has been applied to denote Malay-Muslims who are collectively guaranteed a share of the national wealth (Siddique 1981). The local populations in this study are mainly Malays of Javanese descent in Kuala Langat.

2. Throughout this study, "Malaysia" is used to refer to only the Peninsular segment of the country (i.e., West Malaysia).

3. i.e., different claims to "truth" about working Malay women and what their sexuality may mean to social order.

Chapter 1

1. Thus E.P. Thompson's much-quoted model of class as a "self-making" cultural formation (1963), although commendable for returning to laboring classes their own history, has perhaps overlooked the structured nature of responses by subjects who are also the objects of historical processes.

2. In an arresting piece on English labor history, "Time, Work Discipline and Industrial Capitalism" (1967), E.P. Thompson documents the arduous processes involved in transforming an agrarian population into industrial laborers.

Chapter 2

1. A process of family dispersal and settlement rather in the manner of shifting agriculturalists for whom tolerable population-land ratio, rather than rigid adherence to descent rules, dictated postmarital residence. For an analogous example, see Derek Freeman's ethnographic study of the Ibans (1970).

223

2. See Michael Adas (1981) for a comparative discussion of flight as a customary mode of peasant response to intolerable state expropriation and violence in precolonial and postcolonial Southeast Asian societies.

3. Between 1874 and 1895, direct British rule was introduced into the west coast states of Selangor, Perak, Negri Sembilan, and, on the east coast, Pahang. These "protected" Malay States signed treaties admitting "advice" dispensed by British Residents in each state but giving the crown no jurisdiction in their territories. While in theory the British Resident was restricted to supervising the collection of revenues and general administration outside of "Malay religion and custom," he came to acquire all executive and legislative powers in the name of the sultan. The latter, handsomely pensioned off and elevated to the ceremonial role of symbolising Malay unity, became in effect a British client. For a detailed description of the Residential System in the Malay States, see Sadka (1968), Chapters 6 and 7, and also refer to Ralph Emerson's trenchant exposure of British "direct" and "indirect" rule in the Malay Peninsula (1964).

4. This is perhaps an underestimation. Nevertheless, under the "stabilized" conditions of British rule, the Malay population doubled in the next four years, mainly through encouraging settlement by Malay immigrants from Sumatra, Borneo, and Java. Sadka reports that by 1886 two-thirds of the Malay population in Selangor consisted of "natives of Netherlands India" (1968: 327–328). For a breakdown of the population in the first census taken in 1891, see Table 1. In that year, Selangor had 26,578 Malays (Dodge 1980: 463) but 75,000 Chinese who flooded tin mining camps as the industry and trade expanded rapidly under British control (Jackson 1964: 45–51).

5. The British tax collector stationed in the old royal seat of Kuala Langat reported his plan to increase the Malay population in Selangor:

The neighbourhood of Jugra I propose to populate with 'orang dagang' [traders] and for this purpose suggest the appointment of Haji Tahir as headman . . . I would recommend that [he] receives a regular salary as Immigration agent and be assisted with loans to enable him to make advances to new settlers . . . [I advise] the appointment of a duly authorised agent at Malacca who would meet all steamers arriving from the Dutch territory and by paying the debts of those who are looking for work induce them to come to Selangor (SSF 2546/1886).

6. In 1898, the Malay States under direct British rule were constituted as the "Federated Malay States," in contrast to other states under indirect British administration — the "Unfederated Malay States."

7. See Kernial Sandhu for a historical demography study of the recruitment and employment of Indian immigrants in the Malayan plantation economy (1969).

8. For a recent account of the colonial plantation economy in Deli, North Sumatra, see Ann Stoler's social historical study of confrontations between imported Javanese workers and Dutch estate management (1985).

9. E.P. Thompson (1963) and M. Lazonick (1976) have discussed British upper class perceptions of the "lower orders" in eighteenth and nineteenth century England in unsurprisingly similar terms with regard to their lack of moral rectitude and work discipline. The Methodist Church and mass education became strategic institutions for socializing the laboring classes to the requirements of industrial capitalism.

10. See for instance, Lim T.G.'s (1974) account of peasant protests against colonial discriminatory limits imposed on smallholding rubber production relative to plantations during the years of slumps in the rubber market. Another example of the new social history is Shahril Talib (1983). For an exemplar ethnography of colonialism, see Vincent's fine account of Ugandan "history from the bottom up" (1982).

11. See AR K. Lgt. 135/36. In the early 1930s, hundreds of immigrants from Java and Banjarmasin were provided with land titles, subsidies, and seeds to develop *sawah* lands out of jungle and swamp in the coastal districts north of Kuala Langat. Many *kampung* were founded in this manner by immigrant gangs and ex-contract laborers whom colonial officers thought were more experienced rice growers than local Malays (SAR 1938: 124).

12. Michael Swift, doing fieldwork among Minangkabau peasants in Negri Sembilan during the early 1950s, observed that the economic activities of these *sawah*-rubber cultivators were in large part governed by the rise and fall of world market prices for rubber (1965).

13. "Free" Javanese immigrants were recruited by earler settlers who founded villages by developing holdings and applying for land grants through their leaders. Since the pioneer *kampung* frequently required additional manpower, settlers sent for friends and relatives, offering free travel and lodging in return for two years of coolie labor. After their contract expired, the immigrants worked as rubber tappers or weeding coolies and attempted to occupy land on temporary occupation licenses. Alternately, they cultivated and tended the undeveloped holdings of landowners in return for half-share. Only after they had their own holdings of rubber, coconut, and minor crops did they marry or bring their families over (AR K. Lgt. 386/35). Thus many *kampung* in Kuala Langat developed distinctive cultural identities because of recruitment from home villages in the Netherlands East Indies, the practice of village endogamy, and limited market exchanges (AR K. Lgt. 135/46). Social intercourse with local Malays was rather limited and often marked by mutual hostility, a situation which still persists in symbolic practices, language use, and ethnic endogamy among Javanese villagers throughout the district.

14. Resistance to government policy included covert activities in the Reservations. In Kuala Langat, many villagers broke colonial regulations against leasing their holdings to non–Malays, thus gaining access to external sources of funds. New settlers illegally sold their land titles to Chinese, under the pretext of exorbitant three-year leases, and then left the district (AR K. Lgt. 349/21; K. Lgt. 192/23; SSF 3530/27). Other immigrants borrowed money from

Chettiars and mortgaged their holdings. In 1921, the Assistant Resident of Selangor reported to the FMS administration that he had received numerous petitions signed by village heads, concerning the "financial embarrassment of the poorer classes" who had mortgaged their lands to Chettiars and were threatened with bankruptcy. The official claimed that in the majority of cases, the settlers were "speculators or spendthrifts" and that "cases of genuine hardship [were] in the minority" (SSF2073/21).

Chapter 3

1. Following communal riots in May 1969, in which many youths from Kuala Langat took part, the Malaysian Government introduced the New Economic Policy (NEP) which emphasized massive institutional changes to increase wealth held by the Malay population as a whole vis-à-vis the other two ethnic groups.

2. These fenced-in industrial estates, also known as "export-processing zones" in the Philippines, are usually so situated in parts of developing countries so as to be best served by the national transportation and communications systems. Governments competing to attract the subsidiaries of transnational corporations site their FTZs in the outskirts of cities, at the nodes of road, rail, and air transportation lines, for the rapid exit of manufactured products and sustained inflow of rural labor. These zones are thus geographically "free" as well as "free" of most taxes and duties. In a basic sense, the FTZ is "an alien territory within a national territory" (Tsuchiya 1977), more integrated in the international networks of Japanese, American, and West European corporations than in the local economies.

3. Since the late 1960s, thousands of illegal Javanese and Sumatran immigrants have been flowing into the Malaysian Peninsula, their small crafts easily penetrating the long and permeable coastline. They blend into hundreds of *kampung,* many founded by earlier immigrant Malays, where they constitute a cheap source of labor reserve for the plantation industry increasingly beset by rising labor costs. A large number of them has also moved into the urban centers and married local Malays.

4. Upon the death of the father, who usually has the larger property, it is common practice for his widow to hold his land in trust, using proceeds from the holding to raise the children. Grown, married sons are usually given informal access to their parents' holdings, especially for house-sites. Formal partition of the land rarely takes place so long as one parent is still alive.

5. During the late 1950s the land office had opened up remaining forest reserves in the *mukim* in order to make grants of three-quarter acre lots to families from Sungai Jawa, the largest village in the district. The *kampung* also provided land for local ex-service men who had signed up during the Emergency. However, some of those who had been awarded land titles could not afford to pay the premium and instead sold their shares to rich villagers and civil servants from Kampung Telok. They employed the original titleholders

as regular laborers (*buroh tetap*) to prepare the land and cultivate permanent crops. In 1978, the Selangor government announced that 18,000 acres would be opened under its ''green revolution'' program. Each district would receive about 200 acres for distribution; ''the landless would be given priority'' (*New Straits Times*, June 25, 1978).

6. All currency is given in the Malaysian *ringgit*, which is also symbolized by M $. In the 1979–80 duration of my research, the value of the *ringgit* was M $ 2.22 to U.S. $ 1.

7. *New Straits Times*, Sept. 28, 1981.

8. *New Straits Times*, Oct. 5, 1979; see also *Nadi Insan*, 1979: 18–23.

9. *New Straits Times*, Mar. 8, 1979.

10. See, e.g., *New Straits Times*, Jan. 7, 1982.

11. For an initial discussion of the brokerage role of *kampung* leaders, see S. Husin Ali (1975). Other scholars have noted that the expansion of political party systems into rural Southeast Asian countries has reinforced pre-existing patronage networks in the asymmetrical exchange of government resources for votes (Scott 1977; Kessler 1978: 141–142). Shamsul A. Baharuddin provides an incisive account of ''the politics of poverty eradication'' in post-NEP rural Malay society in which politicians and officials deploy development funds and contracts to secure loyalty to UMNO, as well as to line their own pockets (1983).

12. The current number of immigrants from the Indonesian and Philippines islands to Malaysia is estimated at 430,000. About 37% of them are employed in the plantation sector and 16% engaged in manufacturing industries. See *Far Eastern Economic Review*, April 20, 1984, p.106–111.

13. The ''popular history'' model of laboring class action in the context of capitalist transformation, as most brilliantly developed by E.P. Thompson (1963), is not applicable to many peripheral capitalist societies. Although many Marxist scholars will be disappointed, in Malaysia at least, there are historical and political limits to the forging of ''a working class culture'' among the Malay laboring populations.

Chapter 4

1. The household census of 242 households covered approximately one-third of the total population in Sungai Jawa, a Malay Reservation. I conducted over one-third of the survey, while two local assistants completed the rest. Scheduled interviews elicited information on domestic membership, organization, family history, property, occupations, and budget arrangements. This census provided a statistical profile of the community and operated as a check on data gathered by other methods, such as participant observation and case studies.

A small sample of forty households was selected on the basis of differential land access (landless, landpoor, small, and rich) and willingness on the part of members to impart further information. This sample provided information for time budget studies and a survey of nutritional information.

2. A small but increasing number of time-allocation studies conducted among Asian peasantries has shown that child labor is not uniformly or necessarily of economic value to all rural parents. See, e.g., Mueller (1976) on Taiwanese farm families, and das Gupta (1978) on a North Indian case. Recently, White called for the need to go beyond purely quantitative measures of child labor, urging attention be paid to the subordination of children and their possible evasion of control (1981).

3. Forty households with children ages six years and above were chosen for the recording of daily events. Since cash cropping villagers (excepting rice growers) in Malaysia experience negligible seasonal changes in their agricultural tasks, the time-allocation survey was conducted over a period of only six months, including Ramadan and school holidays, in order to obtain as accurate a measure as possible of the daily activities which reflected the rhythm of work and leisure in Sungai Jawa.

Each household member aged six and above was interviewed about his/her activities on the previous day, from rising to going to bed, one day each week, for six consecutive months. Since village life was much influenced by the clock — for example, timing of school lessons, factory schedules, and the Islamic calls for prayer — the informant's recall of time spent in different activities was relatively accurate. The various types of work and nonwork activities in which villagers engaged in the normal course of a day are grouped under three rubrics in the tables: household maintenance, farm work, and wage labor. The average amount of daily time (in hours) allocated by each age-sex group — girl, boy (between six and sixteen years), woman, man (seventeen years and above) — was calculated by dividing total time alloted by number of informants in that particular group. Thus, the time units given in the tables do not reflect the average time actually expended in a particular task on a "normal day." Rageswari Balakrishna helped conduct the time survey after establishing a fine rapport with the informants. I have no doubt that the data is as accurate as it is socially tolerable to gather.

4. The value of labor power "is the means of subsistence necessary for the maintenance of the labourer." Thus, "the sum of the means of subsistence necessary for the production of labour-power must include the means necessary for the labourer's substitutes, i.e., his children" (Marx 1974: 171–172).

5. A pseudonym. All individuals mentioned in this study are given pseudonyms to protect their privacy.

6. The Federal Land Development Authority is a government agency to settle hundreds of thousands of landpoor Malay families in land-lots newly cleared from the jungle. The families are provided with cash crops and basic housing needs, and are required to repay loans on their holdings from the sale of their crops.

Chapter 5

1. Local Malay cultures in different parts of the country vary according to their adherence to certain sets of customary practices and in their absorption of Islamic principles. For contrasting case studies before and after the Second World War, see Raymond Firth, *Malay Fishermen: Their Peasant Economy* (1966); Rosemary Firth, *Housekeeping Among Malay Peasants* (1966); Michael Swift, *Malay Peasant Society in Jelebu* (1965); and David Banks' *Malay Kinship* (1982).

2. By taking "the native's point of view," Clifford Geertz (1979) emphasized how symbols operate as vehicles of culture within a particular conceptual structure. In his *Reflections on Fieldwork in Morocco* (1979), Paul Rabinow discloses his ethnographic experience as a "dialogic construction" in which informants played a critical and acknowledged role. For another approach which would look beyond native reification of their given cultural categories to an analysis of the interactions between historically conditioned ideas and social phenomena, see Michael Taussig's *The Devil and Commodity Fetishism in South America* (1980).

3. The secular education system is built upon the British model. The pre-university system is divided into a primary school education, graded from Standard (Std.) One through Six, and a secondary school, which is internally-ranked from Form One through Form Six (Lower and Upper levels). Children take their first nationally certified examination at the end of Standard Six. Secondary school students sit for three sets of nationally certified examinations: at the end of Forms Three, Five, and Upper Six.

4. In 1911, a schoolroom was established in Sungai Jawa to instruct village boys in the Koran and in writing the Jawi script and romanized Malay. The Malay teachers were paid by the colonial government to also give instructions in arithmetic, geography, and vegetable gardening, subjects considered adequate from boys who would grow up to be farmers. Girls were gradually admitted to the village school, which also operated as a temporary clinic and dispensary. By independence, approximately one-third of the 400 pupils were female, and they were mainly taught classes in hygiene and sewing. Each year, a handful of children sat for the Standard Six examination. Only one or two boys from the village were chosen to go on to the Kuala Kangsar College, Perak, a prestigious school for training upper-class Malays for the British Civil Service (Source: village school records).

5. Tamil and Chinese children in the district attend other schools, where their own languages, and sometimes English, are taught.

6. In 1979, there were altogether 32 teachers, including the headmaster, in the primary school. Of these, 11 were female teachers. All but one teacher were Malay, and 12 lived in local villages, the rest commuting from town.

7. Benjamin White reports a similar pattern of household resource sharing among Javanese peasants. He notes "a general though not necessarily total

pooling" of resources among members, "since the individuals concerned might retain separate control of different forms of wealth" (1976: 217–218).

8. They had no natural children of their own. During her lifetime, his late wife had neglected to make a will transferring her property to their adopted child. If Islamic law of inheritance were allowed to proceed unmodified, the property would be divided among her surviving siblings, three sisters. (She had no brothers, otherwise they would have been the first claimants after her natural children.) However, the sisters agreed that after having the land transferred to their names they would will the property over to the adopted daughter, whom they felt should rightfully inherit. The daughter had married a petty trader and was then living in Shah Alam.

9. He was not alone in being influenced by American programs shown on *Televeshen Malaysia*. American slang words and media personalities were well-known among villagers, including parents, the vast majority of whom could not speak American or other versions of English.

10. Most men commuting to work in urban centers like Port Klang, Shah Alam, Sungai Way, and Kuala Lumpur used motorbikes. Unless desperately in need of a job, young men refused to take the public transportation, which, in any case, was often not on schedule and very slow. Thus, young educated men starting urban employment insist on first saving for a motorbike, which has also become a powerful symbol of modern masculine identity.

11. In fact, the local nickname of Sungai Jawa was "*Kampung Toyol*," an index of its enviable reputation as a community of enterprising villagers who undoubtedly trafficked in spirits. Indeed, in the *abangan* world of Javanese peasantry (from which the founders of Sungai Jawa derived), Geertz notes that the mischief-making of *tujuls* or "spirit children" helped to make men rich quickly (1964: 16–17). In his view, the *slametan* and spirit beliefs of the *abangan* represented "the triumph of culture over nature, human and nonhuman" (ibid., 28).

Chapter 6

1. The study of family development in agrarian societies began with A. V. Chayanov's construct of household behavior among Russian peasants in the 1920s. He suggested that the biological basis of the family determined its composition at different phases of development, and in thus affecting its producer-consumer ratio was responsible for varying levels of labor productivity and of consumer demands (Thorner 1966: 57–60). Anthropologists elaborated upon the concept of domestic cyclical process. Meyer Fortes's notion of "the developmental cycle of the domestic group" (1970) showed that previously abstracted family "types" (based on descent and residential patterns of African lineages), were in actuality successive phases in the "developmental cycle" of a single general family form in the society concerned (1958: 3). In his view, "political-jural institutions" interacted with physiological changes in the "family cycle" to precipitate structural changes in prescribed cultural ways.

Although Chayanov was concerned with variations in household labor productivity, and Fortes with variations in family structure, their use of the domestic group as the unit of analysis assumed an inevitable unfolding of the family process according to the biological imperative, without considering how external relationships (beyond abstracted cultural norms), might have affected the developmental process. See Jack Goody (1973) for a note on Fortes's work.

2. The *wang mas* was set by the religious authority and usually involved a very small sum, compared to *wang hantaran*, since wedding expenses were used to furnish a bridal suite, pay the *imam* (marriage official) a small fee, and provide a wedding feast. The guests made cash contributions that helped defray the cost of the feast, which in the prewar years were small affairs involving immediate relatives and friends. In marriages to *janda*, i.e., nonvirgins, the bridewealth was minimal and the wedding meal even more modest.

3. A *Haji* is a man who has performed the hajj to Mecca. The female equivalent is *Hajjah*. The village has had a tradition of men — and to a lesser extent, women — performing the pilgrimage in old age. In the past decade, cash income has enabled the well-off and well-placed to undertake the trip in middle age or even earlier. Some *haji* make a second pilgrimage, which they hope will become a spiritual farewell from earthly life.

4. This dual ethnic identity is reflected in daily language; the majority of villagers in Sungai Jawa are bilingual, preferring to use the Javanese dialect when speaking to one another. Among the younger school-going generations, this habit has not taken hold; instead, boys and girls merely understand the dialect but use the national language Malay (*Bahasa Kebangsaan*) in daily speech. Except when dealing with Chinese and Japanese, my daily conversations with village folk, officials, and Tamil workers were all conducted in the *Bahasa*.

5. As we shall see below, actual marriage negotiations concerning bridewealth are conducted by the parents and their representatives, not the engaged couple themselves.

6. The popularity of policemen as husbands among rural women stemmed from their practical recognition that although no high educational qualifications were necessary, the police force was the fastest route to economic security, political power, and high social status for men of *kampung* origins. Since the Emergency, villagers have been well-acquainted with the benefits of such government employment, especially the regular paycheck and the pension.

7. According to Islamic law, women over eighteen years of age could not get married without parental consent *unless* (1) a *wali* (guardian) had been appointed by state authorities in place of her blood kinsmen (e.g., as in the case of the marriage of Malay women of Chinese ancestry adopted in infancy), or (2) she was caught in *flagrante delicto*, in which case the *kadi* acts as *wali*. However, the resolution of individual cases may not be as clear-cut as this statement may imply. I am grateful to William Roff for drawing my at-

tention to this point.

8. Raymond Firth reports that the Kelantanese Malays used credit produced by feasting to purchase capital like boats and nets (Firth 1974: 178–182). In Sungai Jawa, such windfalls can perhaps be invested in livestock but are too limited to purchase desired capital like a motorbike or land. They are nevertheless a significant form of credit internally generated within the village community.

9. Discussions about Malay marriages and divorces at the national level have recently identified a possible contributing factor linked to growing female wage employment. There is the suggestion that the Islamic requirement that husbands are totally responsible for the maintenance of wife and children has met with some resistance when working wives refuse to make cash contributions to the family budget. At the local level, it was not possible to get men to support this view, possibly because it impinges on Islamic rules and their own sense of masculine identity.

Chapter 7

1. See *The Third Malaysia Plan, 1975–80* (1976) for the government program of large-scale state intervention into the rural and urban sectors of the Malaysian economy. Lim Mah Hui (1985) has made a careful study of how state-sponsored programs since 1972 have been directed towards the growth of Malay capital, greatly benefiting individual members of the political elite at the expense of the emergent Malay petty bourgeois class.

2. *Treasury Economic Report,* (1975: 100). The Federal Land Development Authority (FELDA) schemes settled about 31,000 Malay families in cleared jungle reserves between 1957 and 1976, but this number constituted just a fraction of the Malay population which increased by 2.5 million within the same period. In 1975, state officials estimated that the incidence of poverty — defined as living below the standards of good nutritional health and the satisfaction of basic needs — included over 50 percent of rural households (*Third Malaysia Plan,* 1976: 72).

3. For statistics on rural unemployment and the mass urban migration of Malay youths, especially 15- to 19-year-olds, see *Third Malaysia Plan* (1976: 26, 141).

4. That is, about 400,000 in a total population of over one million. See *Sunday Mail,* Sept. 16, 1979.

5. *New Straits Times,* Oct. 14, 1979.

6. In a 1967–68 household census, 17 percent of the Peninsula agricultural work force (excluding unpaid family labor) worked less than 25 hours a week (Blake 1975: 184). This figure decreased to about 9.6 percent by 1974, after the introduction of ''Green Revolution'' programs, especially in the rice-growing areas of Kedah and Perak. Double-cropping and mechanizing of rice production contributed both to short periods of increased labor demands and the

mass outmigration of rural youths (*Third Malaysia Plan,* 1976: 26).

7. *Sunday Mail,* Dec. 2, 1979. See Lim Mah Hui (1980) for his assessment of the implications of these "state capitalist" strategies for ethnic and class politics in Malaysia.

8. See Jamilah Ariffin (1980). For additional, scattered reports on Malay factory workers in Malaysia and Singapore, see also von der Mehren (1973); Linda Lim (1978); Rachel Grossman (1979); Susan Ackerman (1979); Susan Ackerman & Raymond Lee (1981); and Ann-Marie Munster (1980).

9. *Federal Industrial Development Authority,* 1976: 11.

10. *New Straits Times,* Aug. 31, 1979.

11. See Linda Lim (1978); *Southeast Asia Chronicle,* April 1980, pp. 11–13.

12. That is, from 17,200 to 64,000. See Hasan & Sundaram (1980).

13. In recent years, a fiery group of young *ulama* had established a stronghold in the underdeveloped East Coast states, from which they issued demands for the "implementation of an Islamic Economic System." See *Asiaweek,* Dec. 17, 1982.

14. *New Straits Times,* Dec. 8, 1983.

15. See Maier (1970), for the roles Taylorism and Fordism played in validating a new class image, acceptable to bourgeois and social democracy in post–World War I industrial reconstruction of Western Europe.

16. See Dore (1973), for an example of the first view, and Burawoy (1979), for the second.

17. FIDA 1975. See Haraway (1984), for political questions about "sex, race, and class as scientific objects" constituted in structures of domination developed since the nineteenth century.

18. In 1979, I spent two months interviewing the managerial and supervisory staff of all three factories in the Telok FTZ. The management of EJI was the most forthcoming in this exercise. Interviews on their work force, production processes, and corporate policies were mainly conducted in English; occasionally, Malay and Hokkien were used.

19. This statement is misleading. In 1975, Japanese women comprised some 50 percent of the total labor force in Japan. Even with the same educational background as men, women by the age of 35 earned less than one half of men's wages. Moreover, since women cannot be considered part of the permanent labor force, men are the beneficiaries of lifetime employment provided only in large-scale enterprises (Cook & Hayashi 1980: 1–14; Matsutomo 1981: 62).

20. In 1979–80, the basic production processes in semiconductor manufacturing transferred to Malaysia by electronics industries included the following steps: selection of pellets, pin insertion, mounting, bonding, molding of components, and quality control testing and packaging. The first four processes required continual use of the microscope for the intricate wiring and

assembly of the microcomponents. In the mounting section, an operator was expected to process an average of 2,500 microchips per day, although some workers reached a target of 4,600. In the bonding section, operators assembled between 3,200 and 6,000 pieces in the eight hour daily shift.

21. See Braverman 1974, Chapter 4, for a discussion of the development of Taylorist "scientific management" in American industries. In his view, Taylorism achieved its goal of adapting labor to capital needs through (1) the progressive deskilling of the labor force, and (2) the extreme fragmentation and control of successive steps of the production process.

22. The interview, like all others, was conducted in Malay. Whenever an English term was used, it is italicized in the quote. Altogether, I conducted 35 structured interviews with female operators and some male technicians in their homes. The interviewees were chosen on the basis of their willingness to be interviewed, and they included workers from EJI (16), ENI (17) and MUZ (2).

23. Such employment practices were also evident among American electronics companies based in Penang.

24. Not unexpectedly, the only other area of female-dominated activity in the corporation is the typist pool, which came under the administrative division. Most of these jobs, particularly those in finance, accounting, and public relations work, were filled by outstation Chinese women. A few Malay women took typing classes after their factory shift to compete for these jobs from the outside, but only a mere handful were successful.

25. Thus, it is misleading to claim that in societies undergoing rapid capitalist development, preexisting "traditional patriarchy" is "at the bottom of women's subjection to imperialist exploitation" (Lim 1983: 78–79, 86). Furthermore, it remains questionable whether capitalist relations of production are "progressive" or necessarily produce "liberation from patriarchy" (ibid. 84–89) a process which in any case cannot be measured by employment opportunities alone.

26. See Chie Nakane (1967), for a succinct analysis of the Japanese peasant household, the "frame" of which she maintains has been reproduced within modern Japanese corporate life.

27. See Zawawi and Shahril (1983), for a discussion of how Malay male workers in plantations resist the harsh treatment of supervisors by using tactics which range from emotional persuasion to physical attacks.

28. A government requirement for all large enterprises with a sizeable Muslim labor force was the setting aside of a prayer room and the right of Muslim workers to perform prayers during work hours.

29. Max Weber defined "traditional authority" in two senses: (1) "personal authority" of an individual "which he enjoys by virtue of his traditional status," and (2) "the sanctity of the order and attendant powers of control as they have been handed down from the past" (1964: 341).

30. This system should not be confused with the Japanese collective decision making process called *ringi sei*, whereby decisions were arrived at after the discussion, approval/disapproval of each segment of the corporate hierarchy. This long, drawn out process involved no single clear-cut authority or responsibility for the decisions made. In EJI, the "grievance procedure" merely mimicked the *ringi sei* in collectivizing complaints from the shopfloor without involving the lower ranks in decision making.

31. For a discussion of contrasting management disciplinary techniques between Japanese and American companies located in Malaysia, see Ong (1984).

Chapter 8

1. For instance, Linda Lim (1978) and Patricia Kelly (1980) have discussed processes of market segmentation whereby third world women are subordinated in the new international division of labor. However, they tend to reduce "patriarchal" or male-supremacist notions to cultural ephiphenomena which could be used by capitalist enterprises to justify or enhance the subjugation of labor to capital.

2. As Mark Poster has pointed out, Foucault's own discourse on the history of "sexual politics" does not offer a basis to consider sexuality in a given society except within a general framework. The different sexual practices of social groups cannot simply be explained on the basis of a totalizing view of discourse (1984: 136).

3. *The Star,* May 19, 1978.

4. *The Star,* Feb. 16, 1979.

5. *New Straits Times,* Feb. 16, 1979.

6. *The Star,* April 4, 1980.

7. *New Straits Times,* Oct. 17, 1981.

8. *The Malay Mail,* June 14, 1982.

9. *New Straits Times,* Aug. 30, 1979.

10. See also Strange 1981: 23–26.

11. ABIM leaders were mainly graduates of local universities — Universiti Malaya, Universiti Kebangsaan, and the MARA Institute of Technology — and their recruitment drives had penetrated the civil service, police, military, professional organizations, and schools. In 1982, the ABIM leader Anwar Ibrahim "defected" to the government by accepting one of the five vice-presidencies of the UMNO party. Since this political maneuver by its most charismatic leader, ABIM has lost some of its moral fervor and sense of direction as a major political force critical of government policies.

12. See Nagata (1981: 416–423); *Far Eastern Economic Review,* Mar. 3, 1983. For other interpretations of the *dakwah movement* in Malaysia in the late 1970s, see Lyon (1979); Kessler (1980).

13. *New Straits Times,* Dec. 2, 1979.

14. See footnote 13 above.

Chapter 9

1. *Sunday Mail,* Jan. 27, 1980.

2. Jamilah Ariffin notes that newspaper reports of abandoned infants out-side urban FTZs indicated the inability of unwed factory women to cope with critical life situations (1980: 56). These factory women in cities probably did not have easy access to female kin, the basic source of emotional and social support in rural society.

3. For a description of the indigenous status classificatory system in the Malay states, see Gullick (1958) and Milner (1982). Social rank and prestige were derived from the political system based on the sultanate. In Telok, the traditional strata of *raja, orang besar,* and *rakyat;* were still regarded as culturally salient even though the traditional prestige system has been restructured and emasculated under British colonial rule and modern state formation. For in-stance, the term *orang besar* applied to surviving members of aristocratic fam-ilies has been bestowed on contemporary power holders of "common origins": civil servants and elected representatives who constitute the up-per stratum of rural society (A. Kahar Bador 1973).

4. See e.g., Wolf (1969); Scott (1976); Nash (1979); Taussig (1980).

5. For a report on "hysteria-exam blues link," see *New Straits Times,* Oct. 23, 1981.

6. For media interpretations of "mass hysteria" among factory women see *Asiaweek,* Aug. 4, 1978; *Sunday Echo,* Nov. 27, 1978; *Mimbar Sosialis,* June/July 1978.

7. See Linda Lim (1978) for one view of this incident.

8. *Sunday Echo,* November 27, 1978.

9. *New Straits Times,* Sept. 26, 1980.

10. However, in their motivations the Malay workers were comparable to the Luddites in that it was not the machines per se which they objected to, but the new relations of production of which the machines were part (see Hobsbawm 1964: 11).

Glossary

MALAY WORDS USED in TEXT*

adat customary sayings, practices and law

adik-beradik siblings

akad nikah marriage contract

akal intelligence, logic

bagi dua arrangement whereby owner and tenant each holds half-share in product of land or livestock capital

bagi nafkah under Islamic practice, maintenance — shelter, food, clothing — paid in cash and kind by husband to wife

Bahasa Kebangsaan National Language of Malaysia, i.e., Malay

baju kurong loose tunic and sarong worn by Malay girls and women

bantah argue, dispute, contest

bapa angkat foster father

bebas at liberty; not restrained in speech and behavior

bidan Malay village midwife

bomoh Malay spirit-healer

budak budak children; also maidens

bujang unmarried man or woman

bumiputra "sons-of-the-soil," legal definition of Malay-Muslims who enjoy special rights under the Malaysian constitution

bunga "flower," euphemism for disguised interest on investment

buroh kasar manual (unskilled) laborer; **buroh tetap** — laborer
hired to work on a piece of property

caci criticise, scold, abuse

dakwah proselytizing activities carried out by Islamic
revivalists; the advocates and movements
associated with these activities

datuk grandfather; honorary title for a man of high status;
ancestral male spirit associated with a sacred place

dukun synonym for **bomoh,** but with suggestion of black magic
practice; i.e., sorcerer

guru teacher

Haji A Muslin man who has performed the hajj

Hajjah A Muslim woman who has performed the hajj

hantu spirits, often harmful to human beings, associated with a
place, animal, or deceased person

hawa nafsu passion, carnal desires

janda widow, divorcée; woman who has no husband due to his
death or a divorce

jual tenaga sell labor power; engage in wage labor

kadi judge in Muslim courts and affairs

kaki foot; **kaki lima** — "five-foot-way" or sidewalk; with
negative symbolic connotations such as: **jolli kaki** —
footloose behavior, having a swinging time; shaking legs,
not working; **kaki arak** — alcoholic

kampung village; **ketua kampung** — village headman

keadilan justice, fairness

kebebasan lack of customary restraint; unseemly independence

kebun garden; used here for a commerical crop holding or an
estate under one hundred acres

keluarga family, parents, and children; in a wider sense,
category of relatives descended from the same ancestor

kenduri feast, usually marking rite-of-passage ceremony or
religious occasion

kerajaan government; body of civil servants

keras harsh, unyielding behavior and language

kerja work; in village discourse, the term was used to mean employment with steady income; it includes: **kerja kampung** — employment in the village; **kerja kontrak** — contract work; **kerja sendiri** — self-employment

khalwat spatial seclusion of a man and a woman not married to each other; a situation which may be construed as evidence of illicit sexual intimacy

kongkongan shackles; to be held in captivity

kotor dirty, obscene; also used as noun — filth

kramat sacred abode of spirit

kuasa authority; power

kuli manual laborer; unskilled worker

langsuir whinnying banshee that attacks pregnant women

lemah semangat weak spiritual constitution

madrasah school set up by *kijaji* for Koranic instruction

majikan management of a company

makan eat; consume; **makan gaji** — make a living from earning wages; **makan sekali** — eat together, to have a joint budget; **makan suku** — eat separately, even though living under the same roof

malu shy, shameful; shame

mandur foreman, overseer of labor gang

manusia human being; humanity

mukim subdistrict; smallest administrative unit, headed by a **penghulu**

orang human being; people, persons in general; **orang asing** — aliens; **orang asli** — native, aboriginal people; **orang besar** — big men, i.e., aristocratic leaders in indigenous political systems; **orang biasa** — commoner, ordinary people; **orang dagang** — traders; **orang Islam** — Muslims; Islamic people; **orang kampung** — villagefolk; **orang kaya** — rich people; **orang luar** — aliens, outsiders; **orang miskin** — poor folk;

orang sederhana — ordinary people, i.e., those who consider themselves in middling circumstances; **orang susah** — people who have difficulty in making a living.

pegawai officer, executive in a government office or private enterprise

pembangunan development, especially economic development

pemborong labor contractor

pemuda young man; generally unmarried youths; **Pemuda UMNO** — UMNO Youth Faction

pemudi young unmarried woman

penghulu lowest government administrator, in charge of the mukim

penyakit histeria hysteria affliction

penyakit jiwa spiritual illness

pesaka inheritance, usually landed inheritance

pinangan marriage proposal

pokok belanja main source for covering daily expenses

pontianak female demon which harasses women in childbirth

rakyat citizens; people

Ramadan fasting month in Islamic calendar

ringgit Malaysian dollar, valued at US 45 cents in 1979

rugi losing, to be cheated of gain

rumah tangga household

salaam peace salutation, greetings

sawah wet rice field

sekolah school

slametan ritual feast seeking peaceful negotiation of some stressful passage in everyday life, e.g., childbirth

sosial Malay version of "social"; in local parlance, unrestrained relations between single men and women

sultan Muslim ruler of a state

surau Islamic prayer room or house

syaitan Satan, the Evil One

takut fearful, anxiously respectful

tanah land, earth; **tanah hidup** — live land, i.e. cultivated and used for living; **tanah mati** — dead land, i.e. uncultivated land; **tanah modal** — landed wealth or capital; **tanah pesaka** — landed inheritance

tanam modal to "plant capital", such as investing in land

tani farmer; peasant

tekanan pressure, oppression

tidak apa "it doesn't matter"; an unconcerned, unhurried attitude

timbang rasa sympathy

toyol mischievous spirit raised by owner to steal on his behalf

tugas responsibility, duty

tukang tebus labor contractor

tumpang to "squat", i.e., lodge temporarily with relative or friend; also to squat on someone's land as a hired laborer

ulama learned Islamic scholar who engages in Koranic instruction and proselytizing

ustaz Islamic teacher trained at government-sponsored institutions

wajib duty-bound or obligatory practice

wakil rakyat people's representative, member of Parliament

wali Islamic guardian of bride, usually her father

wang hantaran Cash payments by groom for wedding expenses; **hantaran** for short

wang mas cash or gold payment from groom to bride as part of the marital exchange

wanita women; female; **Wanita UMNO** — women's faction of the UMNO

zinah illicit sexual intercourse

---

* The spelling follows the common system adopted by Malaysia and The Republic of Indonesia. Some words were defined by consulting the dictionary *Kamus Lengkap*, by Awang Sudjai Hairul and Yusoff Khan. Petaling Jaya, Malaysia: Pustaka Zaman Sdn Bhd., 1977.

Bibliography

OFFICIAL COLONIAL RECORDS
THE NATIONAL ARCHIVES OF MALAYSIA
PETALING JAYA

Annual Report, Kuala Langat (AR K. Lgt.), 1946
Federal Council Proceedings (FCP), 1913
Federated Malay States, Annual Report (FMSAR), 1900
Federation of Malaya Annual Reports (FMAR), 1950-55
Selangor Annual Reports (SAR), 1932–1938, 1948
Selangor Secretariat Files (SSF), 1886–1912

MALAYSIAN GOVERNMENT PUBLICATIONS
KUALA LUMPUR

Department of Statistics. 1972.

Community Groups.

Federal Industrial Development Authority (FIDA). 1975.

Malaysia: The Solid State for Electronics.

———. 1976.

Malaysia: Your Profit Centre in Asia.

Jabatan Pertanian Selangor. 1966, 1978.

Laporan Tahunan.

Ministry of Finance. 1975, 1976.

Treasury Economic Reports.

Third Malaysia Plan, 1976-1980.

243

Selangor State Development Corporation (SSDC). 1976.

Investment Brochure.

The Government Press. 1976.

The Third Malaysia Plan. 1975–80, (TMP).

BOOKS AND ARTICLES

A. Kahar Bador. 1973.
"Social Rank, Status-Honour and Social Class Consciousness among the Malays." In *Modernization in Southeast Asia,* edited by Hans-Dieter Evers. Singapore: Oxford University Press.

Ackerman, Susan E. 1979.
"Industrial Conflict in Malaysia: A Case Study of Rural Malay Female Workers." Unpublished manuscript.

Ackerman, Susan E. & Raymond Lee. 1981.
"Communication and Cognitive Pluralism in a Spirit Possession Event in Malaysia." *American Ethnologist,* 81: 789-799.

Adas, Michael. 1981.
"From Avoidance to Confrontation: Peasant Protest in Precolonial and Colonial Southeast Asia." *Comparative Studies in Society and History,* 23 (2): 217–247.

Banks, David. 1982.
Malay Kinship. Philadelphia: Ishi Publications.

Bauer, Peter. 1948.
Report on a Visit to the Rubber-growing Smallholdings of Malaya, July–September, 1946. London: Her Majesty's Stationery Office.

Becker, Gary. 1965.
"A Theory of the Allocation of Time." *The Economic Journal,* LXXV:493-517.

Berger, John. 1984.
And our faces, my heart, brief as photos. New York: Pantheon Books.

Bingswanger, H.P. et al., eds. 1980.
Rural Household Studies in Asia. Singapore University Press.

Bird, Isabella. 1967.
The Golden Chersonese. Kuala Lumpur: Oxford University Press [org. pub. 1883].

Blake, David. 1975.
"Unemployment: The West Coast Example." In *Readings in*

Malaysian Economic Development, edited by David Lim. Kuala Lumpur: Oxford University Press.

Boserup, Ester. 1970.
Women's Role in Economic Development. London: St. Martin's Press.

Bourdieu, Pierre. 1963.
"The Attitude of the Algerian Peasant Toward Time" In *Mediterranean Countrymen: Essays in the Social Anthropology of the Mediterranean,* edited by Julian Pitt-Rivers. Paris: Mouton.

———. 1977.
Outline of a Theory of Practice. Translated by Richard Nice. Cambridge University Press [org. pub. Paris, 1972].

———. 1984.
Distinction: A Social Critique of the Judgement of Taste. Translated by Richard Nice. Cambridge, Ma.: Harvard University Press [org. pub. Paris, 1979].

Braverman, Harry. 1974.
Labor and Monopoly Capital: The Degradation of Work in the Twentieth Century. New York: Monthly Review Press.

Burawoy, Michael. 1979.
Manufacturing Consent: Changes in the Labor Process under Monopoly Capitalism. University of Chicago Press.

Clifford, Hugh. 1927.
In Court and Kampong. London: The Richards Press.

Cook, Alice H. & Hiroko Hayashi. 1980.
Working Women in Japan: Discrimination, Resistance and Reform. Ithaca: New York State School of Labor and Industrial Relations.

das Gupta, Monica. 1978.
"Changing Social Relations and Population: Rampur." In *Population and Development,* edited by G. Hawthorn. London: Frank Cass.

de Certeau, Michel. 1984.
The Practice of Everyday Life. Berkeley: University of California Press.

de Josselin, Jong, P.E. 1960.
"Islam versus *Adat* in Negri Sembilan (Malaya)." *Bijdragen,* 116(1): 158-203.

Djamour, Judith. 1965.
Malay Kinship and Marriage in Singapore. London: Athlone Press.

Dodge, Nicholas. 1980.
"Population Estimates for the Malay Peninsula in the 19th Century, with special reference to the East Coast States." *Population Studies*, 34 (3): 437–75.

Dore, Ronald. 1973.
British Factory—Japanese Factory: The Origins of National Diversity in Industrial Relations. Berkeley: University of California Press.

Drabble, J.H. 1973.
Rubber in Malaya, 1876–1922: The Genesis of the Industry. Kuala Lumpur: Oxford University Press.

Emerson, Ralph. 1964.
Malaysia: A Study in Direct and Indirect Rule. Kuala Lumpur: Oxford University Press [org. pub. 1937].

Engels, Frederick. 1972.
The Origins of the Family, Private Property and the State. New York: International Publishers [org. pub. 1884].

Evenson, Robert. 1978.
"Time Allocation in Rural Philippine Households." *American Journal of Agricultural Economics*, 60(2): 322–330.

Firth, Raymond. 1966.
Malay Fishermen: Their Peasant Economy. New York: W.W. Norton [org. pub. 1946].

———. 1974.
"Relations between Personal Kin (*Waris*) among Kelantan Malays." In *Social Organization and the Applications of Anthropology*, edited by Robert J. Smith. Ithaca: Cornell University Press.

Firth, Rosemary. 1966.
Housekeeping Among Malay Peasants. New York: Humanities Press [org. pub. 1943].

Fortes, Meyer. 1958.
"Introduction." In *The Developmental Cycle in Domestic Groups*, edited by Jack Goody. Cambridge University Press.

———. 1970.
Time and Social Structure and Other Essays. New York: Humanities Press [org. pub. 1949].

Foucault, Michel. 1979.
Discipline and Punish: The Birth of the Prison. Translated by Alan Sheridan. New York: Vintage Books [org. pub. Paris, 1975].

————. 1979a.

"On Governmentality." *Ideology and Consciousness* (Autumn 1979): 5–21.

————. 1980.

The History of Sexuality, Volume I. Translated by Robert Hurley. New York: Vintage Books [org. pub. Paris, 1976].

Freeman, Derek. 1970.

Report on the Iban. New York: Humanities Press.

Gay, Jill. 1983.

"Sweet Darlings in the Media: How Foreign Corporations Sell Western Images of Women to the Third World." *Multinational Monitor,* 4(7): 19-21.

Geertz, Clifford. 1964.

The Religion of Java. New York: The Free Press.

————. 1973.

"Thick Description: Toward an Interpretive Theory of Culture." In *The Interpretation of Cultures: Selected Essays,* by Clifford Geertz. New York: Basic Books.

————. 1979.

"From the Native's Point of View: On the Nature of Anthropological Understanding." In *Interpretive Social Science: A Reader,* edited by Paul Rabinow and William M. Sullivan. Berkeley: University of California Press [org. pub. 1976].

Gluckman, Max. 1958.

Analysis of a Social Situation in Modern Zululand. Manchester University Press [The Rhodes-Livingstone Papers, no. 28].

Goffman, Erving. 1959.

The Presentation of Self in Everyday Life. New York: Anchor Books.

Goody, Jack. 1973.

"Introduction." In *The Character of Kinship,* edited by Jack Goody. Cambridge University Press.

Grossman, Rachel. 1979.

"Women's Place in the Electronic Circuit." *Southeast Asia Chronicle,* 66: 2-17.

Gullick, J.M. 1958.

Indigenous Political Systems of Western Malays. London: Athlone Press.

Hannerz, Ulf. 1985.
"The World System of Culture: The International Flow of Meaning and its Local Management." Unpublished manuscript.

Haraway, Donna. 1984.
"Class, Race, Sex as Scientific Objects of Knowledge: A socialist-feminist perspective on the social construction of productive knowledge and some political consequences." In *Women in Scientific and Engineering Professions,* edited by Violet Haas and Caroline Perucci. Ann Arbor: University of Michigan Press.

Hasan, O.R. & Sundaram, Jomo. 1980.
"Wage Trends in Peninsular Malaysian Manufacturing, 1963–1973." Paper presented at the 6th Convention of the Malaysian Economic Association, May 1980, Penang.

Hill, R.D. 1967.
"Agricultural Land Tenure in West Malaysia." *Malayan Economic Review,* 12 (1):99–116.

Ho, Robert. 1967.
"Labour Inputs of Rubber Producing Smallholders in Malaya." *Malayan Economic Review,* 12:79–89.

Hobsbawm, Eric. 1964.
Labouring Men: Studies in the History of Labour. London: Routledge & Kegan Paul.

———. 1971.
"Class Consciousness in History." In *Aspects of History and Class Consciousness,* edited by I. Meszaros. London.

———. 1977.
The Age of Capital 1848–1875. London: Sphere Books Ltd. [org. pub. 1975].

Jackson, James C. 1964.
"Population Change in Selangor State, 1850–1891." *Journal of Tropical Geography,* 19:42–57.

———. 1968.
Planters and Speculators: Chinese and European Enterprise in Malaya, 1786–1921. Kuala Lumpur: University of Malaya Press.

Jamilah Ariffin. 1980.
"Industrial Development in Peninsular Malaysia and Rural-Urban Migration of Women Workers: Impact and Implications." *Jurnal Ekonomi Malaysia,* 1: 41-59.

Kelly, Maria Patricia Fernandez. 1983.
For We Are Sold, I and My People: Women and Industry in Mexico's Frontier. Albany: State University of New York Press.

Kessler, Clive S. 1977.
"Conflict and Sovereignty in Kelantan Malay Spirit Seances." In *Case Studies in Spirit Possession,* edited by Vincent Crapanzano and V. Garrison. New York: J. Wiley and Sons.

———. 1978.
Islam and Politics in a Malay State: Kelantan 1838–1969. Ithaca: Cornell University Press.

———. 1980.
"Malaysia: Islamic Revivalism and Political Disaffection in a Divided Society." *Southeast Asia Chronicle,* 75: 3-11.

Khazin Mohd. Tamrin. 1980
"The Javanese Involvement in the Economic Development of British Malaya." Paper presented at the 8th Conference of the International Association of Historians of Asia, August 25–29, 1980, Kuala Lumpur.

Kusnic, Michael & Judith DaVanzo. 1980.
Income Inequality and the Definition of Income: The Case of Malaysia. Santa Monica: The Rand Corporation Monograph R–2416.

Lazonick, M. 1976.
"The Subjection of Labor to Capital: The Rise of The Capitalist System." *Review of Radical Political Economy,* X, no. 1.

Lee, George. 1973.
"Commodity Production and Reproduction among the Malayan Peasantry." Journal of Contemporary Asia, 3, (4): 441-456.

Lenin, Illych. 1964.
The Development of Capitalism in Russia. Collected Works, Vol. 3. Moscow: Progress Publishers.

Lewis, Ioan M. 1971.
Ecstatic Religion: An Anthropological Study of Spirit Possession and Shamanism. Harmondsworth: Penguin Books.

Lim, Linda. 1978.
Women Workers in Multinational Corporations: The Case of the Electronics Industry in Malaysia and Singapore. University of Michigan, Occasional Paper no. 9.

———. 1983.

"Capitalism, Imperialism and Patriarchy: The Dilemma of Third World Women Workers in Multinational Factories." In *Women, Men and the International Division of Labor*, edited by June Nash and Patricia Maria Fernandez Kelly. Albany: State University of New York Press.

Lim Mah Hui. 1980.

"Ethnic and Class Relations in Malaysia." *Journal of Contemporary Asia*, 10(1-2): 130-154.

———. 1985.

"Contradictions in the Development of Malay Capital: State, Accumulation and Legitimation." *Journal of Contemporary Asia*, 15(1): 37-63.

Lim Teck Ghee. 1974.

"Malayan Peasant Smallholders and the Stevenson Restriction Scheme, 1922-1928." *Journal of the Malayan Branch of the Royal Asiatic Society (JMBRAS)*: 105-119.

———. 1977.

Peasants and their Agricultural Economy in Colonial Malaya, 1874-1941. Kuala Lumpur: Oxford University Press.

Lukács, Georg. 1982.

History and Class Consciousness: Studies in Marxist Dialectics. Translated by Rodney Livingstone. Cambridge, Mass: MIT Press [org. pub. Berlin, 1968].

Lyon, Margo. 1979.

"*The Dakwah* Movement in Malaysia." *RIMA*, 13(2): 34-45.

Maier, Charles S. 1970.

"Between Taylorism and Technocracy: European Ideologies and the Vision of Industrial Productivity in the 1920s." *The Journal of Contemporary History*, 5(2): 27-61.

Mamdani, Mohammad. 1973.

The Myth of Population Control: Family, Caste and Class in an Indian Village. New York: Monthly Review Press.

Marx, Karl. 1974.

Capital, Volume I. New York: International Publishers [org. pub. 1867].

Matsutomo, Sheila. 1981.

"Women in Factories." In *Women in Changing Japan*, edited by J. Lebra et al. Stanford University Press.

Maxwell, W. W. 1884.
"The Laws and Customs of the Malays with Reference to the Tenure of Land." *JMBRAS*, XIII (1884): 75–220.

Milner, Anthony C. 1982.
Kerajaan: Malay Political Culture on the Eve of Colonial Rule. Tucson, Arizona: University of Arizona Press.

Minge-Kalman [Minge-Klevana], Wanda. 1978.
"A Theory of the European Household Economy during the Peasant-to-Worker Transition." *Ethnology*, 17 (12): 183–196.

———. 1980.
"Does Labor Time Decrease with Industrialization? A Survey of Time-Allocation Studies." *Current Anthropology*, 21 (3): 279–298.

Mueller, Eva. 1976.
"The Economic Value of Children in Peasant Agriculture." In *Population and Development*, edited by R.G. Rider. Baltimore: The Johns Hopkins University Press.

Munster, Anne-Marie. 1980.
"Export of Industries and Changing Structures of the International Labor Market." Max Planck Institute of the Social Sciences, Starnberg. Unpublished manuscript.

Nagata, Judith. 1981.
"Religious Ideology and Social Change: The Islamic Revival in Malaysia." *Pacific Affairs*, 53 (Fall 1981):405–430.

Nakane, Chie. 1967.
Kinship and Economic Organization in Rural Japan. New York: Athelone Press.

Nash, June. 1979.
We Eat the Mines and the Mines Eat Us: Dependency and Exploitation in Bolivian Tin Mines. New York: Columbia University Press.

Ong Aihwa. 1984.
"Capitalist Discipline and Cultural Discourse: Industrialization in Export-Processing Industries, Malaysia." Unpublished manuscript.

Ooi Jin-Bee. 1959.
Rural Development in Tropical Areas, with Special Reference to Malaya. Special Issue of *Journal of Tropical Geography*, 12.

Poster, Mark. 1984.
Foucault, Marxism and History: Mode of Production versus Mode of Information. Cambridge: Polity Press.

Rabinow, Paul. 1979.
> *Reflections on Fieldwork in Morocco.* Chicago: Chicago University Press.
—————. 1985.
> "Discourse and Power: On the Limits of Ethnographic Texts." *Dialectical Anthropology,* 10 (1 & 2): 1-13.

Ramsay, A.B. 1956.
> "Indonesians in Malaya." *Journal of the Malayan Branch of the Royal Asiatic Society,* 29 (1): 119-124.

Rathborne, A.B. 1898.
> *Camping and Tramping in Malaya.* London.

S. Husin Ali. 1964.
> "Social Stratification in Kampung Bagan." *JMBRAS* (1964): 1-170.

S. Hussein Alatas. 1977.
> *The Myth of the Lazy Native.* London: Frank Cass.

Sadka, Emily. 1968.
> *The Protected Malay States, 1874–1895.* Kuala Lumpur: University of Malaya Press.

Sandhu, Kernial. 1969.
> *Indians in Malaya: Immigration and Settlements, 1876–1959.* London.

Schultz, T.P. 1980.
> "An Economic Interpetation of the Decline in Fertility in a Rapidly Developing Country: The Case of Taiwan." In *Rural Household Studies in Asia,* edited by H.P. Bingswanger et al. Singapore University Press.

Scott, James C. 1976.
> *The Moral Economy of the Peasant: Subsistence and Rebellion in Southeast Asia.* New Haven: Yale University Press.
—————. 1977.
> "Patron-Client Politics and Political Change in Southeast Asia." In *Friends, Followers and Factions,* edited by S.W. Schmidt et al. Berkeley: University of California Press.

Shahnon Ahmad. 1972.
> *No Harvest but a Thorn (Ranjau Sepanjang Jalan).* Translated by Adibah Amin, Kuala Lumpur: Oxford University Press [org. pub. 1966].

Shahril Talib. 1983.
"Voices from the Kelantan Desa 1900-1940." *Modern Asian Studies*, 17(2): 177-195.
Shamsul A. Baharuddin. 1983.
"The Politics of Poverty Eradication: The Implementation of Development Projects in a Malayan District." *Pacific Affairs*, 56: 455-476.
Siddique, Sharon. 1981.
"Some Aspects of Malay-Muslim Ethnicity in Peninsular Malaysia." *Journal of Contemporary Southeast Asia*, 3 (1): 76-87.
Stoler, Ann L. 1985.
Capitalism and Confrontation in Sumatra's Plantation Belt, 1870-1979. New Haven: Yale University Press.
Strange, Heather. 1981.
Rural Malay Women from Tradition to Transition. New York: Praeger.
Strathern, Marilyn. 1981.
"Culture in a Netbag: The Manufacture of a Subdiscipline in Anthropology," *Man*, (n.s.) 16: 665-88.
Swift, Michael. 1965.
Malay Peasant Society in Jelebu. New York: Humanities Press.
———. 1967.
"Economic Concentration and Malay Peasant Society." In *Social Organization*, edited by Maurice Freedman. London.
T. Shamsul Bahrin. 1967.
"The Pattern of Indonesian Migration and Settlement in Malaya." *Journal of Asian Studies*, 5: 233-257.
Taussig, Michael. 1980.
The Devil and Commodity Fetishism in South America. Chapel Hill: The University of North Carolina Press.
Thompson, Edward P. 1963.
The Making of the English Working Class. New York: Vintage Books.
———. 1967.
"Time, Work Discipline and Industrial Capitalism." *Past and Present*, 38 (Dec. 1967): 56-97.
Thorner, Daniel. 1966.
"Chayanov's Concept of Peasant Economy." In *The Theory of Peasant Economy*, edited by David Thorner et al. Homewood, Ill.: The American Economic Association Series.

Tsuchiya Takeo. 1967.
> "Introduction." In *Free Trade Zones and Industrialization of Asia.* Special Issue of AMPO: Japan-Asia Quarterly Review. Tokyo.

Vincent, Joan. 1982.
> *Teso In Transformation: The Political Economy of Peasant and Class in Eastern Africa.* Berkeley: University of California Press.

von der Mehren, Fred R. 1973.
> *Industrial Policy in Malaysia: A Penang Micro-Study.* Rice University Program for Developmental Studies, Occasional Paper. Houston.

Weber, Max. 1958.
> *The Protestant Ethic and the Spirit of Capitalism.* Translated by Talcott Parsons. New York: Charles Scribner's Sons [org. pub. 1946].

———. 1964.
> *The Theory of Social and Economic Organization.* Edited and translated by Talcott Parsons. New York: Free Press [org. pub. 1947].

White, Benjamin N. 1976.
> *Production and Reproduction in a Javanese Village.* Columbia University Ph.D. dissertation.

———. 1982.
> "Child Labor and Population Growth: Some Studies from Rural Asia." Development and Change, 13: 587-610.

Williams, Raymond. 1977.
> *Marxism and Literature.* Oxford: Oxford University Press.

Winstedt, Richard. 1981.
> *The Malays: A Cultural History.* Revised and updated by Tham Seong Chee. Singapore: Graham Brash (Pte) Ltd. [org. pub. 1947].

Wolf, Eric. 1969.
> *Peasant Wars of the Twentieth Century.* New York: Harper and Row.

———. 1982.
> *Europe and the People Without History.* Berkeley: University of California Press.

Zawawi Ibrahim & Shahril Talib. 1983.
> "Neither Rebellions nor Revolutions: Everyday Resistance of the Malay Peasantry Under Capitalist Domination." *Ilmu Masyarakat,* 2 (Apr.-June): 25-41.

NEWSPAPERS AND NEWS JOURNALS

Asiaweek (Hong Kong)

Berita Harian (Kuala Lumpur)

Far Eastern Economic Review (Hong Kong)

The Malay Mail (Kuala Lumpur)

Mimbar Sosialis (Kuala Lumpur)

Nadi Insan (Kuala Lumpur)

New Straits Times (Kuala Lumpur)

Southeast Asia Chronicle (Berkeley, Ca., United States)

The Star (Kuala Lumpur)

Suara Melayu (Kuala Lumpur)

Sunday Echo (Penang)

Sunday Mail (Penang)

·

Index

Spirits of Resistance and Capitalist Discipline: Factory Women in Malaysia
Aihwa Ong

Why are Malay women workers periodically seized by spirit posses-sion on the shopfloors of modern factories? In this book, Aihwa Ong captures the disruptions, conflicts, and ambivalences in the lives of Malay women and their families as they make the transition from peasant society to industrial production.

To discover the meaning that the market economy and wage labor hold for Malay peasants, Ong conducted anthropological field work in an agricultural district in Selangor, Peninsular Malaysia, which is undergoing rapid proletarianization. Weaving together history, ethnography, and quantitative analysis, she addresses many ques-tions pertaining to peasants and state policies. The book shows how the diverging roles of young men and women are increasingly chan-nelled, by educational and labor market pressures, toward confor-mity with corporate culture and capitalist discipline.

A unique feature of this book is the portrayal of Malay women workers in Japanese factories, caught between their culture and the culture of capitalism. Ong argues that cultural values and practices — both Islamic-Malay and foreign — are reworked and reconstituted in the industrial hierarchy. Her vivid accounts of hysterical episodes, violent incidents, and women's self-perceptions provide insights in-to their attitudes toward capitalist relations.

By illuminating the encounter of Malay peasants with global in-dustrial production, the book also throws light on the attitude of neophyte wage workers elsewhere in the Third World.

Aihwa Ong is Associate Professor in the Department of Anthro-pology, University of California, Berkeley.

SUNY Series in the Anthropology of Work
June Nash, Editor

0-88706-381-0

State University of New York Press